PATTERNS OF
emotions

patterns of / EMOTIONS

A NEW ANALYSIS OF ANXIETY AND DEPRESSION

CARROLL E. IZARD

Department of Psychology
Vanderbilt University
Nashville, Tennessee

WITH CHAPTERS COAUTHORED BY

EDMUND S. BARTLETT
Orange Memorial Hospital
Orlando, Florida

ALAN G. MARSHALL
Blue Ridge Mental Health Center
Ashville, North Carolina

ACADEMIC PRESS • New York and London • 1972

ACADEMIC PRESS, INC.
111 Fifth Avenue, New York, New York 10003

United Kingdom Edition published by
ACADEMIC PRESS, INC. (LONDON) LTD.
24/28 Oval Road, London NW1

LIBRARY OF CONGRESS CATALOG CARD NUMBER: 72-82657

PRINTED IN THE UNITED STATES OF AMERICA

Contents

Contents

Contents

Contents

Preface

Since the dawn of the species *Homo sapiens*, the emotions have played an essential role in human adaptation and personality functioning. The individual human being has always had some awareness and some understanding of his or her own emotions and their importance. Much of this awareness and understanding seems intuitive rather than rational or logical, and thus a person often has difficulty sorting out, labeling, and verbalizing his emotions or emotional experiences.

While people have always been concerned with emotions, scientists have only recently begun to apply their knowledge, skills, and methods to this area. At last, there are a number of encouraging signs which point toward the development of a science of the emotions—a science which will consider the discrete fundamental emotions of human experience as worthy of study.

Hopefully, a science of the emotions will enhance, rather than replace, the individual's intuitive grasp of his inner life. Furthermore, scientific advance in this area should facilitate the individual's effort to reflect on his emotions and the part they play in his life—his perceptions, his thoughts, his memory, his actions, and his relationships with other people.

The Face of Emotion (Izard, 1971) presented a general conceptual framework for the study of the personality, a theory of the emotions, and evidence for the universality of the fundamental emotions of interest, joy, surprise, distress, anger, disgust, contempt, shame, and fear. It also discussed the role of these emotions in human development and the use of emotion concepts in the assessment and treatment of human problems.

Patterns of Emotions was a necessary sequel. The delineation and measurement of the fundamental emotions led to the discovery that emotions frequently, probably typically, occur in combinations and patterns. This approach also made possible the analysis of complex emotional experiences in terms of discrete fundamental emotions.

The principal purpose of *Patterns of Emotions* is to present a theoretical and empirical analysis of anxiety and depression—phenomena experienced in some degree by everyone and in crippling intensity by many. These two human problems have claimed far more of the attention of clinical psychologists, psychiatrists, social workers, psychiatric nurses, and the related helping professions than any others—probably more than all others combined. Yet, these phenomena are still often conceived and treated as global, unitary states or processes. In the present work they are defined, in the framework of differential emotion theory, as combinations or patterns of interacting fundamental emotions and bodily feelings. The differential emotion theory of anxiety and depression is compared with psychoanalytic theory, cognitive theory, and biogenetic theory. A number of studies are presented which support the differential emotion analysis of anxiety and depression.

Finally, the book presents studies of various life situations in which a particular fundamental emotion is dominant. What has been found repeatedly is that, in each such situation, the dominant emotion occurs in a pattern of dynamically related fundamental emotions. The patterns for a variety of commonly experienced and universal emotion situations are presented and discussed.

Acknowledgments

My wife, Barbara Sinquefield, has continually given me a very special kind of love which helps keep my own anxieties and depressions within manageable limits, and she and my children Cal, Camille, and Ashley continue to provide both challenge and insight for my study of human emotions.

Dr. Hans Strupp, Department of Psychology, Vanderbilt University, read the sections on psychoanalytic theory and made helpful comments. Dr. John Davis, Departments of Pharmacology and Psychiatry, Vanderbilt School of Medicine, served as a critic for the chapters dealing with the neurophysiology and biochemistry of the emotions.

A number of graduate students in psychology have helped in various ways. Edmund Bartlett and Alan Marshall coauthored chapters. Frank Dougherty helped with the development of the Differential Emotion Scale. Robert Speth proofed the chapters dealing with neurophysiology and biochemistry and made valuable suggestions and improvements.

Literally hundreds of Vanderbilt undergraduates have contributed directly or indirectly to this volume. In my course on the emotions, in independent study, and in honors research they have brought creative energies and enthusiasm. Bill Kotsch, a senior honors student, occupies a special place in the research program on the emotions. He has participated effectively since his sophomore year. Term papers on anxiety by Harold Simpson II and Robbi Slocum, and on depression by Stuart McCarthy and Robert Harris, were quite helpful.

Dorothy Timberlake, Business Manager, Department of Psychology, set up the bibliography, and she and Jackie Caldwell,

Acknowledgments

Administrative Assistant, have graciously and efficiently provided the support necessary for the preparation of the manuscript. Pat Burns, Sue Clark, Carol Darien, Penny Adgent, Pat Harris, and Debbie Keller helped with the typing and proofing.

CHAPTER ONE

The Emotions and Their Neurophysiological Substrates

An increasing number of psychologists and other behavioral scientists are accepting emotion as a legitimate field of inquiry. Nevertheless, much of the research in the area is fragmented, and different facets of emotion are sometimes presented as though they were the whole of it. In *The Face of Emotion* (Izard, 1971), I presented a comprehensive theory of emotion and personality together with supporting cross-cultural, developmental, and clinical evidence. Here, I shall review a few points that are essential to formulations and evidence contained in the present volume.

I. A WAY OF CONCEPTUALIZING THE EMOTIONS

The term "emotion" used in a general sense or without modifiers is necessarily imprecise. Yet, even as a general term it has usefulness. To describe a state or process as emotion distinguishes it from other general classes of phenomena such as cognition and locomotion. These latter terms are likewise imprecise. To say that a given process is "cognition" does not tell us whether it is perception, associative learning, thought, memory, or a combination of these and other types of cognition. Such imprecision does not render the term "cognition" useless. Rather, it means that theory and research in the area of cognition will require differentiation among facets and types of cognition. The case for the term "emotion" is similar. It may refer either to a discrete fundamental emotion or to a pattern or combination of emotions.

1

A. FUNDAMENTAL EMOTIONS

The fundamental emotions are interest, joy, surprise, distress, anger, disgust, contempt, shame (shyness, guilt), and fear. Each of these emotions has unique motivational properties of crucial importance to the individual and the species, and each adds its own special quality or significance to life experiences. Each emotion has an inherently adaptive function. They are termed fundamental because each of them has *(a)* a specific innately determined neural substrate, *(b)* a characteristic neuromuscular–expressive pattern, and *(c)* a distinct subjective or phenomenological quality. No one of these three facets constitutes emotion. Each is an emotion component. A complete emotion or complete emotion process requires all three, though socialization may greatly diminish the expressive pattern in both duration and intensity. In a sense, each fundamental emotion is a system made up of its three components and their interactions. The fundamental emotions have already been identified and defined empirically at the expressive and phenomenological levels (Izard, 1971). In the ensuing pages they will be further defined, particularly with respect to their interrelationships (emotion–emotion dynamics and patterning) and their relationship to certain nonemotional processes.

In addition to the three principal components of an emotion, there are a number of other organs and systems that become involved during emotion. Of particular importance are the endocrine, cardiovascular, and respiratory systems. For a long time it has been known that emotion is accompanied by changes in the autonomic nervous system and in the visceral organs (e.g., heart, blood vessels, glands) which it innervates. Unfortunately, a great deal of research has mistakenly treated autonomic–visceral processes as though they constituted emotion. Some eminent investigators who once did this do so no longer (e.g., Pribram, 1970), but many still do. The fact that autonomic–visceral processes accompany emotion does not mean that they define it. Some of them also accompany physical exertion. Under well-understood conditions, the fact that they accompany emotion may mean that they can serve as relatively reliable indicators of the presence of emotion. As we shall see later, the indicators in current use usually point to emotion in the general or imprecise sense rather than to a discrete fundamental emotion. At present there is only tentative evidence for discrete emotion-specific autonomic–visceral patterns, and we have this for only a few of the fundamental emotions. Autonomic–visceral patterns may be quite

2

helpful in the study of emotion in general and in the study of discrete emotion when it is possible to use other evidence, e.g., facial patterning and phenomenological self-report, to identify the particular fundamental emotion or emotions.

Two kinds of phenomena militate against the study of fundamental emotions separately. First, emotion tends to involve the whole organism rather than to remain a process confined to a single system. For example, the activation of sympathetic mechanisms that accompany one emotion may activate other sympathetic mechanisms that subserve other emotions. This point will· be discussed further in a later section. Second, emotions tend to occur in certain combinations or patterns. Discrete fundamental emotions undoubtedly occur in the life of an individual, but they probably exist separately for only a very short time before other emotions are activated. Moments of experience characterized by a single fundamental emotion are relatively rare in terms of the total time they occupy, and they are very difficult to obtain for sufficient duration and under conditions required for systematic study.

B. PATTERNS OF EMOTIONS

The *combinations* or *patterns of emotions* that will be dealt with most extensively in this book are anxiety and depression. These terms have been conceived in science and in popular thinking as unitary concepts and often viewed as discrete emotions. The theory and evidence to be presented in this book run counter to this conceptualization and favor the position that anxiety and depression are combinations or patterns of two or more fundamental emotions. The evidence also suggests that, while the fundamental emotions are the principal constituents, somatic and cognitive components are also involved. Cognitive components may be represented most effectively as attitudes, or psychological phenomena wherein emotion and cognition themselves join or interact.

It is tempting to simplify the nomenclature and refer to phenomena such as anxiety and depression as complex emotions. The problem with this is that "complex emotion" tends to signify a single though complicated process. It has the ring of entity and unity. To be accurate, the term "complex" should be used in this context only as a noun, as is the case for the terms "combination" or "pattern." In most cases, "combination" and "pattern" are preferred to "complex," since they imply greater possibility of independence among interacting parts. Thus, in the present theoretical framework,

3

it is preferable to speak of phenomena like anxiety as a *combination of emotions* or as a *pattern of emotions*. The awkwardness created by constant use of the preferred phrases, together with other language problems or deficits in this area, has led me to the ungrammatical use of "emotion" as a noun modifier. In this way, the slightly shorter terms such as *emotion pattern* may be used interchangeably with "pattern of emotions."

My theory suggests that certain emotions tend to interact, cycle, or alternate with sufficient regularity to be identified as relatively stable patterns. I have maintained that fundamental emotions have unique motivational–experiential characteristics. The occurrence of a particular emotion in a combination of emotions does not change its essential or genotypic properties, but its interactional effect and the consequent observable behavior may differ in different patterns. Fear in combination with interest produces alternating approach and avoidance behaviors. Fear in combination with guilt yields only avoidance or withdrawal behaviors. Anger in combination with contempt may produce destructive aggression, while anger in combination with interest may yield constructive criticism or other socially responsible and less apparently aggressive action. These illustrations may be somewhat oversimplified, but they point out how the organism's functioning in relation to a specific emotion (e.g., fear-related functioning) may result in different behaviors. Unless we are aware that the underlying genotypes (fear–interest combination versus fear–guilt combination) are different and that both fear and interest are motivational, we may look at the behavior and draw the wrong inference about *fear.*

Both the biological nature of the individual emotions and experiential learning in person–environment interactions help determine the characteristics of a particular pattern. The characteristics of a pattern are the qualities, intensities, and durations of the configural emotions. Emotion–emotion dynamics have been discussed extensively by Tomkins (1962, 1963), and the concepts of patterning, interaction, and mixing by Izard (1971). These concepts will be explored further and evaluated empirically in this book.

II. NEUROPHYSIOLOGICAL AND BIOCHEMICAL CONSIDERATIONS

Experts in neurophysiology and biochemistry generally agree that the internal processes associated with phenomena like anxiety and depression are not completely understood. While neither

4

discipline claims a panacea, both seem to have something to offer. However, in making this observation, I am not implying that we should consider neurochemical mechanisms and functions as the primary determinants or "causes" of emotions. I believe that under certain conditions they may be either first- or second-order determinants of emotions, but I doubt that ordinary cause–effect logic is applicable here, particularly if we are thinking in terms of simple linear relationships. Relationships among the cognitive, neurochemical, neuromuscular, and affective variables involved are highly complex. The relationships among emotion-related variables may even appear to be circular. Gellhorn (1965) found that hypothalamic reactivity, cortical arousal, muscle tone, and sympathic discharge were all positively intercorrelated. We can avoid the stigma of the term "circularity" and increase the precision of our formulations if we think of the variables in emotion as having *interactive* relationships.

Since emotion is a function of living organisms, we know it has neurochemical substrates, and both personal experience and scientific investigations tell us that experiential emotion has a variable accompaniment of bodily changes. Regardless of their place in a causal sequence, a knowledge of their role and their interactions with the other variables involved should help in the understanding and management of the emotions.

An understanding of the neurophysiological mechanisms and functions associated with the emotions requires a brief overview of the nervous system. (For a more detailed review see Gellhorn and Loofbourrow, 1963, and Gellhorn, 1968, two of the principal sources for the present summary.)

A. OVERALL ORGANIZATION OF THE NERVOUS SYSTEM

The nervous system consists of the brain, the spinal cord, and the peripheral nerves. The brain and spinal cord make up the central nervous system (CNS), sometimes called the neuraxis.

The peripheral nervous system consists of 12 pairs of cranial nerves extending from the brain and 31 pairs of spinal nerves extending from the spinal cord. Peripheral nerves subserve afferent or sensory functions, conducting impulses from specialized peripheral receptors to the CNS, and efferent or motor functions, conducting impulses from the CNS to the voluntary striate muscles of the skeletal-muscular system and to the smooth muscles of the viscera and glands.

The nervous system has segmental and suprasegmental parts and, more importantly for our purposes, a division into somatic and autonomic systems. For the study of emotions, we shall be most concerned with certain parts of the brain—the limbic lobe, the hypothalamus, and the areas of the neocortex most closely associated with these structures—and with the autonomic nervous system.

B. SEGMENTAL AND SUPRASEGMENTAL PARTS

The CNS may be divided functionally into segmental and suprasegmental parts, in keeping with the fact that a vertebrate animal is an organization of segments. Segmental action of the vervous system consists of receptor–effector links or reflex arcs that are confined to one segment of the organism. Both the smooth and striate muscles involved in emotion are regulated in part by such reflex arcs. However, in the primates and most of all in man, "the segmental centers have come to depend heavily on impulses from other parts of the central nervous system, particularly the brain, for facilitation [Gellhorn & Loofbourrow, 1963, p. 24]."

Viewed in evolutionary perspective, the decrease in independence in segmental functions in vertebrates has been accompanied by a dramatic increase in encephalization (brain growth). This line of development has not only moved the important centers of action and control upward to the head but, at the same time, has moved them forward. The most important receptors and sensory organs have moved closer together and to the front of the head, the face. These developments have placed the face and the newest part of the brain in close proximity. One important consequence of all this has been the emergence of the face not only as the site of the human being's most highly developed sense organs but as the undisputed supreme center of social communication.

The nerves that conduct impulses to and from the face are examples of cranial nerves. The facial or VIIth cranial nerve is primarily the efferent or motor nerve whose branches innervate all the superficial musculature of the face. The VIIth nerve and the facial muscles are immediately responsible for the emotion-specific patterns that constitute the behavioral-expressive component of the emotions and that furnish the principal communicative cues that inform observers of the emotional condition of the behaving person. The trigeminal or Vth cranial nerve is the afferent or sensory nerve for the face. It furnishes the brain with feedback on the emotion

6

pattern in the facial muscles. Since theory and evidence indicate that this is the most highly differentiated feedback available to the brain, it follows that this feedback is crucial in the mediation of the experiential or phenomenological component of a discrete or specific emotion. (For a further discussion of this point see Izard, 1971.)

In a sense, the facial and trigeminal nerves are segmental. They are confined entirely to one segment, the head. However, since they are involved in both peripheral and central aspects of the emotion process, they also have suprasegmental characteristics. Their emotion-related functions undoubtedly result in the recruitment of other neural structures involved in the complete emotion process.

Emotion-related tension in the muscles of the torso and limbs may be partially a segmental process, particularly in cases of emotional disorder. This may help account for the fact that such tension seems so unreasonable and intractable. Drugs furnish only temporary relief and may do so via central processes without real change in the tone of the affected muscles. Jacobson (1938, 1964, 1967) has pioneered special (nondrug) relaxation techniques that have proved effective. Some of these techniques have been employed with success in behavior therapy. I have presented a system of therapy and emotion control that combines some of the techniques of Jacobson and behavior therapy in the framework of differential emotion theory (Izard, 1971, Chap. 15).

C. THE SOMATIC AND AUTONOMIC NERVOUS SYSTEM

Another functional division of the nervous system is that between the neural structures of the skeletal-muscular system and the visceral-glandular system. The former involves the striped or striate muscles responsible for posture, locomotion, and all external body movements included in environmental exploration and manipulation, and in work and play. The somatic nervous system plays an important role in emotion, since it innervates the facial and postural muscles that execute the expressive patterns of the emotions. These patterns are highly important both as a source of feedback to the brain in the intraorganism emotion process and in interorganism emotion communication. The visceral-glandular system involves the muscles of the iris of the eye, and of the heart, blood vessels, gut, and glands—the internal organs vitally related to such life processes as homeostasis (maintaining chemical equilibrium), metabolism and nutrition, energy mobilization, and other emotion-related functions.

7

The somatic nervous system is clearly divided from the autonomic only in the case of motor or efferent nerves. The nerves which innervate the muscles of posture, locomotion, and limb movement are strictly somatic. Somatic motor neurons have one other unique characteristic. Each of these neurons extends from the CNS where its cell body is located to the skeletal muscle fibers which it innervates.

There is no sharp somatic–autonomic distinction among sensory nerves. Afferent nerves may branch out to both striate and smooth muscle.

D. FUNCTIONS OF THE AUTONOMIC SYSTEM

The autonomic nervous system enjoys some degree of functional independence. However, as Gellhorn and Loofbourrow (1963) observed, it is not as autonomous as its name implies. Its functions are often influenced by the somatic system, sometimes quite markedly, as in the case of striate muscle relaxation procedures.

The autonomic nervous system not only innervates a different type of muscle than the somatic system; it has other structural and functional differences as well. In contrast to the type of single-neuron innervation of the somatic system, innervation by the autonomic system always involves a chain of two neurons in the link between the CNS and the smooth muscle of the organs innervated by the autonomic nervous system. This structural characteristic may contribute to the relative slowness of response of the internal organs. For example, in emotion, the striate muscles of the face and body respond much more rapidly than do visceral–glandular structures. Similarly, the return of the latter to base line functioning is much slower. The two-neuron type of innervation may also contribute directly or indirectly to the relatively stronger tendency of sympathetic neurons to recruit other neurons into the action. It is well established that, once a single organ innervated by the sympathetic nervous system is stimulated, activity in other organs innervated by the sympathetic nervous system usually changes also. This sometimes gives the impression that the autonomic nervous system functions as a whole. The apparent tendency to wholistic functioning has made it extremely difficult for investigators to study the various autonomic functions separately, for purposes of determining their individual roles in different emotions.

II. Neurophysiological and Biochemical Considerations

While the tendency of the sympathetic system to act wholistically is observable under certain conditions, it is not correct to conclude that the sympathetic system or even one of its major subdivisions always functions as a whole. For example, it is quite possible for a part of the sympathetic system to act relatively independently of, and perhaps counter to, another part (Gellhorn, personal communication).

Since the advent of the James–Lange theory, considering particularly the emphasis given by Lange, the autonomic nervous system has traditionally been considered the nervous system of the emotions. The obvious involvement of the autonomic nervous system in emotion processes has kept the tradition alive. Even many investigators who no longer look to the autonomic nervous system for determinants of emotion still turn to autonomic functions for indicants of emotion. With some exceptions, indicia that are specific to a particular individual emotion are very difficult to identify. This does not mean that there are no emotion-specific neurochemical substrates. More likely it means that a particular single emotion in isolation from other emotions is rarely obtained in the laboratory, and when it is obtained it probably does not remain the only emotion for very long. Many factors, including the character of the autonomic nervous system, converge to make emotional experience a combination or pattern of emotions rather than the "pure" experience of any single emotion. It is possible to have one emotion relatively dominant for a period of time, and this probably accounts for the occasional success in neurochemical studies that attempt to differentiate between emotions. One way to increase the likelihood of success in such studies would be to set up conditions wherein the two target emotions have relatively nonoverlapping patterns.

The concept of the patterning of emotions will be discussed in subsequent chapters. We shall see that at the phenomenological level, or the level in which emotion can be symbolized and reported by the subject, we have strong evidence that human experience is most typically characterized by a patterning of emotions rather than by a single emotion. This kind of evidence is consistent with the known characteristics of the structure and functioning of the autonomic nervous system, which is responsible for a number of things involved in emotion and in maintaining emotion processes over time.

1. The Sympathetic and Parasympathetic Divisions of the Autonomic Nervous System. The autonomic nervous system has two functional subdivisions, the sympathetic and parasympathetic systems. According to Gellhorn and Loofbourrow (1963, p. 29), the contrasting locations of the ganglia provide the most important anatomical distinction between the two systems. Most of the ganglia of the sympathetic system are close to the spinal cord in the thoracic and lumbar regions. The ganglia of the parasympathetic system lie near or within the effector organs themselves.

This anatomical difference undoubtedly contributes to some of the differences in functional characteristics of the two systems. For one thing, it suggests that the parasympathetic system is relatively more segmental in character, being under less direct and immediate influence of the CNS. This would mean that emotions involving predominantly the sympathetic system (e.g., fear) might be expected to respond more readily to a brain function like cognition (appraisal, memory, reasoning) than would an emotion (e.g., distress) involving predominantly the parasympathetic system. Indeed, our everyday experience tells us that fear usually passes more readily than distress. Distress, as seen in intense sadness or grief, changes relatively slowly. Similarly, clinical evidence indicates that fear-related emotional disturbances (e.g., anxieties, phobias) yield much more readily to relationship or predominantly verbal (cognitive) psychotherapy and conditioning–learning techniques than do distress-related disorders (e.g., depressions). Even the behavior therapy technique of desensitization, which is actually heavily dependent on cognitive input and on relaxation of somatically innervated and voluntarily controlled muscles, works much better with anxieties than with depressions.

The biochemistry of the two systems demonstrates another important distinction between the sympathetic and parasympathetic systems. The difference is in the hormonal or chemical message required for the transmission of neural impulses. The integration of the various body processes into meaningful patterns of experience and behavior requires both nervous and hormonal-chemical messages. Hormones play a crucial role in neural transmission at the synapse, the structure which connects one neuron to another. While the end-knobs of some neurons may secrete their own excitatory or inhibitory chemical transmitter, much neural activity is known to depend on hormones from the endocrine system. A case in point is the sympathetic nervous system. The principal chemical transmitter of the sympathetic system is noradrenaline, a derivative of the medulla of the adrenal gland. By virtue of this fact, sympathetic transmission is said to be adrenergic.

The parasympathetic system secretes its own chemical transmitter, acetylcholine. In this way, too, the parasympathetic system is relatively more segmental and autonomous. These characteristics undoubtedly contribute to some of the observable differences between parasympathetic and sympathetic emotion processes. The parasympathetic system is said to be cholinergic.

We have already noted that the autonomic nervous system tends toward general rather than specific action. This is more characteristic of the sympathetic division than the parasympathetic. Stimulation of the sympathetic system has more widespread effects than is the case for the parasympathetic system. Stimulation of the sympathetic system leads to an increase in adrenomedullary hormones, constriction of abdominal vessels with consequent inhibition of activity in the gastrointestinal tract, and an increase in blood pressure, pupil dilation, contraction of the nictitating membrane, and piloerection.

2. The Autonomic Nervous System and the Emotion Process. Of greatest interest to the purposes of this book is the relationship of the autonomic nervous system to emotion. While it has long been known that autonomic activity is concomitant with emotion, we still have much to learn about the relationships between autonomic functions and discrete emotions. I prefer to think of the autonomic nervous system as part of the structure underlying the emotion process. The conception of the autonomic nervous system as playing a role in a *process* gets us away from linear cause–effect logic. Yet I think it is worthwhile to conceptualize patterns of autonomic activity for each emotion. I believe this in spite of the fact that I also strongly believe that emotions most typically occur in patterns. Even in patterns, a single emotion may be dominant. Knowledge of the neurology and biochemistry of the "dominant" emotion should prove theoretically and clinically useful.

Although we cannot describe many emotion-specific autonomic patterns, some relationships between the autonomic nervous system and emotion are apparently fairly well established. Available evidence suggests that the sympathetic system dominates in fear. Observational and experimental evidence have shown that fear is accompanied by such sympathetic effects as facial pallor, constriction of blood vessels, and reduction of activity in the gastrointestinal tract. Sympathetic effects that anyone can easily observe, even in relatively mild fear or apprehension, are sweating of the palms and dryness of the mouth.

11

In contrast, the parasympathetic system dominates in distress—feelings of sadness, dejection, and defeat. Tears, part of the prototypic distress response of crying, result from increased parasympathetic activation of the lacrimal glands. Distress is also accompanied by other parasympathetic effects such as decrease in blood pressure and heart rate and increase in tone and activity of the gastrointestinal tract. Distress is also characterized by a loss of tone in the striate muscles. When one feels sad or defeated, the face sags and the body becomes limp. The loss of tone in the muscles of expression and action, and the consequent feeling of droopiness, are evidence of decreased sympathetic activity, which may be viewed as a reciprocal or coordinate function of the increased and dominant activity of the parasympathetic system.

While the fundamental emotions of fear and distress appear to be associated primarily with sympathetic and parasympathetic activity, respectively, all emotions are not necessarily so closely identified with only one of the two systems. In addition to opposing functions and reciprocal relations that may always be present, both systems may be actively involved in certain fundamental emotions. And surely both are involved in many of the patterns of emotions that characterize day-to-day life.

Some evidence suggests that the fundamental emotion of anger involves both sympathetic and parasympathetic activity. Sympathetic discharges effect increased heart rate and blood pressure and a reduction of blood flow through the kidney. These actions are part of what has been called the emergency response, the preparation for attack or defense. They mobilize available energy by increasing blood supply to the muscles of action. At the same time, anger is accompanied by parasympathetic discharges that increase blood flow and secretory activity in mucous membranes of the gastrointestinal tract. Blood flow may also be increased in the face (flushing), in the bladder, and, for females, in the vagina (Gellhorn & Loofbourrow, 1963, p. 72).

The net effect of the coordinated actions of the sympathetic and parasympathetic systems in anger enables the organism to defend itself or to attack the threatening agent with increased vigor (sympathetic discharges) while continuing the gastrointestinal business of digestion, which is essential for maintenance and endurance of the organism. Conceivably, this arrangement came about in the evolutionary process as a result of the organism's having to defend itself at eating time, which was not always scheduled according to contemporary conventions but, rather, whenever the hunt was successful. This could help explain why our contemporary rigid schedule of eating, together with our unpredictable periods of anger, resentment, or hostility, lead to increased gastrointestinal secretions at times when all they have to work on is the mucous tissue itself. The result reverses the intended maintenance and endurance functions and increases the likelihood of tissue deterioration and debilitation in the form of lacerations and ulcers.

Joy, like anger, probably involves both sympathetic and parasympathetic activity. Parasympathetic discharges cause the often observable increased vascularity in the face (flushing) during joy. When we "jump with joy" we are experiencing the direct and/or indirect effects of sympathetic discharge. In mild or more passive states of joy, the parasympathetic system probably dominates, while in more active states of joy there is increased, if not dominant, sympathetic activity. Since parasympathetic discharges increase vascular and secretory activity in the gastrointestinal tract, eating in a mildly joyful mood is a happy combination indeed.

At least in some situations, "jumping with joy" may also signify the presence of other emotions or attitudes. We may literally or metaphorically jump joyfully over or on a defeated opponent, in which case joy and anger may be mixed. Also, the smile of triumph and the sneer of contempt may have psychological similarity as well as physiological and physiognomic–expressive similarity.

In contrast to anger, we have noted that fear is accompanied by predominantly sympathetic activity. In anger, the two systems coordinate. The sympathetic system mobilizes energy for environmentally directed action, primarily by its influence on the cardiovascular processes. Concomitantly, the parasympathetic system increases its organismic-support activities by its influence on gastrointestinal processes. In fear, the sympathetic system predominates in both cardiovascular and gastrointestinal processes. This suggests that a fear situation is even more an emergency than an anger situation and calls for more radical energy mobilization and action. Thus there are both decreased blood flow to the gastrointestinal tract and increased blood supply to the muscles that effect action in the external environment. The decrease in blood flow to the gastrointestinal tract minimizes the energy used by this important internal process and maximizes the available energy for what could be a life-or-death struggle with outside forces. The frightened organism, except where extreme fear paralyzes, is optimally prepared for flight.

Or, if it is cornered, it has maximum strength for a fight, though its endurance might not be as great as in anger because of the slowing down of nutritional processes.

For a contest or combat that tests both strength and endurance, a combination or alternation of anger with fear would be optimal; the fear phase provides maximum bursts of strength, the anger phase facilitates the processes required for endurance. In some situations, there may be advantages in eliciting dynamically related additional emotions such as contempt, often associated with anger in human experience, and interest-excitement, which readily alternates with fear because of its similar neurophysiological and psychological characteristics.

E. THE LIMBIC LOBE

Of great importance in emotion is the limbic lobe (sometimes called the rhinencephalon, limbic system, limbic ring), a complex cortical structure and one much older phylogenetically than the neocortex. The limbic lobe forms a border around the rostral brain stem at the hilum of the cerebral hemispheres. The limbic lobe is virtually submerged by the neocortex and white matter of the hemispheres. As its topographical position implies, it has vast interconnections with the neocortex (upper brain centers) on the one hand and the subcortical structures (lower brain centers) and the brainstem reticular formation on the other.

In an early contribution to the neurophysiology of emotion, Papez (1937) drew attention to the limbic area. He proposed that the hippocampus and the gyrus cinguli, together with the hypothalamus and their interconnections (the Papez circuit), constituted the anatomical basis of the emotions. Partly because of the interrelationships between the limbic lobe, hypothalamus, and autonomic system, Papez has typically been identified with the visceral theory of emotion. This theory sees the visceral-glandular activities not as accompaniments of emotion but as emotion proper. As Pribram (1970) pointed out, this is not an altogether correct classification of Papez's position. Papez (1951) saw the role of the limbic and midbrain areas in posture and in other aspects of somatic expression as essential functions in emotion. He drew explicit similarities between his position and Bull's (1951) motor attitude theory of emotion.

According to MacLean (1949), the principal subdivisions of the limbic lobe (or "visceral brain" as MacLean called it) are the

14

hippocampal gyrus, the fornix, the parasplenial gyrus, the precuneus, the cingulate gyrus, the amygdala, the subcallosal gyrus, and the pyriform lobe. The mammillary body of the hypothalamus and the anterior thalamic nuclei are subcortical structures closely associated with the limbic lobe.

Of importance in understanding the roles and functions of the limbic lobe is the fact that the system of limbic circuits receives most of its afferent influx not from the classical "specific" afferent pathways but from diffuse pathways from the reticular formation and spinal cord. This may be further evidence of the tendency for emotional circuitry to produce general or global effects.

MacLean (1954, 1968, 1970) has done extensive investigations on the structures and systems that he has called the "limbic ring." He maintains that these brain centers constitute the neural circuitry in emotion and emotional expression and control the bodily changes in emotion processes.

In his latest statement, MacLean (1970) delineated subdivisions of the limbic ring that he thought served distinct purposes. The lower part of the ring, which is fed by fibers descending from the median forebrain bundle and olfactory bulb through the amygdala and which contains the hippocampus, serves feelings and emotions related to survival functions, e.g., feeding, fighting, and self-protection. The upper part of the limbic ring, which is fed by fibers from the median forebrain and olfactory bulb via the septum and which contains the cingulate gyrus, serves emotions related to social and sexual functions. MacLean reported evidence suggesting that neural perturbations or eruptions in the limbic system could produce symptoms observed in psychotic processes such as depersonalization and paranoid states.

In Arnold's (1960b) view, the limbic system, which constitutes a functional division of the brain, consists of the subcallosal, cingulate, retrosplenial, and hippocampal gyri and the island of Reil. She maintained that the limbic cortex is part of a more complex functional unit, the estimative system. The limbic lobe component of the estimative system mediates the experience of liking or disliking, a vital step in the sequence of events that lead to emotion. The limbic lobe is also responsible for the appraisal of objects as harmful or beneficial. The hippocampal and cingulate gyri of the limbic lobe play a role in the mediation of the "felt impulses to definite action," which is Arnold's definition of emotion proper. Arnold proposed that the hippocampal gyrus of the limbic lobe functions in the mediation of the visceral-glandular activities that accompany emo-

15

tion, emotion expression, and emotion-related action. The hippo-campus, via its role in memory, also plays a part in the appraisal of the impulse to action and in the choice of action. However, Arnold indicated that integrated or directed action was a function of the motor and premotor areas of the neocortex, together with the extrapyramidal structures involved in body movement.

Pribram (1970) has interpreted some of the evidence from his laboratory as essentially supporting and extending Arnold's (1960b) formulations of the role of certain limbic structures. He indicated that the hippocampus together with the amygdala con-stitute the anatomical basis for an important appraisal function. The amygdala provides a kind of sensitivity "to what is relevant, salient, correct—to what is the right response to make in a problem [p. 49]." The hippocampus helps determine when something has become non-salient. The two structures together provide for a sequence of pro-cesses "which allow us to appraise the amount of uncertainty [p. 51]." This is very much like Arnold's notion of "appraisal of the impulse to action" and "choice of action" that she attributed in part to the hippocampus.

Papez, and to a lesser extent MacLean, may have over-emphasized the role of the limbic lobe and underemphasized the role of the neocortex in emotion. Both Arnold (1960b) and Gellhorn (1968) have suggested that the neocortex is ultimately responsible for the subjective experience of emotion. MacLean's more recent work (1968, 1970) has suggested that relationships between the visual cortex and the posterior hippocampal gyrus may help us understand the processes involved in visually elicited emotions. Gell-horn (1968) maintained that the imminence of the role of the neocortex is evident from the prolonged afterdischarge following emotional arousal and the goal-directedness of emotional behavior.

F. THE HYPOTHALAMUS AND ITS INTERACTIONS WITH THE NEOCORTEX AND LIMBIC LOBE

The hypothalamus has long been recognized as the most important subcortical structure in the emotion process. Gellhorn has consistently marshalled evidence and arguments to support the hy-pothesis that the hypothalamus is important in several facets of emotion, including emotional integration. He holds that its position of preeminence is due to its unique relationship to the rest of the nervous system. The hypothalamus also has a unique relationship with the endocrine system, particularly via its role in the functioning of the pituitary gland.

The early contributions of Bard (see Gellhorn & Loofbourrow, 1963, p. 59) showed that the hypothalamus was essential for the full expression of rage. In human beings, I consider rage a high intensity of the fundamental emotion of anger. The full *expression* of rage has been observed in decorticate animals, but only fragments of the expression appeared after removal of brain areas that included the hypothalamus. The common application of the term "sham rage" to rage expression in decorticate animals is misleading. The term should not be taken to mean that the rage, or rather the rage expression, was not genuine. To be more precise, we should abandon the term "sham rage" and describe the response of the decorticate animal to rage elicitors as the *expressive component* of rage. In this description, there is no implication that the *felt* or *experiential component* of the emotion should be present. Rather, it recognizes the fact that one or two of the three components of emotion can exist without the complete emotion process (see Izard, 1971, Chap. 7). In the decorticate animal, the felt or experiential component is missing since the absence of the neocortex precludes the integrated emotional feeling or experience.

The strategic location of the hypothalamus at the base of the brain, behind the optic chiasma and above the pituitary (the "master" gland of the body), bespeaks its powerful regulatory role in the neurophysiological functioning of the organism. Gellhorn and Loofbourrow (1963) thought there was probably no organ of greater importance to the well-being of the individual.

The hypothalamus is the chief center for the control of the autonomic nervous system. The sympathetic system is activated by stimulation of the posterior and lateral regions of the hypothalamus, and parasympathetic effects are obtained by stimulation of the anterior parts.

Hypothalamically induced sympathetic effects are confined to excitation of visceral organs. Gellhorn (cited in Gellhorn & Loofbourrow, 1963, p. 35) has demonstrated that stimulation of the posterior hypothalamus can lead to sympathetic effects that are inhibitory in the gut and bladder and excitatory in the cardiovascular system. It is the sympathetically induced adrenomedullary secretion that effects the inhibitory action on the bladder. While different sympathetic and parasympathetic effects can be obtained by stimulation of different areas of the hypothalamus, Gellhorn and Loof-

17

bourrow were careful to point out that the sympathetic and parasympathetic zones overlap and that stimulation of the hypothalamus often leads to mixed effects.

There is considerable evidence that hypothalamic discharges affect the somatic nervous system as well as the autonomic nervous system. The variety of motor responses accompanying emotion in animals (e.g., the angry cat's hissing, growling, biting, and unsheathing of claws) can be mediated by hypothalamic activity, as demonstrated in experiments with decorticate animals. Although the motor responses of anger contrast sharply with those of fear (e.g., crouching and mewing), the latter are apparently accompanied by highly similar predominantly sympathetic discharges. This distinction between these emotions at the somatic or behavioral–expressive level and presumed lack of clear differentiation at the hypothalamic–autonomic level led Gellhorn and Loofbourrow to conclude that the somatic system composed of the somatic nervous system and striate muscles has a greater variety of emotion-specific patterns than does the autonomic system consisting of the autonomic nervous system and viscera. A number of other theorists and investigators have agreed with this conclusion (see Izard, 1971).

It is now well established that the striate muscles of the face, innervated by the somatic nervous system, are intimately involved in emotion (Izard, 1971). While these muscles are largely under the control of cortical centers, their actions in emotional expression in human beings are undoubtedly influenced directly or indirectly by downward discharges of the hypothalamus. Also, hypothalamic discharges probably affect in some way the different postural attitudes of the emotions and the well-known changes in somatic muscle tone (see Jacobson, 1967) that occur in emotion and relaxation.

Upward discharges of the hypothalamus probably play a role in all the foregoing hypothalamically influenced activities. The upward discharges from the hypothalamus tend to activate the whole cerebral cortex, which means that virtually all functions would be affected to some extent. This brings us back to an observation made early in this chapter: Emotion tends to influence the whole organism and all its functions and actions. More particularly, the effects of upward hypothalamic discharges on the motor area of the cortex lead to increased pyramidal discharges and hence to intensification of the actions of the organism (Gellhorn & Loofbourrow, 1963, p. 76).

While the hypothalamus exerts an excitatory influence on the cerebral hemispheres, the cerebral hemispheres in turn exert an inhibitory influence on the hypothalamus. The frontal cortex has the principal role in inhibiting hypothalamic activity. It is this inhibitory function of the cortex that misled a number of theorists to the conclusion that the emotions were mainly lower-order disruptive phenomena which in noble *Homo sapiens* should be eliminated from higher-order mental processes (appraising, thinking, remembering, reasoning) and tightly controlled in relation to all human functions. Among other things, this erroneous view of the place of the emotions in the individual and in the species overlooked the fact that the cortex also excites the hypothalamus. Hence the proudest product of brain evolution, the neocortex, may *instigate* emotion. Gellhorn and Loofbourrow (1963, p. 77) cited an experiment which demonstrated that sensory impressions experimentally induced directly on the cortex could result in emotional excitement.

Crucial to an understanding of limbic-hypothalamic inter-actions is the fact that limbic forebrain structures mediate a large part of the neural influx received by the hypothalamus. A number of experiments have demonstrated the close relationships between units of the limbic lobe (e.g., fornix, hippocampus, amygdala, cingulate gyrus) and the hypothalamus (see Gellhorn & Loofbourrow, 1963, pp. 60-65).

Stimulation of the fornix where it penetrates the hypo-thalamus evokes manifestations of rage. Stimulation of the hippo-campus, which has many interconnections with the hypothalamus, has been found to lower the rage threshold in cats. Other studies (Gellhorn & Loofbourrow, 1963) found that well-organized angry defense or attack behavior was sometimes evoked by stimula-tion of the hippocampal area near the amygdala. In the cat, the hippocampal–amygdaloid interconnections apparently form the neural substrate for a general defense pattern consisting of growling, hissing, and flight. Gellhorn and Loofbourrow (1963, p. 63) cited two studies which reported that stimulation of the amygdala in human beings led to subjectively felt or experiential fear. Consistent with this finding, ablation of the amygdala and overlying cortex in cats led to increased sexual and other pleasurable behavior and decreased aggressiveness and fear.

G. HYPOTHALAMIC–PITUITARY INTERACTIONS

As already noted, the hypothalamus and pituitary glands have important interconnections and interrelations. Indeed, Gellhorn and Loofbourrow (1963) concluded that the hypothalamus itself

19

elaborates certain hormones which "in large measure determine the secretory activity of both the anterior and posterior pituitary and thereby profoundly influence the endocrine balance of the entire organism [p. 85]." The anterior pituitary secretes a "trophic" (nourishing) hormone for each of the glands of the endocrine system. In this way the pituitary exercises a high degree of control over the growth and normal activity of the various glands of internal secretion. The influence of the hypothalamic–pituitary interactions on the emotions and emotion-related activities are obviously of considerable importance, particularly in regulating the intensity and duration of emotion processes.

H. THE ERGOTROPIC AND TROPHOTROPIC SYSTEMS

Gellhorn (1970) has recently described two general neurophysiological systems—the ergotrophic and the trophotropic—which provide a broader framework for the differentiation of the emotions. (Gellhorn attributed the original delineation of these systems to W. R. Hess.) The ergotropic system mediates the more energetic and vigorous organismic and organism–environment interactions. For example, extreme and active joy as well as rage are mediated by this system. The ergotropic system is characterized by sympathetic dominance, cerebral excitation, cortical desynchronization, and increased activity and tone of the striate muscles. Ergotropic effects can be obtained by stimulation of the posterior hypothalamus (or by its release via removal of the cortex), the reticular formation, certain areas of the limbic lobe, and by visceral receptors and chemoreceptors that activate the posterior hypothalamus. In general, frequent and strong stimuli are more likely to evoke ergotropic effects.

The trophotropic system mediates those functions concerned with comfort, maintenance, drive pleasures (feeding, sex), and recuperation of the organism. The trophotropic system is characterized by parasympathetic dominance, sleeplike potentials, cortical synchronization, and a decrease in activity and tone of the striate muscles. Trophotropic effects may be obtained by stimulation of the anterior hypothalamus, septum, hippocampus, intralaminar nuclei of the thalamus, or the caudate nucleus. The basal forebrain, the orbital surface of the frontal lobe, is very important in the trophotropic system. Stimulating it directly or by way of the IXth and Xth cranial nerves produces trophotropic effects. These effects are also produced reflexively via somatic and visceral receptors. By comparison with the ergotropic system, the trophotropic system responds to weaker, lower-frequency stimulation. Activity of the neural mechanisms of the trophotropic system tends to produce relaxation of the striate muscle system and to sustain and enhance the drive pleasures associated with the satisfaction of hunger, contact, and sex needs. With respect to the emotions, mild or passive states of enjoyment as well as distress are associated with trophotropic dominance.

Certain of the fundamental emotions are apparently associated primarily with one or the other of the two systems. As we have indicated, the ergotropic system predominates in fear, extreme joy, and anger, while the trophotropic system predominates in mild or passive joy and distress. In other emotions, both systems are quite active, with neither being clearly and continuously dominant.

Of course, both systems may be said to be involved in all emotions through their reciprocal relationship. Some emotions seem to involve first one system then the other, depending on the organism–environment interaction. I have already noted that anger involves both the sympathetic and parasympathetic nervous systems, aspects of the ergotropic and trophotropic systems respectively. The degree to which anger is ergotropic may depend on the degree to which the organism is engaged in defense or attack behaviors on the one hand, and fulfilling maintenance needs while sustaining a readiness-for-action attitude on the other.

Gellhorn and Loofbourrow (1963) indicated that the sympathetic system dominated in fear; this supports the notion of ergotropic dominance. However, in a more recent publication, Gellhorn (1970) said, "Sudden fear elicits mainly trophotropic effects (often followed by compensatory discharges of the ergotropic system) ... [p. 71]." It is as though suddenness of onset is a determining factor. I find this puzzling. It seems rather difficult to conceptualize measureable differences in the onset of an emotion like fear, the activation of which, according to Tomkins (1962), is distinguished from that of other emotions by the steepness of the gradient (suddenness) of stimulation. Tomkins suggested that surprise, or startle, was activated by the steepest gradient of all, and he characterized it as a channel-clearing or resetting affect. In view of this, I suggest that the trophotropic effects which Gellhorn observed may have been associated not with "sudden" fear but with surprise or startle—a state in which organismic activity is temporarily halted or slowed, as would be the case with trophotropic dominance. If the object which activated surprise or startle proved to be frightening, then the ergotropic system would come into play. A surprise–fear sequence would explain how both the trophotropic and ergotropic systems could be called into play in a very brief span of time, with each subserving a discrete fundamental emotion.

Of course, there remain many puzzling problems. Is fear that sustains flight and fear that virtually paralyzes the skeletal muscles and immobilizes the organism dominated by one and the same system? The same question can be asked for active and passive joy and for mild anger and rage, though as already indicated there is some evidence that different systems are involved in these latter within-emotion distinctions.

The extent to which the concepts of ergotropic and trophotropic systems will help in advancing a differential neurophysiology of the emotions remains a challenge for empirical investigation. At the present time, the wisest course may be to expect one-system dominance in certain emotions and two-system involvement in others. In the latter case, the search for the pattern of interaction and balance of the two systems will be important. Considering the wholistic nature of emotion and the psychobiological unity of the person, I believe that the concept of ergotropic–trophotropic interactional patterns may be the best framework for structuring empirical investigations.

I. CORTICAL INTEGRATION
AND THE PSYCHOBIOLOGICAL UNITY OF THE PERSON

It is useful to remind ourselves that while man feels, thinks, and acts, he is not three beings, nor does he possess three totally independent mechanisms for accomplishing these three types of functioning. He is one being. And in the adaptive, effectively functioning person, feeling, thinking, and acting are smoothly integrated. This penultimate of integration is accomplished by the intricate and harmonious interactions of many organs and systems, but the crucial integrative mechanism is the phylogenetically newest part of man's brain—the neocortex. (The neocortex is the top layer of gray matter covering the cerebral hemispheres.)

Emotion itself, like thinking and acting, is also a correlate of the interactions of the chemical and electrical products and activities of numerous organs and systems. However, as in thinking and acting, in the experiencing of a qualitatively distinct fundamental emotion, the neocortex is the ultimate integrator. Before final integration of an emotional experience in the neocortex, many other mechanisms are involved.

J. THE BIOLOGICAL STUDY OF DISCRETE EMOTIONS AND PATTERNS OF EMOTIONS

Before concluding this chapter, I should like to point out an element of uncertainty in some of the evidence and interpretations that have been presented. While some theoretical and empirical evidence support the assumption that each fundamental emotion has its own characteristic nervous and biochemical substrate, most of the experiments on this theme have not had careful controls or monitors to assure us that the measured physiological activity was a function of a single emotion. The frequent occurrence of patterns of emotions, the highly complex cortical–limbic–hypothalamic interactions, the sensitivity of the anterior–posterior hypothalamic balance or relationship, and the intricacies of sympathetic–parasympathetic interactions call for great care and patience in the search for emotion-specific neural and biochemical patterns. The pattern for a single emotion may be very complex, representing cortical, limbic, hypothalamic, sympathetic, and parasympathetic activity. The pattern for interacting emotions would be even more complex.

Yet, if all the preceding factors are taken into account as well as possible, the search for neurochemical patterns may be a worthwhile challenge. It will be essential to seek equal precision in neurophysiological and psychological measuring. Careful control and monitoring of the experiential–phenomenological component of emotion should go hand in hand with the greatest possible precision in neurophysiological measures. It is possible that considerable progress can be made by dealing forthrightly with the frequently occurring phenomena of emotion–emotion interactions and patterns of emotions, seeking to identify relatively common or stable patterns and considering the physiological measures as a function of the combination of emotions in the pattern. By comparing partially overlapping combinations or patterns we may be able to assay single emotions. Techniques such as hypnotic induction, carefully structured imaging, and others may enable us to study discrete emotions. Some work may best be done with children. Even under optimal conditions, the single emotion is likely to hold the field for only a very brief time, and measuring procedures should be adapted accordingly.

III. SUMMARY

This work builds on existing theory and evidence that differentiate a number of fundamental emotions subserved by innate neural mechanisms. Each emotion has neurophysiological, neuro-muscular-expressive, and phenomenological components, and each has unique motivational value and significance for the individual.

A distinction is made between the concepts of fundamental emotions and patterns of emotions. Patterns consist of two or more fundamental emotions in combination and interaction. Discrete emotions retain their essential genotypical characteristics when they occur in patterns. However, behavior related to specific emotions may differ in different combinations. For example, fear-related behavior may differ depending on the emotion with which fear is combining and interacting. Day-to-day experiences are typically characterized by patterns of emotions, and some patterns occur with sufficient regularity to warrant their study as identifiable phenomena.

Emotions, like all functions of the organism, have neural and biochemical substrates. I do not consider neural and biochemical substrates as emotion or as "cause" or "determinants" of emotion. Their natural or spontaneous functioning may instigate emotion, but in general they are viewed as the neuroanatomical and biochemical bases of emotion.

The nervous system is divided into segmental and supraseg-mental parts. Some emotion components and emotion-related mechanisms have segmental properties; others have suprasegmental properties. In man, there are probably few if any strictly segmental mechanisms in emotion.

The nervous system also can be divided into somatic and autonomic systems. In my theory, both are important to the emotions. The somatic system innervates the facial-postural striate muscles that are involved in the expressive component of emotion and in the important face–brain feedback process. The autonomic nervous system innervates visceral and glandular organs whose activities typically accompany emotion and emotional behavior.

The autonomic nervous system can be divided into sympathetic and parasympathetic divisions. Existing theory and evidence suggest that there are some fairly reliable relationships between activity in the autonomic nervous system and specific emotions. Certain emotions seem to be primarily associated with sympathetic activity while others are primarily associated with parasympathetic activity. A number of emotions involve both sympathetic and parasympathetic activity, and perhaps all of them do to some extent either through direct or reciprocal action.

24

III. Summary

The limbic lobe is one of the most important brain areas in emotion processes. It has numerous interconnections with the brainstem reticular formation, which serves as an amplifier in emotion processes, and with the neocortex, which integrates emotion. Limbic structures are also clearly interrelated to the hypothalamic emotion centers and to the autonomic nervous system, which innervates the visceral-glandular organs involved in emotion. These structural relations signal the importance of the limbic system in emotion. Papez and MacLean suggested that the limbic system was *the* anatomical basis of the emotions. Somewhat more conservatively, Arnold maintained that it mediates liking and disliking and plays some role in mediating visceral–glandular activity, emotional experience, and emotion-instigated action.

The hypothalamus is singularly important in controlling the autonomic nervous system and the pituitary gland. It also plays a role in emotional expression, emotional integration, and in the intensification of emotion-related actions. In the emotion process, the hypothalamus exerts an excitatory influence on the cerebral hemispheres. In turn, the cortex exerts an inhibitory influence on the hypothalamus.

The neocortex may also instigate emotion processes by downward discharges to the hypothalamus and limbic lobe. The neocortex is the ultimate integrative mechanism. The emotion process cannot be complete without it. The neocortex integrates the functions of the emotion, cognition, and motor systems and thus effects the psychobiological unity and functional integrity of the individual.

My distinction between emotion as a general, imprecise term and the concept of fundamental emotion as a specific, more precise term, and my distinction between fundamental emotions and patterns of emotions are given some support by the available evidence. The fundamental emotions have been defined empirically at the neuromuscular-expressive and phenomenological levels. This, together with tentative evidence from neurophysiology and biochemistry, suggest there should be emotion-specific neurochemical substrates. The frequency with which people describe themselves, and are described by clinicians, as anxious or depressed suggests that emotions often occur in combinations or patterns. Clinical evidence at the phenomenological level and the close and intricate interrelationships between the structures and mechanisms that subserve different emotions at the neural and biochemical level support the validity and usefulness of the concept of patterns of emotions.

25

The Neurophysiology and Biochemistry of Fear and Anxiety

One of the purposes of Chapters Two through Five is to attempt to bring a higher degree of order into a complex and frequently confusing subject that is of crucial importance in behavioral science, in personality and social research, and in clinical practice. I shall begin by presenting an overview of the four chapters on anxiety.

Chapter Two will deal with the neurophysiology and biochemistry of anxiety. It will discuss the neurophysiological concept of ergotropic–trophotropic balance, in relation to differential emotion theory. In reviewing the biochemical research on anxiety, particular attention will be given to the concept of a norepinephrine–epinephrine ratio, a concept that is quite compatible with the notion of anxiety as a combination of interacting fundamental emotions.

In Chapter Three, I shall attempt a conceptual or substantive analysis of anxiety. First, I shall present a formulation of anxiety as a variable combination of interacting fundamental emotions. Next, I shall examine the substance of previous definitions of anxiety, searching especially for discrete emotion concepts or connotations. Then, I shall elaborate my pattern of emotions theory of anxiety by placing it in the context of a larger theory of emotion and behavior. To accomplish this, I shall present my definition of emotion, the emotion system, and the emotion process. The complex of phenomena which I call the emotion process will be illustrated by looking at the problem of activating an emotion. Another aspect of the emotion process will be dealt with by looking at the ways in which emotion and emotion components combine and interact to produce such phenomena as those we call anxiety and depression.

In Chapter Four, I shall compare some of the major theories of emotion and anxiety with that of my own. In particular, I shall compare my theory with three different versions of a cognitive theory of emotion—those of Lazarus, Epstein, and Janis. In this chapter, I shall attempt to show how these different conceptions of the nature of anxiety and emotion have important implications for the way emotion is treated in research and in clinical practice. The two contrasting theoretical frameworks place emotion in highly different positions with respect to its importance in personality, interpersonal, and intergroup functioning.

Chapter Five will present an empirical analysis of the concept of anxiety and of the concepts of certain fundamental emotions that I hypothesize as possible components of anxiety. The principal analytical tool will be the Differential Emotion Scale, an instrument derived from differential emotion theory and partially validated through factor analytic and other research methods. A version of the Differential Emotion Scale will be combined with a standard anxiety scale and the resulting instrument will be used in the empirical studies to be reported in Chapter Five. First, the factor structure of the Differential Emotion Scale will be compared with that of the combined emotion and anxiety scale. Second, the combined scale will be used to compare an anxiety situation with various discrete emotion situations (fear, distress, guilt, anger, shyness, and interest). An analysis of the free-response descriptions of these anxiety and emotion situations will also be presented. Finally, Chapter Five will develop the concept of patterns or profiles of fundamental emotions and demonstrate its use as a means of differentially assessing the affective–motivational experiences of persons in different situations.

The theory and evidence presented in Chapter One indicate that the neurophysiology and biochemistry of emotion are far from simple. When we consider anxiety, which we view as a pattern or combination of several emotions and emotion-related processes, we are indeed dealing with a highly complex concept. The sheer complexity has made for some incomplete and contradictory experimental results. Yet, some degree of consistency among findings exists.

I. NEUROPHYSIOLOGICAL CONSIDERATIONS

Two principles should prove helpful in interpreting and organizing the neurophysiological, psychophysiological, and biochemical research on anxiety. First, as we shall see in the first part of this chapter, Gellhorn has marshaled considerable supporting evidence for his conception of anxiety as characterized by the simultaneous and antagonistic functioning of both the ergotropic and trophotropic systems. This would mean the simultaneous functioning of the sympathetic and parasympathetic nervous systems. While sympathetic reactions may typically be more prominent, their measurement and interpretation might be complicated by concomitant heightened parasympathetic activity.

Second, in terms of differential emotion theory, anxiety consists of a pattern or combination of several fundamental emotions and emotion-related processes. This guarantees complexity at the neurophysiological and biochemical level. While phenomenologically mild to moderate fear is the most prominent emotion, the emotions of distress, guilt, shyness, anger, and interest may also be involved. Distress is trophotropic and parasympathetic, anger and interest are ergotropic and sympathetic.

In this chapter, we shall consider the neurophysiology of both fear and anxiety. The reasons for this are several. First, the two concepts are often equated or inadequately differentiated in the literature. Second, fear is a prominent component of anxiety. Third, there is the possibility that the alternation in experience of intense fear and mild to moderate fear may produce neurophysiological and biochemical activities very like those in anxiety. This follows from my assumption that intense fear is trophotropic in nature and moderate fear ergotropic.

For an extensive treatment of fear, the reader is referred to Gray's *The Psychology of Fear and Stress* (1971). Gray presents a good summary of work on the inheritance of fear, sex differences in fear behavior, the effects of early environment on fearfulness, and the role of fear in sexual and avoidance behavior.

A. THE NEUROPHYSIOLOGY OF ACUTE (SUDDEN, INTENSE) FEAR

Gellhorn (1965, 1967) has presented a detailed analysis of the neurophysiological basis of fear and anxiety. He began by making

29

a distinction, a very important one for his theory, between acute fear and chronic fear. By implication, acute fear is more intense and sudden in onset than chronic fear. He equated chronic fear with anxiety.

Gellhorn described acute fear as one in which the trophotropic syndrome prevails: Electroencephalogram (EEG) potentials are slowed, the parasympathetic system dominates, and striate muscle tone is inhibited or decreased. Typically, heart rate and blood pressure decrease. The loss of sympathetic vasomotor tone is one mechanism by which the ergotropic–trophotropic balance is shifted to the trophotropic side. Acute fear is also associated with increased excretion from the adrenal medulla, a matter which will be discussed in the next section.

Although the trophotropic syndrome predominates in acute fear, according to Gellhorn, ergotropic discharges occur. Pupillary dilation, sweating, and increased blood flow through the muscles indicate ergotrophic activity.

Gellhorn (1965) reviewed studies of circulation in acute fear which supported his position that acute fear is a trophotropic state. These investigations showed that acute fear results in decreases in minute volume of the heart and blood pressure and sharp increases in vagal activity. Acute fear is sometimes accompanied by vomiting, and retching and vomiting are expressions of trophotropic discharges. Retching and vomiting can be elicited by stimulation of the anterior (parasympathetic, trophotropic) area of the hypothalamus. One of the studies reviewed by Gellhorn showed that stimulation of the anterior hypothalamus at threshold intensity shifted the ergotropic-trophotropic balance to the trophotropic side and produced symptoms of fear. In the light of these studies, Gellhorn reversed Cannon's interpretation of the cause of voodoo death and hypothesized that voodoo death resulted from circulatory collapse brought about by great increases in trophotropic discharges. It should be noted that the voodoo victim apparently thinks his survival is hopeless and his doom inevitable.

Consistent with the foregoing formulation, Gellhorn (1965) reported evidence showing that willed inhibition or voluntary cessation of movements could result in fear. Such inhibition of movements has three important effects:

(1) It tends to shift the trophotropic–ergotropic balance to the trophotropic side by limbic–hypothalamic processes and/or by reduction in proprioceptive feedback. (2) Since the inhibition of muscle activity does not prevent the development of strong central ergotropic discharges, the

latter tend to overflow into the trophotropic system as a critical level of excitation is reached. (3) This overflow is facilitated by the shift in balance (1) and accounts for the change in the emotional state from rage to fear [pp. 505–506].

B. SUBACUTE FEAR

Gellhorn apparently views subacute fear as an emotion that has a discernible and sudden onset but less intensity than acute fear. It may be considered as mild to moderate fear. While the ergotropic system functions in acute fear, it is more effective in subacute fear. Although Gellhorn maintained that subacute fear, like acute fear, is characterized by a shift in the ergotropic–trophotropic balance to the trophotropic side, he indicated that in subacute fear secondary compensatory ergotropic reactions may overshadow trophotropic responses. Thus, mild to moderate fear may be considered an emotion that involves both the trophotropic and ergotropic systems to a considerable extent. The fact that ergotropic indicia may be more prominent may justify considering it an ergotropic emotion; some evidence for this view was presented in Chapter One. Perhaps the final test will have to be in terms of the relative effects of the trophotropic and ergotropic discharges on the functioning and actions of the organism as a whole.

Gellhorn considered subacute fear as an emotional state quite similar to what Funkenstein (1955) and his associates called "anger-in," an adrenergic (adrenalin facilitated) state which contrasts with "anger-out" (aggressiveness), a cholinergic (nonadrenalin facilitated) state. The comparison may be an unfortunate one. Funkenstein and his colleagues depended on mild stressors and laboratory induction techniques that rarely if ever produce a pure emotion (Izard, 1971; Tomkins, 1962). Furthermore, anger-in was thought to bear some resemblance to depressive mood, and depression, as we shall see in the next section, must be considered a complex pattern or combination of emotions. There is considerable evidence that inner-directed anger or hostility is usually a component of depression.

C. THE NEUROPHYSIOLOGY OF CHRONIC FEAR (ANXIETY)

Gellhorn defined anxiety simply as chronic fear. A number of psychologists (see Levitt, 1967; Spielberger, 1966) also have equated anxiety with fear. As we shall see in the following chapters, there is much evidence that militates against a concept of anxiety as a unitary concept, as a single pure emotion or entity of any sort. Theory and evidence also have been presented (Izard, 1971; Lazarus, Averill, & Opton, 1970; Tomkins, 1962) which indicate that pure emotion is relatively rare in day-to-day life, almost impossible to create in the laboratory, and typically fleeting when it does occur. Therefore, *chronic* fear appears to be an unsatisfactory definition of anxiety. When fear characterizes personality functioning over a long period of time, other fundamental emotions undoubtedly accompany the fear or alternate with it.

While Gellhorn's psychological definition of anxiety may be incomplete, his neurophysiological analysis may well represent a significant contribution. His formulation does not preclude the existence of simultaneous and/or alternating fundamental emotions in anxiety. To understand Gellhorn's neurophysiological analysis of anxiety it is necessary to remember that the antagonistic ergotropic and trophotropic systems typically function in a balanced and reciprocal fashion. Normally an increase in ergotropic activity is accompanied by a decrease in trophotropic activity and vice versa. Normal behavior breaks down and anxiety neuroses develop as a result of simultaneous upward discharges of the ergotropic *and* trophotropic systems. The reciprocity of the two systems fails and their concurrent functioning creates conflicting demands on the organism. Gellhorn (1965) recognizes, to use his own words, different "patterns of anxiety [p. 499]." First, there is the excitatory form characterized by restlessness, hyperactivity, sympathetic responses, and ergotropic dominance. Second, the inhibitory form is characterized by hypoactivity, parasympathetic responses, and trophotropic dominance. In the excitatory form, which Gellhorn thought the most common, both the ergotropic and trophotropic systems are active, but the balance is on the ergotropic side.

Gellhorn presented considerable evidence for the notion that anxiety is characterized by both ergotropic and trophotropic activity, with typically ergotropic dominance. He pointed out that normally in the waking state the ergotropic system is dominant and responsive primarily to environmental stimuli. If the stimuli are sufficiently stressful and frequent, sympathetic activity increases and parasympathetic activity decreases. Trophotropic–parasympathetic discharges may be kept in the picture by virtue of the fact that the individual responds periodically to some of the stressful stimuli with acute fear. Since acute fear is primarily trophotropic, even transient or fleeting states of acute fear would serve to sustain the trophotropic side of the simultaneous and antagonistic ergotropic–trophotropic functioning. However, the same effect could obtain as a result of the distress component of anxiety.

Another way in which trophotropic discharges occur, according to Gellhorn, is through spillover or overflow of excitation from an overloaded ergotropic system. When stressful stimuli bombard the organism and excitation of the ergotropic system reaches a critical level, the excitation overflows into the trophotropic system. Gellhorn cited Richter's forced swimming experiments as evidence for the notion of the overflow of excitation. Wild rats forced to swim without possibility of rest or escape died within a few minutes. Their initial activity indicated response to ergotropic discharges, but evidence at autopsy (gross hypothalamic lesions) suggested that intensive trophotropic discharges occurred along with strong ergotropic excitation.

Gellhorn also used observations from experimental neuroses to support his position. He noted that most of the procedures used to induce experimental neuroses—difficult discrimination, massive pain, nociceptive stimulation applied during an alimentary conditioned reflex—involve both the ergotropic and trophotropic systems. For example, a common method used to induce experimental anxiety neurosis is the application of an unconditioned stimulus (US) such as shock or an air blast while the animal is eating. Such a US acts mainly on the ergotropic system, and since it is applied during eating there is concomitant heightened trophotropic activity (Gellhorn, 1967). According to Gellhorn, it is just such simultaneous functioning of the two antagonistic systems which destroys their reciprocity and produces pathological behavior, including anxiety and neurosis.

There are two other considerations in the neurophysiology of anxiety. First, hereditary factors affect hypothalamic tuning and ergotropic–trophotropic balance. Second, there are idiosyncrasies in the patterns of somatic symptoms in anxiety. Apparently, in some cases muscle tension is paramount, in others cardiovascular and gastrointestinal symptoms dominate. A test of this hypothesis by Brandt and Fenz (1969) will be discussed in the next section.

D. PSYCHOPHYSIOLOGICAL STUDIES OF ANXIETY

As indicated in Chapter One and the foregoing section, differential emotion theory defines anxiety as a variable pattern of interacting fundamental emotions. Since each fundamental emotion is assumed to have some distinct neurophysiological and biochemical substrates, the physiology of anxiety cannot be a simple and fixed formula. Indeed, the complex ergotropic–trophotropic mixture described by Gellhorn, which appears consistent with the differential emotion theory of anxiety, seems highly probable.

Differential emotion theory holds that fear is typically the predominant emotion in anxiety. As already noted, some investigators equate anxiety with fear. It is possible that the degree of consistency that does obtain in the findings from psychological studies is due to the prominent common denominator of fear. Similarly, consistent findings from physiological studies may result from the fact that investigators have typically measured simply indices of physiological arousal, with rarely any effort to sort out ergotropic–sympathetic from trophotropic–parasympathetic effects. More often than not, only sympathetic responses are measured, and most typically anxiety involves increased sympathetic activity.

In considering the findings from psychophysiological studies of anxiety, several points need to be kept in mind. First, as discussed in Chapter One, there is some evidence to indicate that mild to moderate fear may be an ergotropic emotion. Thus, indices of sympathetic arousal could signify either fear or the complex state of anxiety, or conceivably some other emotion such as anger. Second, virtually no investigators have followed Alexander's (1950) suggestion that anxiety symptoms could be sorted into sympathetic and parasympathetic types. Investigators have usually been satisfied to show general physiological or autonomic arousal.

A number of studies relating to anxiety (not distinguished from fear) support the notion that anxiety is characterized by sympathetic arousal. Levitt's (1967) review of physiological studies led him to conclude that anxiety indices were primarily sympathetic reactions. Studies reviewed by Martin (1961) showed that systolic (central) blood pressure and heart rate increase in fear or anxiety. However, Buss's (1961) critique of some of the studies cited by Martin reiterates a note of caution regarding oversimplification of the physiology of anxiety. It is also important to keep in mind that these investigators made no effort to test for heightened trophotropic activity or for simultaneous ergotropic–trophotropic functioning.

Mikhail (1969) used rats to examine the effects of conditioned anxiety on ulceration and stomach acidity. Anxiety was conditioned through random electric shock, food deprivation, and bodily restraint. The rats were sacrificed after the anxiety conditioning to examine for ulcers and acidity. Mikhail found no significant differences between experimental and control animals. He concluded that the inhibitory effects of the sympathetic activity on gastric secretions (associated with anxiety) do not provide support for a positive relationship between conditioned anxiety and gastric ulceration.

Contradicting the findings of Mikhail, Brady (1958) showed that stress or conditioned anxiety can produce ulcerations in monkeys. Brady used an avoidance-learning paradigm, with electric shock as the unconditioned stimulus (US). The experimental monkey was termed an "executive monkey" since learning to press a lever enabled it to anticipate and avoid the shocks. A control monkey received shocks at the same time as the experimental monkey, but the former had no means of preventing the shocks. The executive monkey died from acute ulceration after 23 days on a 6-hour-on, 6-hour-off schedule of exposure to the possibility of being shocked. The autopsy of the control monkey showed no abnormalities. From an extension of the study, Brady learned that one critical variable in producing ulceration was the relation of the length of the stress period to that of the rest period. Comparing Brady's experiment to Mikhail's, it seems that for ulceration to result the animal must have some control over his negative stimulation and that the stress-nonstress cycle must have some relationship to the cycles of gastrointestinal activities. Differences between species of subjects also may have been a factor in the difference between the findings of Brady and Mikhail.

Zimmerman (1968) did a study indirectly bearing on anxiety. He differentiated light sleepers from deep sleepers on the basis of sound awakening thresholds. He demonstrated that light sleepers showed more anxiety and conflict on personality tests. Furthermore, he demonstrated that light sleepers (presumably high anxiety subjects) scored higher on the sympathetic indices of heart rate, respiration rate, skin potential reactivity and delta wave amplitude. However, none of the differences between the groups were statistically significant.

Bauman and Straughon (1969) conducted an experiment to determine whether IPAT Anxiety Scale scores related to base skin resistance (BSR) during conditions of stress and nonstress. Subjects were 60 students selected from the upper, middle, and lower 15% of IPAT anxiety scores. Anxiety was induced by electric shock. A psychogalvanometer recorded BSR. The experimenters discovered that BSR was not related to IPAT Anxiety Scale scores, yet BSR did follow the predicted outcome, being lowest during the experimental stress condition and highest during nonstress, thus suggesting that BSR is a useful index of the anxiety state. According to the authors, this result casts doubt on whether anxiety as a personality trait is a useful concept.

Barrett (1972) has recently reported some interesting physiological studies involving measures of both impulsiveness and anxiety. He prefaced his report with the thought that patterns of psychophysiological responses over longer time periods were more meaningful than specific responses to specific stimuli. This notion was supported by an orienting response experiment (Barrett, 1972) in which subjects with different levels of impulsiveness and anxiety listened to 45 presentations of a 1000-Hz tone for 30, 60, or 90 msec. The different groups of subjects did not differ in terms of specific (immediate) responses—galvanic skin response (GSR), BSR, EEG, heart rate, and respiration. However, subjects high on impulsiveness and low on anxiety habituated the EEG after the autonomic nervous system measure, while the opposite was true for the subjects low on impulsiveness and high on anxiety.

Fenz and Epstein (1965) factor analyzed the Taylor Manifest Anxiety Scale and derived three subscales: items relating to autonomic arousal, items relating to symptoms of muscle tension, and items relating to feelings of fear and insecurity. They concluded that manifest anxiety was primarily composed of a general factor of anxiety (feelings of fear, insecurity, etc.) and a specific factor of striated muscle tension.

In a follow-up study, Brandt and Fenz (1969) selected a group of subjects whose autonomic arousal scale scores were higher than their muscle tension scale scores and a second group with the opposite relationship between these scale scores. The investigators attempted to induce three periods and three levels of stress. They measured skin resistance, heart rate, frontalis electromyograph (EMG), and eyeblink. They found consistent, though not always significant, differences between the two groups on all measures. They interpreted their results as evidence for the notion that individuals show idiosyncratic patterns of physiological activity in response to stress and that the autonomic and muscle tension scales provide some basis for predicting types of physiological response patterns.

Further refinement of concepts and measurement techniques should provide a basis for continued progress in neurophysiological studies of anxiety. In particular, the concepts of anxiety as a pattern of emotions and as simultaneous heightened ergotropic–

trophotropic functioning together with improved physiotechnology promise significant contributions.

II. BIOCHEMICAL CONSIDERATIONS

The neurophysiological mechanisms involved in anxiety are directly related to the biochemistry of this pattern of emotions. The hypothalamic system and the balance of the ergotropic–trophotropic systems influence the secretion of hormones by the endocrine glands (see Chapter One and Gellhorn & Loofbourrow, 1963).

For many years it has been known that the endocrine glands are involved in emotion processes. Of greatest importance is the adrenal gland. It has two distinct parts, the cortex, which secretes corticosteriod hormones, and the medulla, which secretes adrenalin or epinephrine. Both the adrenocortical and the adrenomedullary hormones have been associated with anxiety. A third hormone or neurohumor which figures, at least indirectly, in the biochemistry of both anxiety and depression is noradrenalin or norepinephrine. Norepinephrine is thought to be secreted mainly by the nerve endings of the sympathetic vascular system. It has a direct positive relationship with outer-directed anger or hostility, a factor which, according to differential emotion theory, may be involved in both anxiety and depression. Not inconsistent with this notion is the fact that evidence from biochemical studies suggests the possibility that the relationship between hostility, anxiety, and depression may be partially a function of the norepinephrine–epinephrine ratio. The possibility that there exist emotion-specific patterns of hormones continues to inspire a number of investigators.

A. EPINEPHRINE LEVEL, NOREPINEPHRINE–EPINEPHRINE RATIO, AND ANXIETY

Gellhorn (1965) summarized evidence from a number of studies which showed that experimentally induced fear in which no attempt is made to escape the situation increases epinephrine without changing norepinephrine level. Furthermore, most of the conditions which increase epinephrine usually decrease cerebral cortical reactivity and ergotropic reactivity of the hypothalamic system. Similarly, decreasing the excitability of the sympathetic division of the hypothalamus decreases the norepinephrine–epinephrine ratio.

Put another way, an increase in epinephrine and a concomitant decrease in the norepinephrine–epinephrine ratio are associated with a shift in the ergotropic–trophotropic balance to the trophotropic side. At the phenomenological level, this condition might be experienced as an increase in acute fear or in distress and a decrease in anger or aggressiveness.

Some of the early studies attempting to show emotion–hormone relationships were those of Funkenstein (1955). In one of these studies, he found that psychotics who were typically either depressed or frightened showed significantly stronger responses (e.g., sharp drop in blood pressure) to mecholyl (a parasympathetic stimulant) than did psychotics who are typically angry or hostile. He concluded that the emotional content of patients' psychoses was significantly related to their physiological reactions. In a follow-up study he investigated normal subjects (medical students) during a stressful period (waiting to hear about internship applications) and found similar results. Students who were angry at others for the stressful situation had a mild response to the parasympathomimetic agent and those who were angry at themselves (depressed) or afraid (anxious) had a strong reaction. In subsequent studies Funkenstein and his associates produced evidence that these two types of reaction were associated with different hormonal secretions. They found that when subjects responded to stress with anger toward others (outer-directed anger), their physiological reactions were like those induced by injection of noradrenalin (norepinephrine). When the same subjects reacted with fear, their responses were like those induced by injection of adrenalin (epinephrine). Similar findings have been reported by Ax (1953), Schachter (1957), Martin (1961), and Breggin (1964). Furthermore, a recent review by Fehr and Stern (1970) generally supports the notion that fundamental emotions such as anger and fear have specific and distinct hormonal and autonomic patterns.

B. THE CORTICOSTEROIDS AND ANXIETY

Gellhorn (1965) noted that steroid level in the blood increases during anxiety. He argued that the positive relationship between these hormones and the ergotropic system was further evidence that strong ergotropic discharges occur in anxiety. Consistent with this conclusion, Wehmer (1966) induced anxiety by means of a film that portrayed Australian aboriginals conducting phallic mutilation rites, including subincision of the penis of pubescent boys. Wehmer's subjects showed both an increase in plasma 17-hydroxycorticosteroids (17-OH-CS), heart rate, and in self-reported negative emotions.

Brady (1970) has conducted a series of experiments along this line. In one paradigm he induced "anxiety" in rhesus monkeys by superimposing an aversive conditioning procedure (US = shock) on a lever-pressing performance which yielded food reward. The monkey was first trained to press a lever to obtain food. Then, there was a series of conditioning trials in which a 3-min horn signal was terminated contiguously with shock. This latter procedure produced what Brady called conditioned anxiety. Typically the conditioned anxiety suppressed the lever-pressing response and markedly increased the 17-OH-CS level in the blood. This finding was replicated by Brady and other investigators.

C. EXPERIMENTS MEASURING BOTH
CATECHOLAMINES AND CORTICOSTEROIDS

In experiments similar to those described in the foregoing paragraph, Brady showed that the "conditioned anxiety" not only increased the 17-OH-CS level, it also greatly increased the norepinephrine level. There was little or no change in epinephrine level. When cardiovascular measurements were added in later experiments, there was an initial decrease in heart rate and blood pressure followed by an increase in both. One might speculate that the shock US initially produced acute fear, trophotropic dominance, and increased epinephrine secretion, followed by anger and aggressive reaction which was accompanied by ergotropic dominance, sympathetic discharges, and increased norepinephrine secretion.

In a second series of experiments, Brady focused not on procedures which have suppressive effects but on changes in avoidance behavior. In these studies, the monkey had to learn to press a bar every 20 sec in order to avoid shock. After conditioning, the avoidance behavior was accompanied by twofold to fourfold increase in corticosteroid levels and marked increase in the norepinephrine level with no significant change in the epinephrine level.

Another of Brady's experimental paradigms is of particular interest for the biochemistry of anxiety. The basic procedure is that described in the preceding paragraph, with the addition of unavoidable shocks programmed every minute of the session. In this case, there were highly significant increases in both epinephrine and norepinephrine levels. In a modification of this procedure that put the monkey in a conflict situation, there were again increases in both epinephrine and norepinephrine. These findings appear quite consistent with Gellhorn's (1965) position that anxiety involves both the trophotropic and ergotropic systems and, at the phenomenological level, both fear and anger.

III. SUMMARY

The neurophysiology and biochemistry of anxiety is made highly complex by the fact that it involves a pattern of different emotions, some of which are associated with ergotropic, sympathetic, and adrenocortical activity and others with trophotropic, parasympathetic, and adrenomedullary activity.

Almost all theorists agree that fear is an important component of anxiety. Acute fear is apparently associated with trophotropic–parasympathetic dominance and an increase in the adrenomedullary hormone, epinephrine. There are grounds for considering mild to moderate fear an ergotropic–sympathetic emotion; hence, the mobilization and maintenance of energy for defense, escape behavior, or flight.

Anger is another emotion that many theorists consider a component of anxiety. Anger is primarily an ergotropic–sympathetic emotion. With both anger and fear in the picture, it is clear why anxiety would be characterized by both ergotropic and trophotropic discharges, adrenocortical (steroid), and adrenomedullary (epinephrine) activity.

Anxiety may also involve distress, guilt, shyness, and interest. Some of these are probably ergotropic, others trophotropic. The neurophysiology of distress is probably the best known. Most of the evidence suggests that it is primarily a trophotropic emotion.

Most physiologically oriented students of anxiety have typically measured indices of general arousal under stress or anxiety inducing conditions. Usually they find evidence of heightened sympathetic activity; e.g., increased heart rate, blood pressure, and skin conductance.

A number of studies have shown that both catecholamine and corticosteroid levels change during anxiety. The most convincing and pertinent experimental work is that of Brady. Under conditions that would be expected to induce both fearful and aggressive responses and in simulated conflict situations, monkeys showed an increase in corticosteroids and in both epinephrine and norepinephrine levels. These hormones or neurohumors may be involved in feedback or interactive processes which affect the central nervous system (CNS) integration of the components of emotion.

The neurophysiological and biochemical evidence appears generally consistent with the differential emotion theory definition of anxiety as a pattern of emotions. Since the pattern involves contrasting (sometimes conflicting) emotions such as fear and anger, anxiety is characterized by both ergotropic–sympathetic–adrenocortical activity and by trophotropic–parasympathetic–adreno-medullary activity. The simultaneous discharges of these sets of antagonistic systems mark a breakdown in their normally recip-rocal relationships. In view of this, it is readily understood why the anxious organism is less efficient, less effective, and more prone to maladaptive behavior.

CHAPTER THREE

Anxiety as a Variable Combination of Interacting Fundamental Emotions

I. INTRODUCTION

At the outset of this chapter on theory, I want to say something about the difference between my use of the term "anxiety" in a previous work (Izard & Tomkins, 1966) and my use of the term in this book. The difference calls for a new perspective and a new attitude toward the concept.

Izard and Tomkins (1966) asserted that the term "anxiety" was something of a catchall term for all things related to negative, disruptive, or disturbing affects and was also credited with a sometime facilitative effect on learning and performance. We proposed to end the confusion created by such an ambiguous omnibus by equating anxiety with fear, the latter being considered a primary or fundamental emotion that could be defined unequivocally. This tactic clearly failed. There are at least two reasons for the failure. First, most clinicians continued to be convinced that there was something that could be more or less regularly identified as anxiety which had characteristics not explicable by the concept of fear. Second, a number of researchers using multivariate methods showed that anxiety, at least as measured by current anxiety scales, was not unidimensional.

It is true that a number of investigators, apparently quite independently, have decided that they should equate anxiety with fear. But even in these cases, the operational definitions of anxiety and research procedures often involve emotions other than fear.

43

The problem of defining anxiety may be viewed as a rigidity in conceptualizing. The term "anxiety" as an explicator of malfunction and disadaptation has acquired tremendous psychological inertia. Although some scientists have indicated that anxiety is best conceived as a single emotion (fear), neither in theoretical formulations nor in empirical research have any of these scientists clearly separated as different variables the several fundamental emotions that are typically involved in their experimentation.

In 1966 we also suggested that, aside from fear, whatever else anxiety had come to mean to different researchers and investigators should be given more specific and appropriate labels. In particular, we advocated the use of other emotion concepts such as distress and shame—emotions that were seen as frequently interacting with fear. This second tactic, which could succeed only if yoked to the first, was also doomed to failure.

To clarify the record, the Izard–Tomkins chapter in *Anxiety and Behavior* (Spielberger, 1966) must be viewed as a chapter on the emotion of fear and not on anxiety. This is so because anxiety did not come to equal fear in the minds of many who read and write and talk about anxiety and who contribute to its definition.

Lazarus and Averill (1972) generally support our point that there are several discrete emotions that must be considered in the analysis of behavior. They speak of the need to distinguish anxiety from other fear-related emotional syndromes and of the possibility of different kinds of anxiety. Yet, their theory is not based on a clear conceptual differentiation of fundamental emotions, and they conceive of emotion as response while we view it as a process influencing and interacting with other personality and interpersonal processes.

In 1966 we argued that the intraindividual emotion process had three components—neurophysiological, behavioral–expressive, and phenomenological or subjective. This form of conceptualizing emotion (and anxiety) is now present to one degree or another in a number of theories, some of which are presented in Spielberger (1972). In 1966 we also argued for the need to study each of the discrete fundamental emotions. As already indicated, this idea is now being expressed by a number of theorists and investigators, some of whom were contributors to the Spielberger volumes.

In 1966 we maintained that emotion was not a response but a process capable of operating without a stimulus in the usual sense of that term. This idea, though vaguely implicit in some of the other contributions to the Spielberger book and elsewhere, remains characteristic only of our position.

In the empirical studies reported in the present volume, I attempted to analyze anxiety for whatever it is in contemporary behavioral science and in the thinking of people in general. I began by looking at the extant substantive definitions of anxiety, many of which had been collected in a recent review (Mallama, 1970). I found myself rather quickly reverting to the type of thinking that led to my tactical errors of 1966. For all who are willing to see, the literature on anxiety is manifestly clear on one point—*anxiety is not a unitary concept*. And much of the confusion in anxiety theory and research is linked to the tendency to treat it as unitary. Anxiety does not refer to a single class of antecedent conditions, or to a single class of neurophysiological, behavioral–expressive, and subjective–experiential events, or to a single class of consequent acts.

It was disappointing to find that some writers who have contributed heavily to the literature on the assessment and treatment of anxiety have contributed little to the substantive definition of the concept. Wolpe (1966), who like many clinicians, believes that anxiety is central to most neuroses, defines anxiety as an emotional habit associated with autonomic arousal and involving a "primitive (subcortical) level of neural organization [Wolpe & Lazarus 1967, p. 12]." He does not really give a substantive definition of anxiety, but his writing leads one to believe that the concept comprises most of the maladaptive emotional responses that constitute neurosis.

Many writers, particularly those inclined to controlled experimental studies in the laboratory, simply start writing about anxiety as though everyone knows what it is, but they go on to describe one or more of a wide variety of inventories or other indices to indicate that they have indeed measured anxiety. Spence and Spence (1966), who may epitomize the effort to bring anxiety within the framework of s-r theory and into the laboratory for controlled experimentation, use the term anxiety in a rather loose way when they leave behavior theory constructs and symbols aside and speak in substantive terms. They wrote: "The Manifest Anxiety Scale (MAS) was devised as one method of selecting subjects differing in emotional responsiveness . . . [p. 294]." The test was made up of items which "describe both the physiological reactions reported by individuals suffering from anxiety reactions and the accompanying subjective reports of worry, self-doubt, anxiety, and so forth [pp. 294–295]." This contributes very little to a substantive analysis of anxiety, yet the MAS as much as any other measure has been the standard for defining anxiety operationally.

Although there are a few investigators who speak loosely of anxiety as fear or as a kind of fear, anxiety is never really treated as a single emotion, either in terms of verbal definition or in terms of the sundry operations used to measure it. Anxiety as it has been used by theorists and investigators over the years is indeed a complex of negative emotions. It now appears that our only chance of understanding this term as it has been variously used in the literature is to see it as a complex of emotions or emotion-related concepts and to abandon forever the notion that there is a unitary phenomenon of anxiety. *Anxiety is not unipolar, unidimensional, or unifactor in nature.*

One reason why emotion and concepts like anxiety have been treated as global, undifferentiated phenomena is due in no small measure to the fact that a chief source of data has been the maladjusted, neurotic, or psychotic individual whose behavior seemingly invited the oversimplified explanatory concept of "emotional disturbance," which implies that emotion has the character of a general, undifferentiated phenomenon. The situation has not been greatly improved in some of the recent laboratory studies in which artificial or contrived stressors are presumed to elicit true and pure emotional states, such as "anxiety." Such errors of oversimplification were enhanced and supported for more than a decade by those theorists and researchers who placed all emotion on a single dimension called activation or arousal and by those clinically oriented theorists who viewed "anxiety" as a unitary concept that explains virtually all maladjustment and some aspects of effective adjustment. Apparently the effects of certain theorizing and evidence (Gellhorn, 1964; Izard & Tomkins, 1966; Nowlis, 1965; Pribram, 1967; Sprague, Chambers, & Stellar, 1961; Tomkins, 1962; Zuckerman, 1960) have gradually had some effect in reducing the tendency to consider all emotion on the single dimension of activation or arousal. However, the error of viewing anxiety as the central if not single source of all psychopathology remains quite common.

Indeed, the ránge of substantive or dynamic elements that can be found in a survey of definitions of anxiety is great enough to help account for a variety of adjustment problems and other behaviors. However, such a range of different substantive elements supports my conception of anxiety as a variable combination of fundamental emotions and their interactions.

46

II. A CONCEPTUAL ANALYSIS OF ANXIETY

I maintain that all complex emotion processes such as love, hostility, depression, and anxiety contain as elements two or more of the fundamental emotions or their components. In particular, I propose that anxiety includes fear and two or more of the fundamental emotions of distress, anger, shame (including shyness and guilt), and the positive emotion of interest–excitement. As already indicated, this formulation is implicitly supported by several writers in the field—the survey of theoretical and operational definitions of anxiety will show that all the above fundamental emotions have been included by more than one author. The complete list and the a priori definitions of the fundamental emotions are presented in Table 5-1, page 84.

A. EMOTION CONCEPTS IN PREVIOUS DEFINITIONS OF ANXIETY

In his early writings, Freud (1917) did not think it necessary to give a complete description of the emotional component of anxiety since "every one of us has experienced this sensation [p. 392]." Of course, Freud took special pains to point out that the first anxiety experience involved an involuntary separation from the primal love object, the mother or mother-figure. One of Freud's early observations is especially interesting in light of my contention that each emotion has a neuromuscular component and of my conception of anxiety as a multivariable concept. Freud stated that the phenomenological component of anxiety resulted from "perceptions of motor innervations that have occurred and direct feelings of pleasure and unpleasure [p. 395]."

Sarason, Davidson, Lighthall, Waite, and Ruebush (1960) considered test anxiety to be a result of the following emotional sequence. In order to avoid real danger, the child has to repress hostility toward a parent for one or more previous testlike evaluations. Next the child feels guilty for his hostility toward his usually beloved parent. The guilt has to be relegated to the unconscious as much as possible, but when it does become conscious such as in the test situation the child's negative feelings put him in a self-derogatory attitude. Ultimately the self-derogating attitude leads the child to doubt his ability in the testing situation, and to compound the uncertainty the child tends to fantasize about the parent's retaliation for the child's hostility.

47

In this analysis by Sarason, the anxiety experience involves the fundamental emotions of fear, shame or guilt, distress, and anger. One could reasonably account for the phenomena observed by Sarason by assuming that fear is associated with the danger of punishment and failure, shame or guilt with self-derogation and feelings of inadequacy, distress with alienation from parents or loved ones, and anger with an interpersonal situation that has demanding and apparently hostile characteristics. It is quite feasible to argue that this combination of emotions and behaviors can well be called anxiety. What Sarason did not recognize is that experiences from other person–environment interchanges that could equally well be called anxiety might involve some, though not all, of the above emotions. Nor did he point out that anxiety might be reported in situations involving the same emotions in different sequences and different interactions. However, there is considerable overlap in the substance of Sarason's definition of anxiety and mine.

Grinker and Spiegel's (1945) involvement with combat-experienced soldiers was probably instrumental in convincing them that the cause of anxiety, especially in war, was a fear of losing the self, an object of love. They specified a fear component and implied a distress component in the idea of loss of a loved object.

According to Sullivan (1953), anxiety can be characterized by a feeling (always unpleasant) that "all is not going so well, or a noticing of some disturbance in the activity or postural tone in one of the zones of interaction—a change in one's 'facial expression' or in one's voice, as examples—a feeling of tightening up in some skeletal muscles, a disturbance of the action of one's belly, a realization that one has begun to sweat [p. 378]." In the adult, Sullivan maintained, anxiety is a "complex" emotion, and though he claimed not to know the components, he suggested "embarrassment, shame, humiliation, guilt, and chagrin." He thought that these "emotions" were "elaborated from anxiety by specific early training." These component or derivative feelings add up to essentially one emotion, shame–humiliation, which in conscious experience may take the form of guilt, shyness, or shame (Tomkins, 1962).

May (1950) has defined anxiety as diffuse apprehension, differing from fear in its vagueness and objectlessness, and as a state that is associated with feelings of uncertainty, helplessness, and threat to the core or essence of personality. As Epstein (1972) suggested, this definition tends simply to redefine anxiety as a type of great and intense fear. The other substantive aspects of the definition actually appear to involve emotion–cognition interactions—feelings of uncertainty, helplessness, and threat to the essence of the personality. Certainly the latter would have to be considered an admixture of cognition and emotion.

Epstein's own analysis of anxiety did not clearly and explicitly involve different fundamental emotion concepts. However, from experimental and illustrative situations which he uses to elucidate anxiety, one can easily infer the presence of distress and shame.

Spielberger (1966) and Levitt (1967) have essentially equated anxiety with fear. However, here again a close look at the substance of these investigators' writings and experimentation suggest that they too sometimes implicitly or explicitly include other emotions in their thinking and research on anxiety.

More recently Spielberger, Lushene, and McAdoo (in preparation) referred to anxiety as "complex emotional reactions." Though still emphasizing the fear or fearlike component of anxiety, these authors seem to have allowed for the possibility of other fundamental emotions being involved.

Basowitz, Persky, Korchin, and Grinker (1955) distinguished between shame anxiety and harm anxiety. In one sense this can be seen as another way of saying that shame and fear exist as separate components of anxiety. A number of theorists and investigators have linked shame and guilt with anxiety either by including them in their definitions of anxiety or by dealing with them as overlapping concepts.

Mosher (1966) defined guilt and anxiety as related concepts that have some independence. He has developed measures of guilt that correlated only .65 with the Taylor MAS. This is a lower correlation than would be desirable if the two instruments were supposed to measure the same construct. It is considerably lower than the correlation between two anxiety measures such as the MAS and the Spielberger–Gorsuch–Lushene (1970) anxiety scale, STAI.

Katz and Zigler (1967) discussed guilt as a parallel condition to anxiety. With chronological development the individual becomes more capable of self-derogation and of experiencing a wider disparity between real and ideal self-concepts. This increases the capacity for guilt and anxiety.

Maher (1966) saw guilt as a particular instance of anxiety, namely fear of loss of love and other punishments for one's own deeds. Spielberger (1966) alluded to "that special form of anxiety which is guilt [p. 3]."

Punishment may be seen as a common factor tending to link guilt and fear. Wrongdoing can lead to guilt and to the anticipation of punishment or to real punishment. Such punishment can evoke fear. This notion is consonant with some of the thinking of Unger (1962) and Sarason (1966).

Gottschalk and Gleser (1969) have classified anxiety, as they observed it in clinical experience, into six subtypes: death, mutilation, separation, guilt, shame, and diffuse or nonspecific anxiety. In these category terms we can see most of the emotion concepts that I have included in my definition of anxiety.

In his factor-analytic framework, Cattell (1966) views anxiety as a second-order factor. He has specified the first-order components of anxiety as: ego weakness, ergic tension, guilt proneness, defective integration of the self-sentiment, and protension or suspicion (Cattell & Scheier, 1961). In this analysis Cattell has clearly recognized anxiety as a complex of primary factors. My conception is somewhat similar in form, but there are several important differences. I believe factor analysis provides a useful tool in studying the conceptual phenomenology of the emotions, but I doubt that it can specify a fixed set of primary factors that constitute anxiety. My own factor-analytic research has supported the position that what we call anxiety is an unstable and variable set of fundamental emotions, which can sometimes be identified statistically as primary factors. Substantively, some of Cattell's primary factors seem to correspond or overlap with my fundamental emotion concepts; e.g., guilt proneness with shame–humiliation, protension, or suspicion with fear. However, such factors as ego weakness and defective integration of self-sentiment might relate to more than one fundamental emotion and to different emotions for different individuals. Finally, I see fundamental emotions as both structures and processes, and it is their process-nature that makes them somewhat elusive when one tries to pin them down in terms of factor structure. Emotions are highly active and flexible in nature. Human experience is much more frequently characterized by two or more fundamental emotions in a complex interaction than by any pure single-emotion state or experience.

B. VARIABLENESS AND INTERACTIONS
AMONG THE EMOTIONS IN ANXIETY

No single author has included all the posited six fundamental emotions in his definition of anxiety, nor has anyone conceptualized them as discrete yet systemic components of anxiety. It appears to me that all six considered as variable components of a system are necessary for an adequate theory of anxiety, even though all experiences that are described as anxiety may not include all the possible component fundamental emotions.

Indeed, certain individuals may be more guilt-prone and may tend to experience guilt as a very prominent component of a condition that may be anxiety. For others, shyness or distress may be quite important. However, fear is always the dominant emotion in the pattern.

The way the emotion components interact may also vary from individual to individual. A prominent distress component may amplify the fear component in some individuals and the shame component in others. An interest–excitement component may oscillate with fear or shame or inhibit distress.

C. THE EMOTION SYSTEM AND THE EMOTION PROCESS IN RELATION TO ANXIETY

My conception of anxiety derives from a more general theory of emotion and behavior. Let me state briefly the aspects of the general theory that are most pertinent to the conception of anxiety as a variable combination of fundamental emotions.

1. Definition of Emotion. Emotion is a complex process that has neurophysiological, motor–expressive, and phenomenological aspects. At the neurophysiological level emotion is defined primarily in terms of patterns of electrochemical acitvity in the nervous system, particularly in the hypothalamus, the limbic system, and in the facial and trigeminal nerves. The cutaneous nerve supply in the face and the proprioceptors in the facial muscles also participate in emotion at the neurophysiological level. At the motor level, emotion is primarily facial activity and facial patterning and is secondarily bodily (postural–gestural, visceral, and sometimes vocal) activity. At the phenomenological level, emotion is essentially motivating experience and/or experience that has immediate meaning and significance for the person.

My contention that any fundamental emotion has a motor or neuromuscular component and the fact that this component is of crucial importance in the feedback and component interactional processes of emotion and behavior are supported by the research of Malmo (1966) and his colleagues. Among other things, their research points very strongly to the fact that measurements of striate muscle activity are better for differentiating between anxiety patients and controls than the GSR, long considered by many as the best physiological measure of anxiety. Malmo's research has shown that psychiatric patients tend to have somewhat higher muscle-tension levels than normals. Following stimulation calculated to produce startle, patients showed a mean rise in muscle tension similar to that of normals, but while the normals returned to prestimulus level between .2 and .6 of a second, the patients' mean muscle tension level remained elevated significantly higher than that of normals for a period longer than 3 sec. Thus, neuromuscular changes occur in emotion for normals and for anxiety patients, and the evidence indicates that these changes in the motor component of emotion may serve as an index of maladjustment.

When neurochemical activity via innate programs produces patterned neuromuscular responses of the face and body and the feedback from these responses is transformed into conscious form, the result is a discrete fundamental emotion that is both a motivating and meaningful cue-producing experience. Phenomenologically, positive emotions have inherent characteristics that tend to enhance one's sense of well-being and to instigate and sustain approach toward constructive interactions or relations with the involved persons, situations, or objects. Negative emotions tend to be sensed as noxious and difficult to tolerate and as instigating avoidance of and/or nonconstructive interactions or relations. While certain emotions tend to be positive and others negative in import, these terms cannot be applied rigidly to the various emotions without considering other factors.

The emotion system consists of the nine major emotions and their interrelationships. The emotions are: interest, enjoyment, surprise, distress, disgust, anger, shame (including shyness and guilt), fear, and contempt. As I have indicated, five of these (or six, counting shyness and guilt separately) may be components of anxiety—fear, distress, anger, shyness, guilt, and interest.

2. The Emotions as a Personality Subsystem. The concept of the emotion system is important in my analysis of anxiety. While I think it is important to conceive of the fundamental emotions as a system of interacting and mutually influencing components, I would like to caution against thinking of the emotion system as having all the characteristics of any known type of system. I would be particularly careful in considering it as a hydraulic system, a digital system, or as any other kind of computer or electronic system.

Perhaps the most important point here is that by conceiving of the emotions as constituting a system, we accept the principle that each of the fundamental emotions can interact with and influence other fundamental emotions within the system. Furthermore, as any separate fundamental emotion is in itself a system (or subsystem) having its three basic components (neurophysiological, behavioral–expressive, and experiential), we can also assume that one or more of the components of a given emotion may interact with one or more of the components of another or of several other fundamental emotions. It is the assumption of a highly flexible and interactive system of emotions and emotion components that renders feasible my present conception of anxiety.

The bases for describing the emotions as a system have been detailed elsewhere (Izard, 1971; Izard & Tomkins, 1966; Tomkins, 1962) so I shall merely summarize some of the main points. Various emotions are interrelated in dynamic and relatively stable ways on the basis of both their innate and learned characteristics. Some emotions are organized in hierarchical relationship with respect to the gradients of neural stimulation that activate them (see Tomkins, 1962, 1970).

Certain emotions have been considered by various theorists (Darwin, 1872; Plutchik, 1962) as existing in polar relationships. For example, joy and sadness, anger and fear, and other pairs are often considered as polar opposites. Again, I would caution against analogy to an oversimplified model such as the actions and interactions of positive and negative poles in a magnetic field.

Certain emotions tend to have fairly regular relationships under certain circumstances. For example, interest may oscillate with fear as an organism explores some unknown object or situation, and contempt may oscillate with enjoyment to produce some of the heinous effects observed in interracial and intergroup conflicts.

All the emotions tend to have great generality and flexibility as well as other common characteristics, such as their noncyclical nature. Emotions influence or regulate other personality systems, frequently acting as amplifiers or attenuators of homeostatic, drive, cognitive, and motor processes.

The emotion system interacts with other personality systems. The brainstem reticular system serves as a regulator or control for the neural component of emotion, acting either as amplifier or as attenuator. The glandular–visceral system helps prepare the body for determined and directed action and helps sustain the emotion or emotion-related phenomena. The cardiovascular and respiratory systems also interact in important ways with emotion. The major personality systems of cognition and motor activity typically interact with the emotion system in almost all organismic endeavors, and effective personality functioning depends on balance and integration of the activities of these systems.

3. The Emotion Process and the Activation of a Fundamental Emotion. An appreciation of the complexity of the emotion process and its activation is important in understanding the analysis of anxiety as a variable combination of interacting fundamental emotions. An effort toward a complete analysis of the highly complex neurophysiology and phenomenology of the emotion process has been detailed elsewhere (Izard, 1971). Here, I shall simply illustrate its complexity and something of its nature by considering the problem of initiating or activating an emotion. (The various forms of the verb "activate" and the noun "activation" are used here in their more generic sense and not in reference to specific functions of any neural mechanism such as the brainstem reticular system.)

In addition to certain innate releasers and Tomkins' (1962) principle relating to density of neural firing, there are three other principles that may help explain how the different emotions are activated and how it happens that there is some patterning in emotion-related person–environment interactions. First, there is the possibility of innate pathways or neural programs that may be characterized by a selective sensitivity to certain inputs or environmental conditions. The positive emotional responses of infants are more consistently triggered by human than nonhuman stimulation. This principle of selective sensitivity may operate somewhat differently at different ages or stages of development. With increasing maturity, input patterns or environmental conditions can be psychologically simulated through cognitive processes such as dreams and imagination. Producing a particular fundamental emotion by activating an innate neural program subserving (or constituting the neurochemical component of) that emotion would seem to call for *selective* neural stimulation more than for a variation in the intensity of neural stimulation.

As I have shown elsewhere (Izard, 1971), sociocultural phenomena constitute another factor influencing emotion processes. Cultural differences in attitudes toward certain emotions are incorporated during socialization and result in different relationships among the emotions and between the antecedents, concomitants, and consequences of a given emotion.

Another principle that helps explain some of the patterning or consistencies between particular antecedents and particular emotions is learning and idiosyncratic experience. Distress may

54

elicit fear in one individual and shame in another, due to differences in personal experience.

Factors described by any of these principles—selective sensitivity of innate neural programs, changes in density of neural firing, idiosyncratic experience, and socialization—may activate or influence the activation of an emotion and play some role in the emotion process and in emotion-related person—environment interactions.

Elsewhere (Izard, 1971) I have specified several types of person—environment interactions and several types of intraindividual processes that can initiate or activate emotion. These processes include perceptual, hormonal, and skeletal—motor activity as well as memory, imagination, and proprioception.

After the initial activity in the emotion process, the order and loci of second and subsequent steps or phases of the process are partially a function of the site and nature of the initial activity. The emotion process is not a lockstep sequence of cortical, facial, postural, motor, reticular activating system (RAS), ANS, neural, glandular, and visceral activities. There is no fixed number of such activities that is required for activation of any or all of the components of emotion. The emotion process can begin with memory or imagination in the ideation centers of the brain or with perception of, or excitation of receptors by, an external emotion-effective object or event. [The term "perception" is used here to signify stimulation input—the selective or demanded energizing (excitation) of receptors or sense organs. It does not refer to a central, cognitive—interpretive activity.]

Although the problem of emotion activation is quite complex, the complete emotion process is obviously of still greater complexity. The activation of emotion is only the beginning of the process, but it illustrates the intricacy of emotion and its interactions with other personality and person—environment processes.

4. How Emotion and Emotion Components Combine and Interact. Each of the fundamental emotions has distinct components. The components of emotion are largely interdependent, but they also have a degree of independence, especially under certain conditions. A feedback or interaction mechanism is necessary for the integration of the components in the process that produces a complete and discrete emotion. Concomitantly, the integration of emotion components into a particular individual emotion is a fundamental part of the process whereby the discrete emotions are differentiated. Without such integration of components we can have incomplete or undifferentiated emotions. We can have facial pattern-ing without the phenomenological existence of emotion in conscious experience. We can have undifferentiated or nonspecific emotional experience without a particular facial pattern. Finally, we might have facial activity innervated by the VIIth nerve, but interruption of feedback from the face via the Vth nerve or failure of such feedback to achieve awareness. Emotional experience would then have to be based on the slower and grosser feedback from the viscera and/or from postural activity. Such emotion would be gross and vague and would lack the character of a discrete emotion.

Components of two or more emotions may make simul-taneous or rapidly alternating demands on neurophysiological mech-anisms and on consciousness. Such a mixture of the interacting and alternating components of different fundamental emotions could help account for the vagueness and the undifferentiated character so frequently attributed to such elusive concepts as anxiety and de-pression.

I view the emotion component of facial–postural activity (neuromuscular patterning) as crucially important in determining whether we experience an unambiguous fundamental emotion such as fear or a complex combination-interaction of emotions such as anxiety. In infancy and childhood, facial expressions clearly com-municate emotions to others. The proprioceptive patterns of these expressions determine or significantly influence the brain processes that generate the subjective experience of a discrete fundamental emotion. In American culture, as well as in many other cultures, socialization processes typically lead to a diminution or suppression of facial patterning as the individual moves toward later childhood and adolescence. However, the emotion system and the emotion process can still function in essentially the same way as in infancy and early childhood because of developmental changes in the psycho-neurological mechanisms which underlie the development of certain cognitive abilities. When an individual has learned a given facial pattern or pattern of proprioception and is capable of retrieving it from memory, the image of the pattern can operate in a reafferent or inner loop in an analogous fashion to the motor pattern in the afferent or outer loop through the face. The memory image may substitute for or complement the actual motor pattern, or a dimin-ished and micromomentary pattern, in the face.

The pattern of facial activity or the image of the corre-sponding pattern of proprioception is a chief determinant of the specific quality of any felt emotion. If the pattern is that of an innately programmed fundamental emotion there will be a corresponding specific emotional experience. A fundamental emotion will be felt. If the pattern involves elements of two or more innate programs the result will be mixed emotion. If it consists of two or more fundamental emotions in rapid sequence or alternation, the experience will be a pattern or combination of emotions. Such is the case with the anxiety state. It is a mixture, or, at best a variable combination of emotions. It has no fixed neurophysiological structure, no characteristic face, and no singular phenomenology.

The various emotions that constitute anxiety may oscillate in awareness or move back and forth across several levels of awareness. Likewise, at the neurophysiological level, elements of one emotion may interact in various ways with elements of another.

However, two or more fundamental emotions which pattern frequently may produce over time a relatively stable, well-defined emotional experience that may be considered a complex of emotions strongly influenced by learning and experience. If there are certain prevailing conditions that regularly elicit this combination of emotions (pattern of fundamentals), this pattern and its related cognitive–motor behavior may take on the nature of a personality characteristic or trait. One possible result would be a pattern that could be called "trait anxiety," a complex trait subserved by a relatively consistent yet variable pattern of emotions. It is important that the anxiety trait, as the anxiety state, be conceived as a variable combination of interacting fundamental emotions. There is the possibility that the more fixed and stable the combination of emotions in state or trait anxiety, the more likely we are to have psychopathology.

I use the terms "state anxiety" and "trait anxiety" with a high degree of tentativeness. In my view any clinically useful analysis of anxiety calls for a statement of the particular profile or pattern of emotions characteristic of the individual and the experience under consideration. The particular fundamental emotions and emotion interactions involved in what is called anxiety have to be considered as something that varies with individuals and situations. However, as already suggested, it may be possible to delineate certain types or groups of individuals as characterized by an anxiety that is defined as a particular pattern of emotions and emotion interactions that tend to prevail under specifiable conditions.

This formulation of anxiety has implications for psychodiagnostic assessment and psychotherapy and for the analysis and management of interpersonal and intergroup problems. For one thing, therapy or any therapeutic behavior change program dealing with anxiety might best begin with an attempt to analyze the anxiety into its component fundamental emotions, assessing the degree to which each is present and selecting appropriate treatment or management procedures that take each emotion, its interactions, and its motivational-experiential properties into account.

III. SUMMARY

Anxiety theory and research have suffered from inconsistent and inadequate definitions of the concept. For a long time theorists and investigators have tended to think of anxiety as unidimensional. Clinical experience has always run counter to such a conception. The professional attempting to understand and help individuals has never been convinced that anxiety is a singular and simple thing, either in terms of its motivational qualities or in terms of its effect upon adjustment and behavior. A close look at experimental and clinical literature reveals that even authors who spoke of anxiety as unitary often included in their descriptions of anxiety two or more relatively independent components of some sort. A central thesis of this chapter is that anxiety is not unipolar, unidimensional, or unifactor in nature.

Differential emotion theory defines anxiety as a combination or pattern of fundamental emotions including fear and two or more of the emotions of distress, anger, shame (including shyness and guilt), and the positive emotion of interest–excitement. These six emotions are considered as variable components of a complex pattern. The relative importance of these emotions in the anxiety pattern varies with the individual and the situation. Individual variations in the pattern of emotions in anxiety are a function both of hereditary and experiential determinants.

Since anxiety was defined as a pattern of fundamental emotions, the chapter dealt briefly with the definition of emotion and the emotions as a personality subsystem. Emotion was defined as a complex process that has neurophysiological, motor–expressive, and phenomenological aspects. Common characteristics of emotions, such as generality and flexibility, and certain regularities in interrelationships among emotions were discussed as factors that characterize the emotions as a system.

The complexity of the emotion system was illustrated by discussion of several ways in which an emotion or an emotion

58

process can be activated. Selective sensitivity, variations in density of neural firing, idiosyncratic experience, and socialization effects may activate or influence the activation of an emotion and play some role in the emotion process and in emotion-related person–environment interactions.

Finally, a statement was given of the ways in which emotion and emotion components combine and interact. Integrated emotions combine and interact in numerous ways. Moreover, the components of two or more discrete emotions may mix, producing vague and undifferentiated feelings and possibly maladaptive behavior. Anxiety is a pattern or combination of discrete emotions, and in addition, it may include a mixture of the components of two or more fundamental emotions. One of the problems in studying anxiety results from its great complexity. It is a variable combination of elements; it has no characteristic behavioral–expressive component; and it has no singular phenomenology. This formulation of anxiety has implications for psychodiagnostic assessment and psychotherapy and for the analysis and management of interpersonal and intergroup problems.

CHAPTER FOUR

Differential Emotion Theory in Relation to Classical Psychoanalytic and Cognitive Theories of Emotion and Anxiety

To help clarify the position I am taking in this book, I shall draw some distinctions between my theory, classical psychoanalytic theory, and the theories of Lazarus and Averill (1972), Epstein (1972), and Janis (1969). I see the four authors as representing different versions of a cognitive theory of emotion. Thus, the differences in the positions of these authors and my own will also distinguish my position from that of a number of other researchers who are influenced by cognitive theory.

I. THE CLASSICAL PSYCHOANALYTIC THEORY OF ANXIETY

Freud's theory of anxiety is presented rather succinctly in his own work, *Inhibitions, Symptoms, and Anxiety* (1959), and in the translator's introduction to that work. It has also been dealt with by numerous other writers, a good example being May (1950). In view of the relative availability of Freud's theory in his original work and its familiarity through frequent treatment in secondary sources, a brief summary will suffice here. Particular attention will be paid to elements of Freudian theory that have been generally neglected by other writers, especially those elements which bear some relationship to differential emotion theory or to cognitive theory.

4. Differential Emotion Theory

A. THE EGO AS THE SEAT OF ANXIETY

Freud's early theory of anxiety was that repressed libidinal impulses were directly transformed into anxiety. His final view of anxiety essentially reversed this process, and anxiety was seen as the cause of repression rather than vice versa. Since the ego is the mechanism of repression, Freud, in his final view, considered the ego as the seat of anxiety, but he quickly reminded his reader that the ego is identical with the id except that it is a specially differentiated part. The ego is the organized part of the id. It is incorrect to view the ego and the id as always at war with one another, though this may often be the case.

Freud's conception of signal anxiety confirmed his view that the ego was the seat of anxiety. Only the ego can make judgments about a situation of danger and can feel anxiety. The anxiety serves as a signal of potential danger and calls for action aimed at preventing or coping with the situation.

Freud's conception of signal anxiety as a response to threat and his notion that anxiety involves expectation and indefiniteness of object are very similar to concepts dealt with in the cognitive theories to be reviewed later. In the case of signal anxiety, the ego submits to slight anxiety to escape extreme anxiety. Realistic anxiety involves a known danger or object, while neurotic anxiety involves an unknown danger or object.

Anxiety may be either the automatic innate response to a traumatic situation or the response to perceived dangers. Although Freud did not say so, surely the innate anxiety response would not be dependent on the ego or rational process. In the case of perceived danger, anxiety serves as a warning signal. According to Freud, all danger situations involve separation from or loss of a loved object or loss of its love. The most common danger situations are birth, loss of mother as an object, loss of penis or castration, loss of cathected objects, loss of love, or loss of the superego's love.

B. SOURCES OF ANXIETY

Freud almost made a three-way distinction among sources of anxiety: the traumatic situation in which the individual actually suffers some injury or harm, the situation of danger in which physical or psychological harm is imminent, and finally the threat of danger, or as Freud originally stated it, the threat that the danger situation will occur. In the final analysis, Freud distinguished only two situations, the traumatic situation and the danger situation being treated similarly as situations in which anxiety is innately released and takes on the nature of a species-common hysterical attack.

Birth was considered the prototypic danger experience. Apparently the critical factor in this danger experience is separation. Since birth is the prototypic danger from which all other danger experiences arise, one can find in the separation experience the common theme which links all of them.

What constitutes a danger situation changes with age. In early childhood it is the loss of object; during the phallic phase of development it is the castration danger. After the superego develops, social anxiety may become an internal substitute for an external danger, and moral anxiety may develop as a completely endopsychic phenomenon.

Freud noted that anxiety could not be considered as the only result of loss or separation. Mourning or grief also results from loss of object and separation. Freud was not able to draw clear criteria for determining when loss resulted in anxiety and when it resulted in grief or mourning. Freud was generally unsuccessful in distinguishing among what he considered the various unpleasurable affects. He recognized the need for distinguishing among them, but was never successful in doing so.

Although Freud did not clearly say so, he apparently thought that the threat of danger was the result of a cognitive process. As already indicated, Freud believed in innate anxiety, and he did not rule out the possibility of the innateness of the cognitive process involved in signal anxiety, a process that can easily be interpreted as appraisal. The general sense of his statements about perceived threat suggests that he viewed this source of anxiety as the one which allowed for individually learned anxiety responses and individual differences in response to different situations. Freud can therefore be credited with the notions that *(a)* individuals differ in their perception and appraisal of the world about them, and *(b)* what triggers anxiety in nondangerous situations is a result of individual learning.

In his conception of "threat of occurrence of a danger situation" as the source of signal anxiety, Freud laid the foundation for the cognitive theories of emotion and anxiety which will be reviewed in the next section. The threat of the occurrence of a danger situation is a function of the individual's appraisal of the situation. Freud allowed for the possibility that appraisal may be determined or at least influenced by innate processes (mnemic images). Contemporary cognitive theories do not. Freud apparently considered the threat–anxiety paradigm as the one which accounts for most of what many contemporary theorists call "learned anxiety."

Freud thought that signal anxiety was the most ubiquitous and most frequent type. He viewed signal anxiety as having an inherently adaptive function. In foreseeing the possibility of danger, it prepares the individual to prevent the danger situation from occurring. More specifically, he saw signal anxiety as restricting and regulating emotion (discharge) and as facilitating adaptive behavior (operation of normal defenses). However, when defenses are inadequate, anxiety increases, becomes disrupting, disorganizing, and maladaptive. Unrealistic appraisal, perceiving danger where none exists, and inadequate defenses lead to anxiety neuroses.

C. INNATE (AUTOMATIC) ANXIETY AND SIGNAL ANXIETY

One very important aspect of Freudian anxiety theory which has been systematically ignored by subsequent interpreters and followers was Freud's belief that anxiety as experienced in a traumatic situation is innate. When an individual is confronted with a traumatic situation, he responds with what Freud termed automatic anxiety. There can be no doubt that Freud was referring to innate anxiety. He used the terms automatic and innate interchangeably. Freud (1959) assumed that the mechanism of innate anxiety was a mnemic image, a kind of inherited memory which today might be termed engram or innate neural program.

> Anxiety is not newly created in repression; it is reproduced as an affective state in accordance with an already existing mnemic image. If we go further and inquire into the origin of that anxiety—and of affects in general—we shall be leaving the realm of pure psychology and entering the borderland of physiology. Affective states have become incorporated in the mind as precipitates of primaeval traumatic experience and when a similar situation occurs, they are revived like mnemic symbols. . . . In man and the higher animals, it would seem that the act of birth, as the individual's first experience of anxiety, has given the affect of anxiety certain characteristic forms of expression. But, while acknowledging this connection, we must not lay undue stress on it nor overlook the fact that biological necessity demands that a situation of danger should have an affective symbol, so that a symbol of this kind would have to be created in any case [pp. 93–94].*

*From Freud, S. Inhibitions, symptoms, and anxiety. In J. Strachey (Ed.), *The standard edition of the complete psychological works of Sigmund Freud.* Vol. 20, pp. 93-94. London: Hogarth Press, 1959.

I. The Classical Psychoanalytic Theory of Anxiety

Freud's belief that anxiety in traumatic situations was innate was linked to his conception of anxiety as an affect. Freud regarded affects as either universal and innate hysterical attacks or as acquired attacks.

Freud leaned on his conception of an innate component of anxiety in explaining some of the anxieties of small children. He thought that children's fears of "small animals, thunderstorms, etc., might perhaps be accounted for as vestigial traces of the congenital preparedness to meet real dangers, which is so strongly developed in other animals [p. 168]." Anxiety also occurs in children as a result of losing or missing someone who is loved or longed for. This is partly due to the fact that the child's mnemic image of the loved person is intensely cathected. Loss leaves the child at "wit's end" and the expression of anxiety is seemingly its only way to cope. At a deeper level, according to Freud, it is the loss of satisfaction or a "growing tension due to need" which causes the child's anxiety.

In addition to the automatic or innate anxiety with which the individual responds to the traumatic situation, there is, as already noted, anxiety which functions as the signal or response to the threat of occurrence of a traumatic situation. In this case the anxiety signals the individual to avoid or to prepare to deal with an approaching danger.

There can be no doubt that Freud, unlike many of his contemporary admirers, believed that anxiety as well as other negative affects were inherited—innate and universal. It was probably the lingering influence of 19th-century rationalism that led Freud to view the innate response as inexpedient. He saw the automatic and immediate response to a traumatic situation or a situation of danger as inexpedient, and, in contrast, he saw signal anxiety that follows from the threat of imminent or approaching danger as expedient. Though Freud did not make the point explicitly, he apparently considered automatic innately released affect as inexpedient and maladaptive because it was not preceded, restrained, and regulated by rational (cognitive) processes.

Freud's final statement of his theory of anxiety is open to the interpretation that innate factors in the form of mnemic images not only account for automatic or innately released anxiety in traumatic or realistic danger situations, but influence acquired or learned anxiety as well. This may be partly due to the fact that Freud believed that certain animal phobias were innate, and two of the cases on which he leaned heavily in his theorizing, Little Hans and the Wolfman, involved animal phobias. Furthermore, since he believed that the child had a mnemic image of the primal love object (mother image), it is not a far step to believe that the child has a mnemic image of the father, an image which has threatening features. This would certainly help account for Freud's belief in the universality of the Oedipus complex and the fear of castration. Freud thought the animal phobias of Little Hans and the Wolfman consisted of "untransformed fear of castration." The ideas of their anxiety—being bitten by a horse or devoured by a wolf—were distortions of the idea of being castrated by their father. The anxiety in these cases was response to what was perceived as a real danger, and that anxiety brought about a repression of the fear of being castrated by the father. The possibility that Freud (1959) believed in the existence of an innate mnemic image of a potentially castrating father is also supported by his belief that the ego recognizes the danger of castration in any disguise—a horse, a wolf, or whatever.

> The conclusion we have come to, then, is this. Anxiety is a reaction to a situation of danger. It is obviated by the ego's doing something to avoid that situation or to withdraw from it. It might be said that symptoms are created so as to avoid the generating of anxiety. But this does not go deep enough. It would be truer to say that symptoms are created so as to avoid a *danger-situation* whose presence has been signalled by the generation of something traceable back to castration [pp. 128-129].*

At the time when Freud believed that anxiety was the result of the repression of libidinal impulses and the subsequent direct transformation of excess libidinal energy into anxiety, he also believed that instinctual impulses were dangerous. He later changed this view, stating that instinctual impulses were dangerous only insofar as they entailed real external danger, i.e., the danger of castration.

In the framework of differential emotion theory, the terms "acquired anxiety" or "learned anxiety" are misnomers. One does not learn how to feel afraid, distressed, ashamed, or anxious. On the other hand, one may learn to respond with the emotions of anxiety to certain persons, situations, or cues. It would be more accurate to speak of learned or acquired anxiety cues. It is the value or characteristic of the cue that is learned, and the value may be realistically or unrealistically assessed. Freud seemed to have appreciated this distinction, though, to my knowledge, he never made it explicit.

*From Freud, S. Inhibitions, symptoms, and anxiety. In J. Strachey (Ed.), *The standard edition of the complete psychological works of Sigmund Freud.* Vol. 20, pp. 128-129. London: Hogarth Press, 1959.

One might reason that realistic assessment and appropriate emotional response to the threat of occurrence of a danger situation are relatively more influenced by innate factors, whereas unrealistic assessment and inappropriate emotional response may be relatively more influenced by learning. Of course, there is the possibility that an innate mechanism such as a mnemic image could be defective or the information in it ineffectively decoded and processed. Though classical psychoanalytic theory and differential emotion theory differ in significant ways, they are in agreement in seeing both innate and acquired factors as important in anxiety.

II. EMOTION AND BEHAVIOR AS A RESULT OF COGNITION

Lazarus and Averill (1972) imply that emotion must follow from the purely cognitive process of appraisal. They assume that a person or animal proceeds through processes described as primary appraisal, secondary appraisal, and reappraisal, all presumably cognitive functions, without experiencing any emotion. That is quite a bit of cognition to have occur in the face of danger, threat, or provocation prior to any emotion or emotion-related activity. Yet, if cognitive theorists admit that some emotion may follow immediately after primary appraisal and before the other steps in the appraisal process, then the notion that cognition is the sole mediator of emotion appears untenable. Once on the intrapsychic scene, it seems highly probable that emotion will influence the subsequent stages of appraisal and all other organismic processes and activities. It seems highly unlikely that a person can complete an appraisal without some interaction between emotion and cognition.

A weakness in Lazarus and Averill's dependence on cognitive processes as the basis for emotion differentiation in experience and behavior is exemplified in their efforts to distinguish between separation distress and separation anxiety as experienced by the infant and young child. They are undoubtedly correct in arguing that separation distress is more closely related to grief than to fear or anxiety (see also Averill, 1968). I see distress, as defined in Table 5-1 (page 84), as the central emotion in grief, but I do not believe that we can look to cognitive process as the sole means of mediating the experience of distress. Lazarus and Averill acknowledge that the infant can experience separation distress as early as 6 months. Many observers would agree that infants experience distress of some sort almost from the beginning of life, as witnessed by the cry of distress and its ubiquity at birth and in the early weeks following birth. No one would argue that distress in infancy is accompanied by the same symbolic processes as distress in adulthood, but some would agree that infantile distress is a valid distress experience, having psychological structure and significance similar to that of later distress experiences.

If we accept the fact that the infant does experience distress at birth and in the first days of life, then it seems to render untenable the notion that this experience is mediated by symbolic processes of the type described by Lazarus and Averill. As noted earlier, one does not learn how to feel distressed or how to feel afraid. One does eventually associate certain stimuli and certain actions with distress and other stimuli and actions with fear, but this learning process does not mean that the individual learns the meaning and significance of the emotion experience itself. The failure to recognize the utility of conceptual distinctions between the intraindividual emotion process, on the one hand, and antecedent and consequent person–environment or social processes on the other, has created much confusion in emotion theory and research.

Lazarus and Averill see appraisal and subsequent cognition as the activators of emotion. Furthermore, they maintain that the ebb and flow of emotion as well as subsequent coping behavior are a result of changing cognitive activity that arises from new input and from feedback from reaction and reflection, all of which alter the appraisal. The fundamental question that Lazarus and Averill have not answered is what motivates and sustains cognitive activity. They cannot answer this question simply by saying inputs or feedback from reaction and reflection, for this is a circular and overly mechanistic s-r-like formulation. They might say that life itself guarantees cognitive activity, but this would leave unanswered even more critical questions. What guides perceptual–cognitive activity? What determines the selection of sensory data and the focusing of input? Obviously a person or animal does not react to all the data available to the sensory systems and the feedback mechanisms. I propose that the emotions play a crucial role in selecting sensory data and guiding the processing of these data and subsequent activities. As I have argued previously (Izard, 1971), meaningful or purposive perceptual –cognitive processes are initiated and in part sustained and guided by the fundamental emotions, with the emotion of interest often playing a key role.

The principle of the primacy of cognition in organismic functioning also runs counter to general principles underlying phylogeny and evolution. It implies that in the evolutionary process animals had to be able to "think" before they could "feel." The opposite case seems much more plausible. The principle of the primacy of cognition as elaborated by cognitive theorists also requires that cognitive processes generate and guide the coping or problem-solving efforts that an individual makes when the demands he faces are highly relevant to his survival and welfare. I believe with Jolly (1966) and Hamburg (1963) that emotions and emotion processes preceded higher-order intelligence. In evolutionary perspective, it seems highly probable that emotion played a vital role in problem-solving and survival efforts of animals and man. Lack of the experience of anger in the face of a need to defend one's physical self or one's integrity, lack of fear in the face of imminent danger, or lack of interest in the face of a need to perceive and sort out relevant data may well have proved a fatal deficiency in a coping or survival effort.

Of course, cognition plays a great role in influencing emotion and emotion-related behavior, but this role develops through conditioning, learning, and idiosyncratic experience built on a foundation of evolutionary–hereditary mechanisms. In essence, the individual does not learn how to be afraid (a hereditary given), but he learns some of the things to be afraid of and what to do in the face of these things. Putting it another way, an individual expands his flexibility and adaptability as a living organism as he generates more and more cognitions or cognitive mechanisms for influencing emotion and emotion-related behaviors. This is made possible through the acquisition of language and the skills of symbolizing. As required by the innumerable man-made dangers of our era, an individual learns efficiently to rule in or rule out certain situations as fearworthy and as requiring responses appropriate to fear. In this way cognitive processes increase man's freedom by increasing his power to differentiate between situations worthy of increased emotion and action and those that are not.

As I have noted elsewhere (Izard, 1971), the position developed by Lazarus and his associates (Averill, Opton, & Lazarus, 1969) contains many points of similarity with Arnold's system. In turn, Arnold drew some of her concepts from St. Thomas Aquinas. I refer especially to the Thomistic notion that organisms' responses follow from and are guided by cognitive processes. In the fourth article of the *Summa Theologica*, Aquinas (ca. 1266, translated, 1948) observed that animal motion and action follow apprehension. He defined the estimative power as one of the four interior sensitive powers which constitute the part of the soul designated as the intellect. He pointed out that it is the estimative power which enables the animal to apprehend something as harmful or beneficial. Such apprehension may be based on the perception of intention, a process that may be independent of the form or color of the object.

Actually, Aquinas leaned more toward innate (as opposed to environmental) determinism than do contemporary cognitive theorists. He gave as an example of estimative power the sheep's apprehension of the wolf as dangerous. The apprehension, according to Aquinas, is not based on the color or shape of the wolf but on the fact that the wolf is a natural enemy and intends harm. Aquinas pointed out that this natural estimative power in animals is referred to as the cogitative power in man, the power which enables him to discover intentions that define things as harmful or beneficial.

Aquinas defined apprehension as a power or function of intellect which in turn is a power of the soul. Arnold, Lazarus and Averill, and other cognitive theorists follow essentially the same logic, making emotion dependent upon apprehension and recognizing apprehension as an intellective or cognitive function. In this system, the soul or, in more contemporary psychological terminology, cognition and such cognitive functions as estimation and appraisal, tend to take on the quality of an entelechy or autochthonous process which operates without "motivation" or influence from other processes. Therefore, Arnold, Lazarus and Averill, and cognitive theorists of similar orientation (e.g., Epstein, 1972) are essentially in agreement with the 13th-century rationalism of St. Thomas Aquinas. Again, as with Freud, they overlook Aquinas' concept of innateness as a factor in appraisal (apprehension) and emotion. Other than this, I see no useful distinction between the central thesis of the cognitive theorists and Aquinas' proposition that emotions are strong and transient affections, reactions of the sensory–rational being to things apprehended or known.

In contrast to the cognitive theories of emotion, and by way of summary of the differences between differential emotion theory and cognitive theory with respect to the role of cognition, I assume that emotion may be mediated or elicited and influenced not only by cognition but by innate releasers, homeostatic processes, drives, and other emotions or emotion components. I believe that these other emotion activators and regulators can, under certain conditions, operate completely independently of cognition and that they frequently operate with some degree of independence, particularly of conscious cognition. In turn, emotion enjoys the same kind of independence, yet it is continually interacting with and influencing cognition and action.

The rational-man ideology, brought into sharp focus by Aquinas and represented in contemporary behavioral science by cognitive theories of behavior, holds that processes like primary and secondary appraisal and reappraisal and subsequent cognition determine the quality and degree of every emotional response. Furthermore, it maintains that the coping processes are also set in motion by appraisal and cognition. This vitiates or drastically limits the significance of emotion and its role in other important psychological and behavioral processes.

III. EMOTION AS RESPONSE OR RESPONSE SYNDROME

Cognitive theorists have maintained that emotion is really not very important. They see emotion primarily as response, as the result of things rather than as the cause of things. Lazarus and Averill (1972) go so far as to describe emotions as a syndrome, a term typically applied to a set of symptoms resulting from a disease.

Lazarus and Averill describe, as the basic components of the emotion response syndrome, cognitive appraisal, physiological reaction, expressive behavior, and instrumental acts. The breakdown bears some similarity to Izard and Tomkins' (1966) analysis of the components of emotion as neurophysiological, behavioral–expressive, and phenomenological or experiential. However, the similarity between the two theoretical models is more superficial than real in view of the other fundamental differences in conception. Lazarus and Averill emphasize the response quality of emotion and fail to distinguish between intraperson and person–environment activities at the conceptual level. Again and again Lazarus and Averill underscore the point that the essential determinant of behavior is cognition and that emotion is a kind of by-product of cognition and a concomitant of instrumental behavior. This is diametrically opposed to the position of Izard and Tomkins and a number of other theorists who see emotion as having very important motivational characteristics including guidance and cue-producing functions and also the function of giving meaning and significance to life.

In elaborating the concept of emotion as response, Lazarus and Averill actually draw an analogy between emotion and disease. I see this as an unfortunate comparison. There are so many characteristics of disease that have no counterpart in emotion that the analogy seems far more misleading and harmful than enlightening and helpful. Perhaps the greatest contrasting characteristic between disease

71

and emotion is the very fact that disease is considered an abnormal process, typically involving invasion of the organism by foreign bodies with consequent disruption and dysfunction of various organs and systems. Emotion, on the other hand, is a natural and normal subsystem of the person or organism. It requires no invasion of foreign bodies and no stimulation or input from the outside in order for the process to be initiated and to proceed through its course.

Serious conceptual problems result from the overinclusion of relatively independent subsystems in the Lazarus–Averill definition of the emotion response syndrome. They maintain that an emotion syndrome includes instrumental acts and other coping responses. To say that an emotion includes instrumental motor activities reflects Lazarus and Averill's tendency to fail to differentiate between the intraperson emotion process and the activities related to and subsequent to the emotion process.

In my view it would be more nearly correct to say that any emotion such as fear or anger involves a neuromuscular component. This neuromuscular component results in a certain patterning of the muscular–skeletal system. This neuromuscular patterning may take on the appearance of a bodily attitude consonant with withdrawal or movement away from objects when indeed there are externally perceived objects. But in fear, or certainly in anxiety as defined by Lazarus and Averill, there is not always an externally perceived object. There is, in effect, nothing external to the person from which to escape.

The point at issue is that the neuromuscular patterning inherent in the intraindividual emotion process should be conceptually distinguished from instrumental acts or person–environment interaction which, for example, involve the gross movement of the organism toward or away from a person or object. Of course, the neuromuscular patterning inherent in each emotion normally facilitates adaptive action on the part of the person or organism. Nevertheless, the connections between the neuromuscular patterning and the specific motor activities and person–environment interactions that follow must be conceived as being variable and flexible. This conception is necessary in order to explain adequately the degree of flexibility and freedom which the individual has in acting in relation to his emotions. To suggest an invariable connection between emotion and instrumental response, as implicit in Lazarus and Averill's formulation, is to make the kind of mistake made in early s-r psychology and early instinct psychology. It amounts to considering man far more mechanistic and automatic than he really is.

Another problem with Lazarus and Averill's overinclusive definition of emotion or the emotion response syndrome is pointed up by the contention that "most emotions cannot be defined without reference to their objects." They note that Freud used distinctions between sources (objects) of threat as a means of distinguishing between objective anxiety (fear), social anxiety (shame), and moral anxiety (guilt). This is another way of saying that emotion is to be understood as response and that the response cannot be understood without specifying and understanding the stimulus. This takes us back to the search for *the* stimulus and to an inexorably oversimplified s-r psychology. It is a denial of the crucial importance of emotion, an experience defined not by a stimulus but by evolutionary–hereditary processes. It is like saying that the infant does not know how to feel distressed until it can conceptualize the distressing situation or that an individual does not know how to feel angry until he can specify the nature of the provocation. This formulation flatly contradicts the concepts of free-floating anxiety or objectless fear. The concept of objectless fear has long been viable in common sense and clinically. One of the basic types of fear situations is one in which the object is unknown, or at least unfamiliar and undefined. If the unknown or mysterious quality is sensed as dangerous the individual may experience fear, but if it is not sensed as dangerous he may only experience excitement or heightened interest.

In the individual case, it is sometimes important to know what elicits fear, but what elicits fear in a particular individual may tell us nothing about the intraindividual emotion process. It may tell us nothing about the neurophysiology of fear, nothing about the behavioral–expressive component of fear, and nothing about the experience of fear and its meaning and significance for the individual. Thus, as differential emotion theory suggests, there is a place for the study of intraperson emotion per se. The understanding of emotion or emotion process can contribute to the understanding of the person and his social interactions, with or without the specification of a particular stimulus and a particular response that might sometimes be associated as an antecedent and consequence of the emotion.

IV. EMOTION RESPONSE SYNDROME VERSUS INTRAPERSON EMOTION SYSTEM

Lazarus and Averill's (1972) version of cognitive theory devalues the role of emotion in personality and behavior. Perhaps it is because of this that they have difficulty in accepting the fundamental emotions of human experience as discrete and scientificially useful concepts. It may also explain their failure to deal with the intraperson process of emotion as a relatively independent subsystem of personality rather than as part of a syndrome that includes cognition and instrumental acts.

After summarizing their theoretical orientation, Lazarus and Averill raise the question as to whether the commonsense emotion categories represent unitary syndromes. They think not, and there are two reasons why they could easily have reached this conclusion. First, in their examples of commonsense emotion categories they include such disparate terms as anxiety, fear, anger, depression, and love. As I have shown elsewhere (Izard, 1971; Izard, in preparation), two of these, fear and anger, are fundamental emotions that can be represented at the phenomenological level by a single and unique concept; whereas depression and love, like anxiety, represent variable combinations of fundamental emotions that cannot be represented phenomenologically by a single or unitary emotion concept. The other reason why Lazarus and Averill did not recognize discrete emotions is their overinclusive definition of the emotion response syndrome, which fails to disentangle antecedent processes, emotion processes, and consequent processes.

Lazarus and Averill raise the question as to whether there is more than one kind of fear; this question, too, reflects their tendency to confound emotion and emotion-related activities. There is only one emotion process which generates the experience of fear, but there are many stimuli that can touch off this process and many activities that may be learned as adaptive or maladaptive responses to the fear experience.

With respect to the problem of classifying or categorizing emotions or emotional reactions, Lazarus and Averill propose that this be done by examining the response topographies of the emotion. By response topographies they mean the motor or instrumental acts, the subjective manifestations, the patterns of physiological arousal, and the patterns of motor expression. Here again we can see the lack of a clear conceptual separation of emotion process on the one hand and the antecedents and consequences of the emotion process on the other. Experiential emotion and its guidance and cue functions interact with the cognitive and motor systems, but they also enjoy a significant degree of functional independence.

In my view we can most readily find a high degree of consistency in the topography of human functioning if we look at

74

the neuromuscular component of the emotion process. This component is manifested in the expressive features of higher animals and children, and to some extent in the spontaneous expressions of adults. But as we move out into the realm of instrumental responses, as opposed to the emotion process per se, we shall find great variety. We need to acknowledge the fact that there is such a thing as an emotion proper and that the intraindividual emotion process itself has a motor or behavioral–expressive component as well as a neurophysiological and a subjective–experiential component. Using such a framework we can expect to find consistencies among emotion processes on the one hand and to understand the varieties of emotion-related responses on the other.

V. ANXIETY AS ANTICIPATORY REACTION OR AROUSAL

Epstein's (1972) explanatory paradigm for anxiety is similar to that of Lazarus and Averill.

> Given a crisis it is important that the organism rapidly assess the situation and take rapid action. The first step has to consist of perception of danger. This is followed by a state of heightened diffuse arousal that prepares the animal non-specifically for fight or flight. Normally a rapid assessment will be made, and the arousal will support a differentiated motive state, such as fear, and its corresponding action . . . flight . . .

Epstein's theorizing leads him to suggest the desirability of substituting the term "arousal" for anxiety. He does not do this because the experimental literature uses the term "anxiety" to refer both to "anticipatory reaction to noxious stimuli and to certain levels of arousal." The substitution of arousal for the term anxiety would seem to be a step backward in the development of an adequate conceptual framework for the study of the emotions. There is now substantial support both in theory and empirical evidence (Gellhorn, 1964; Izard, 1971, Sprague, Chambers, & Stellar, 1961; Tomkins, 1962) to indicate that arousal or activation is clearly separate and distinct from emotion.

Epstein interprets May's (1950) interpretation of Kierkegaardian anxiety as support for his hypothesis of a complex relationship between expectancy and anxiety. Izard and Tomkins (1966, pp. 122–123) gave an analysis of Kierkegaard's (1844) thought on anxiety and showed how this philosopher's brilliant presentation contained much insight and was a precursor to a theory of discrete emotions. Kierkegaard linked anxiety to the concepts of choice and possibility, and in particular to the possibility of freedom. These concepts have somewhat broader meaning in Kierkegaardian and existential philosophy than does expectancy in Epstein's controlled laboratory studies. Kierkegaard saw possibility, choice, and freedom as the cognitive framework that facilitated creativity. A careful study of Kierkegaard shows that his concept of anxiety is clearly multifactor and, as we indicated earlier (Izard & Tomkins, 1966), it clearly involves an oscillation between the negative emotion of fear and the positive emotion of interest–excitement.

Much of the empirical research that Epstein has reported is framed in terms of manipulating expectancy as the independent variable and using heart rate and skin conductance as dependent variables. Since heart rate and skin conductance are known to vary with a number of emotions, conditions, and situations, he does not claim that these are studies of anxiety.

Epstein has attempted to measure changes in physiological indices during a period in which the subject awaits some noxious and presumably threatening stimulus. The fact that he gets changes in physiological functioning in such a period is no surprise to anyone. The fact that these changes fluctuate or vary at different points in the time interval during expectation or waiting should be no more surprising. As has been shown elsewhere (Izard, 1971; Izard & Tomkins, 1966; Tomkins, 1962), pure emotions are rare and difficult to obtain in the laboratory. If one is obtained, it is probably only a matter of seconds before that emotion elicits other emotions and interacts with cognition. Indeed, such is the nature of anxiety. The first emotion elicited in an anxiety situation may be fear, but fear may quickly elicit distress, shame, or anger. The variations and the physiological responses might be better explained not in terms of the concept of expectancy and changes in expectancy over time, but in terms of changes in emotions and emotion interactions elicited while waiting for a noxious stimulus in a contrived and artificial situation.

Similarly, the variation in intensity of the noxious stimulus, from which Epstein infers variation in threat expectancy, could easily lead to changes at the physiological level for more than one reason. One explanation equally plausible to that of Epstein's is that an individual threatened with a highly noxious stimulus might first feel some fear, while an individual threatened with a mildly noxious stimulus might in fact feel the annoyance and irritation of mild anger.

V. Anxiety as Anticipatory Reaction or Arousal

Epstein, Lazarus and Averill, and other investigators with a cognitive theory orientation seem to assume that once a particular emotion is elicited, this emotion state remains in pure form for a substantial period of time. This appears to be a naive and untenable assumption. One emotion can almost instantaneously elicit another emotion that amplifies, attenuates, inhibits, or interacts with the original emotional experience. When a person begins cogitating the situation that has evoked the emotion and while he waits in anticipation for some noxious stimulus, other emotions are almost certain to be elicited. For example, as a subject contemplates the possibility that the experimenter is playing games with him by manipulating the painful event that may or may not happen to him, he may get angry instead of afraid even though the coming event is presumably threatening and fear producing.

Interestingly, some of the informal investigations which Epstein reported are similar to the systematic studies to be reported in Chapter Five. Epstein has described certain situations to students and asked them to indicate whether they would feel fear or anxiety. While it is unfortunate that Epstein limited the students' choices to these two concepts (fear and anxiety), he did obtain results somewhat similar to my own. He summarized the results as follows: "Some situations are almost unanimously recognized as fear, some as anxiety, and for some there is a division of opinion, suggesting that there is a mixture of the two." The problem with his approach is that we have no basis for knowing exactly what students mean when they use the label of anxiety.

Epstein found that knowledge of the source of threat did not serve as a distinguishing factor between what students labeled as fear and anxiety. He thought that all the anxiety situations had one thing in common: "an inability to direct the arousal produced by threat into an action tendency." This type of evidence and reasoning led Epstein to define fear as "an avoidance motive supporting directed action" and anxiety as "unresolved fear." Alternatively, he defined anxiety as "a state of undirected arousal following the perception of danger."

There is an alternative to Epstein's interpretation. What he terms "undirected arousal" may be seen more accurately as the presence of more than one fundamental emotion, each having its own cue and guidance functions. When the different emotions constitute different and opposing or conflicting motivations, the anxiety state would appear to be undirected and unresolved.

Some of the situations that Epstein gave his students for labeling as anxiety and fear also could be the source of a number of fundamental emotions. Let us look at one example closely.

Now imagine that you have been sent by your mother to buy something at the store. You have heard that there is a vicious dog who lives around the corner and you have often seen him straining at his chain to get you. Usually he is kept in the house but sometimes he gets free. Will he be there when you round the corner? You are approaching the corner and will soon find out. What is your feeling now?

Epstein said his students labeled the feeling in this situation as anxiety. His students' choice would confirm my conception of anxiety if it could be demonstrated that several fundamental emotions would obtain in this situation. Let us look at the possibilities. The individual may feel some distress (discouragement, downheartedness, etc.) over his inability to cope with the threatening situation. This may cause him to recognize some weaknesses or inadequacies in himself as an individual. Such recognition of inadequacy and the possibility of defeat could lead to a feeling of shame. The notion that he may not be able to complete the mission may lead to a feeling of guilt. If similar trips have been made a number of times with success there is even the possibility that the individual approaching the corner may feel some interest or excitement at the possibility of grazing danger without actually being physically harmed or psychologically debilitated. With excitement bolstering his confidence, he might get a little angry at the dog or his owner. Fear certainly may be the most prominent of the fundamental emotions in this situation; but there is the possibility that fear might oscillate with interest–excitement (Izard, 1971; Izard & Tomkins, 1966) and a high probability that the emotions of distress, shame, and anger could also be present. These are the emotions I have hypothesized as components of anxiety.

VI. ANXIETY AS A CONCEPT THAT INCLUDES FEAR, SHAME, AND GUILT

Although Janis (1969) has been strongly influenced by the work of Lazarus and Epstein, he discusses anxiety in terms of three discrete emotions. Janis concluded that anxiety is a concept that "most theorists use as a generic term that includes fear, shame, and guilt [p. 111]." Janis was assuming, and to a large extent correctly so, that most theorists have been strongly influenced by Freud's description of objective anxiety (fear), social anxiety (shame), and conscience or moral anxiety (guilt).

Janis introduced the concept of reflective emotion as a tool for differentiating between normal and neurotic emotional reactions. His concept of reflective emotion is in one sense an extension of Freud and in part a confirmation of Schachter's (1964) and Lazarus' (1966, 1972) positions, Janis considers reflective emotion as generally normal but he recognizes that the distinction between reflective and nonreflective and between normal and abnormal is sometimes thin and tenuous. An emotional state is reflective if it can be influenced by thoughtful reflection. Since reflective emotion is mediated by conscious verbal responses, it tends to be directly correlated with changes in signs of external threat. "In other words, the emotion reflects like a mirror the environmental changes [p. 114]." Reflective emotion tends to increase vigilance and a somewhat conflicting need to seek emotion-alleviating reassurances. These changes lead to changes in cognition and action. Finally, reflective emotion increases the likelihood that the "person will develop a new attitude constituting a compromise between vigilance and reassurance tendencies [p. 115]." Janis' concept of reflective emotion is dealt with in differential emotion theory as cognition–emotion interaction.

After noting that anxiety is a generic term that includes fear, shame, and guilt, Janis, unlike Lazarus, Epstein, and others, proceeded to deal with fear, shame, and guilt as separate phenomena. However, like others, Janis tended to confuse antecedent conditions, emotion, and consequent emotion-determined or emotion-related actions.

Janis recognized the influence of cognition on emotion, thus implicitly accepting the principle of cognition–emotion interaction, but he did not clearly acknowledge the influence of emotion on cognition and action. Furthermore, he did not recognize the principle of emotion–emotion interactions—the power of one emotion to elicit, inhibit, attenuate, or amplify another.

VII. SUMMARY

Although the two positions differ significantly, there are some elements in classical psychoanalytic theory that are quite similar to points in differential emotion theory. In particular, both recognize the important role of innate factors.

Cognitive theorists are even more deeply indebted to psychoanalytic theory, since Freud anticipated the basic paradigm of cognitive theory: Anxiety follows from appraisal, or the perception of the threat of occurrence of a danger situation. However, cognitive theory, like most other contemporary theories of emotion that borrow from Freud, completely ignores Freud's concept of innate affect.

There are several versions of the cognitive theory of emotion and anxiety. Lazarus and his associates have developed what is perhaps the most systematic and extensive formulation. Lazarus and his colleagues view emotion as the result of cognition. Primary appraisal, secondary appraisal, and reappraisal are described as cognitive processes that precede emotion. This view appears to violate observations from both ontogenetic and phylogenetic development. In ontogeny emotional processes appear to precede cognitive processes such as appraisal and reappraisal. From an evolutionary point of view, the cognitive position would require that the animal be able to think or appraise before being able to have emotion. The reverse seems much more plausible.

Differential emotion theory holds that emotion may be mediated or elicited and influenced not only by cognition but by innate releasers, homeostatic processes, drives, and other emotions or emotion components. The emotions enjoy a degree of independence as a separate system within the personality, yet differential emotion theory clearly maintains that emotions or the emotion system continually interact with and influence cognition and action.

Lazarus and his colleagues describe emotion as a response syndrome and draw an analogy between emotion and disease. This seems a most unfortunate and faulty analogy. Emotion or the emotion process requires no invasion of foreign bodies, stimulation or input from the outside, or any malfunction of tissue as is the case with disease. In contrast with the cognitive position, differential emotion theory maintains that emotion is a natural and normal process of the organism or person.

Cognitive theory fails to distinguish between fundamental emotions such as fear and anger and patterns of emotions such as anxiety and depression. This creates both conceptual and methodological problems. It even raises a question as to the utility of distinguishing among emotions at all.

More importantly, cognitive theory fails to distinguish the emotion process from processes that are antecedent, concomitant, or

80

consequent to the emotion process. Since Lazarus' version of cognitive theory makes no distinction between emotion and instrumental response, it actually invites a continued neglect of the study of the subjective experience of emotion. The failure to distinguish clearly among the emotion, cognition, and motor systems also creates very significant taxonomic problems for this field of study.

Epstein would like to define anxiety as arousal, yet there is now substantial theoretical and empirical support for conceiving activation or arousal as a clearly separate system from emotion. In practice Epstein defined anxiety as an anticipatory reaction to a noxious stimulus and to certain levels of arousal. He reported a number of studies showing physiological changes in the face of different kinds of anticipation. Differential emotion theory holds that anticipation of a highly noxious stimulus, a mildly noxious stimulus, and other such experimental manipulations might well lead to different discrete emotions or patterns of emotions and that these in turn might be more direct and parsimonious determinants of the reported physiological changes.

Janis, following Freud, included fear, shame, and guilt in his definition of anxiety. He introduced the concept of reflective emotion (emotion influenced by thoughtful reflections) for differentiating normal and neurotic anxiety and for the study and analysis of anxiety in general. He did not clearly recognize the role of emotion in cognition and action.

The differences between differential emotion theory and cognitive theory are radical. The contrast is between a theory that explains certain key processes of personality and human functioning on the basis of the patterning and interactions of fundamental emotions and a theory that uses cognitive processes to explain behavior, including emotional responses. The crucial questions for the two approaches are these: Are our thoughts and actions determined more by what we know (perceptual data or information) or by how we feel (emotion or, typically, a pattern of emotions)? Are the dynamic and functional relationships between cognition and behavior more fundamental than those between the emotions and behavior?

A crucial deficiency in cognitive theory is its failure to explain the highly important and ever-present phenomena of selectivity and purposiveness or directionality in perceptual–cognitive functioning. I maintain that the person's pattern of emotions subserves selective perception and cognition, with the emotion of interest normally playing a critical role. An emotion or pattern of emotions may be activated or changed as a function of numerous intraperson, social, and person–environment processes.

Following a Thomistic–rationalistic ideology, cognitive theory views perceptual and thought processes as the key determinants of behavior, including emotional behavior. Thus, emotion is viewed as response, often an unwanted response to a troublesome and undesirable stimulus. The emphasis is on the maladaptive–maladjustive emotional response to stressful and frustrating stimuli. This line of reasoning is taken to its logical extreme by Lazarus and Averill who view emotion as a syndrome analogous to a disease process. In virtually complete opposition, I see the emotions as the most important motivating and meaningful experiences of human life and as having inherently adaptive functions.

I believe the differences between differential emotion theory and cognitive theory have implications of great importance to future developments in this area. The single most important implication relates to the place of emotion in the science of man. Generally, cognitive theory relegates it to a relatively insignificant role. In contrast, I see emotion as crucially important in providing motivation and guidance for critical aspects of personality, interpersonal, and intergroup functioning.

CHAPTER FIVE

An Empirical Analysis of Anxiety in Terms of Discrete Emotions

I. INTRODUCTION

I undertook a series of studies in search of empirical confirmation of a central thesis of this book: Anxiety is an unstable and variable combination of interacting fundamental emotions. I say "combination" primarily to indicate that more than one discrete emotion is involved. Certain fundamental emotions or their components may interact with enough regularity to give the appearance of a unity with distinct characteristics and functions, but I suspect the search for such unity will be futile, as was our historical search for a unitary concept of anxiety. The combination is described as unstable and variable because it is susceptible to change in relation to time, persons, and situations, and because the fundamental emotions of the combination may vary in quality and intensity. That is, anxiety may be an interaction of strong fear, moderate distress, and mild guilt or shame, or it may be an interaction of moderate fear, strong guilt, and mild distress, and so on through many possible combinations and interactions.

It should be helpful in understanding the framework for these studies to take a look at the list of fundamental emotions and their definitions. These are presented as Table 5-1. In general, the first term following the number in the left-hand margin of the table corresponds to a relatively lower intensity of the emotion while the second term indicates a higher intensity of the emotion. The adjectives or phrases following the emotion category label are defining terms selected primarily on the basis of synonymity. These are

83

essentially a priori definitions, though some of the defining terms were added as a result of empirical studies. The concepts of fundamental emotions as labeled and defined in Table 5-1 have been used in a variety of studies, both in the laboratory and in cross-cultural research (Ekman, Sorenson, & Friesen, 1969; Izard, 1971; Snyder & Katahn, 1970).

The list of fundamental emotions requires one further explanation. We consider shame–humiliation (number 7 of Table 5-1) to be a fundamental emotion but, as will be evident from data to be presented later, factor analyses of emotion terms representing all fundamental emotions often divide the terms used in the a priori substantive definition of shame–humiliation into two primary factors. The terms of one factor correspond rather well to the concept of guilt (7a of Table 5-1) and those of the other correspond to a concept of shyness (7b of Table 5-1).

Tomkins (1962) maintains, and I agree, that there is one innate neural program for the fundamental emotion of shame–humiliation; yet this emotion may be represented in conscious experience as shame, shyness, or guilt. Since the factor analyses that separated shyness and guilt were based on self-reports (of conscious experience), this neither confirms nor rejects the hypothesis of a single underlying mechanism for these three different emotional experiences. Of course, if I had obtained only one factor for shame–shyness–guilt, this would not have proven anything about the *neurological* basis of the emotion either, and I want to make it clear that I am not making such an inference in those instances where the statistical factors matched the a priori definitions. Such matching

TABLE 5-1

The Fundamental Emotions: A Priori Definitions

1.	Interest-Excitement (I-E):	Concentrating, attending, attracted, curious
2.	Enjoyment-Joy (E-J):	Glad, merry, delighted, joyful
3.	Suprise-Startle (S-S):	Sudden reaction to something unexpected, astonished
4.	Distress-Anguish (D-A):	Sad, unhappy, miserable, feels like crying
5.	Disgust-Revulsion (D-R):	Repugnance, aversion, distaste; feels sickened
6.	Anger-Rage (A-R):	Angry, hostile, furious, enraged
7.	Shame-Humiliation (S-H):	Shy, embarrassed, ashamed, guilty
		a. Guilt: Blameworthy, repentant, guilty
		b. Shyness: Bashful, sheepish, shy
8.	Fear-Terror (F-T):	Scared, afraid, terrified, panicked
9.	Contempt-Scorn (C-S):	Disdainful, sneering, derisive, haughty

does strengthen our theoretical postulate of discrete fundamental emotions as useful scientific concepts at the phenomenological or experiential level.

The central aim of the empirical studies was to delineate the components (discrete emotions) of anxiety at the phenomenological level. To accomplish this aim, two things were necessary—a technique for measuring the emotions of subjective experience and an "anxiety situation." Our approach to the measurement problem was to develop a set of adjective scales that would enable subjects to indicate the degree to which each of the fundamental emotions was present in experience. This instrument will be described in the next section.

The second factor that was needed was a situation that would elicit anxiety in all subjects. Previous research (Allport, 1924; Izard, Wehmer, Livsey, & Jennings, 1965; Tomkins, 1962) suggested that few if any contrived laboratory situations would do the job well. Taking a lead from behavior therapy (desensitization procedures) and some pilot research comparing emotional experiences induced by hypnosis and waking suggestion, I decided simply to instruct subjects to visualize or imagine a situation in which they had personally experienced strong anxiety. The specifics of this procedure will be described later.

II. THE DIFFERENTIAL EMOTION SCALE

The Differential Emotion Scale (DES) (Izard, 1969) is based on premises derived from the theory presented in Chapter Three. In particular, the DES assumes that separate and discrete emotions exist and that each has measurable experiential and motivational properties. Thus, a major aim (ideal) in the construction and refinement of the DES is to develop relatively independent scales or factors corresponding to each of the fundamental emotions. The restrictions common to verbal measures as indices of emotion-determined functioning make for some difficulties (if not limits) on the full achievement of this aim. However, results to date suggest that the aim represents a feasible guiding principle.

A. DEVELOPMENT OF THE DES

The DES is also based on the assumption that for each subjective experience corresponding to a fundamental emotion there is a corresponding facial pattern or expression. From cross-culturally obtained free responses to the facial expressions of the fundamental emotions, six or more adjectives were selected to represent each one of the nine fundamental emotions. The resulting group of 67 items was given to 622 freshmen students during a session of placement and personality testing at Vanderbilt University in September, 1968.

DES instructions and sample items are presented in Table 5-2. The students were given the DES and asked to indicate their present feelings or emotions by using the 5-point scale by each of the 67 emotion terms.

Table 5-3 presents the primary factor loading of each adjective listed by factor. These were taken from the promax rotation of a principal components factor analysis. The factor names were assigned on the basis of the a priori expectations. These results offer strong support for some aspects of my theory, though some items did not factor quite as expected.

TABLE 5-2

Instructions and Sample Items for the 67-Item Differential Emotion Scale

This scale consists of a number of words that describe different emotions or feelings. Please indicate the extent to which each word describes the way you feel at the present time.

Record your answers by circling the appropriate number on the five-point scale following each word. Presented below is the scale for indicating the degree to which each word describes the way you feel.

1	2	3	4	5
very slightly or not at all	slightly	moderately	considerably	very strongly

In deciding on your answer to a given item or word, consider the feeling connoted or defined by that word. Then, if at the present moment you feel that way *very slightly* or *not at all*, you would circle the number *1* on the scale; if you feel that way to a *moderate* degree, you would circle *3*; if you feel that way *very strongly*, you would circle *5*, and so forth.

Remember, you are requested to make your responses on the basis of the way you feel *at this time*. Work at a good pace. It is not necessary to ponder; the first answer you decide on for a given word is probably the most valid. You should be able to finish in about 5 min.

1. downhearted	1	2	3	4	5		26. guilty	1	2	3	4	5
6. astonished	1	2	3	4	5		35. afraid	1	2	3	4	5
18. attentive	1	2	3	4	5		44. joyful	1	2	3	4	5
20. ashamed	1	2	3	4	5		61. angry	1	2	3	4	5

TABLE 5-3

*Factor Content and Primary Loadings from the
Promax Factor Rotation of 67-Item Differential Emotion Scale[a]*

1. *Interest-Excitement*
   .85 attentive
   .80 concentrating
   .74 alert
   .72 engaged in thought
   .67 interested
   .53 contemplative

2. *Enjoyment-Joy*
   .88 joyful
   .88 enthusiastic
   .86 delighted
   .82 happy
   .78 excited
   .70 energetic
   .68 warmhearted
   .66 blissful

3. *Surprise-Startle*
   .81 surprised
   .78 amazed
   .77 startled
   .75 astonished
   .74 shocked

4. *Distress-Anguish*
   .77 sad
   .75 downhearted
   .73 lonely
   .73 discouraged
   .72 upset
   .67 distressed
   .59 emotional

5. *Disgust-(Mixed)*
   .69 feeling of revulsion
   .66 sickened
   .60 contemptuous
   .58 quarrelsome

6. *Anger-Disgust-Contempt*
   .80 irritated
   .79 scornful
   .79 angry

   .77 mad
   .77 feeling of distaste
   .75 bitter
   .74 disdainful
   .73 disgusted
   .72 annoyed
   .71 hostile
   .68 provoked
   .67 feeling of loathing
   .65 feeling of aversion
   .64 defiant
   .62 rebellious
   .61 enraged
   .50 haughty

7. *(Shame)-Guilt*
   .81 guilty
   .75 ashamed
   .69 blameworthy
   .69 repentant

8. *(Shame)-Shyness*
   .91 bashful
   .88 shy
   .71 sheepish

9. *Fear-Terror*
   .91 afraid
   .91 scared
   .89 fearful
   .87 frightened
   .78 jittery
   .66 shaky
   .52 anxious
   .52 inadequate

10. *Contempt-Scorn*
    .74 sarcastic
    .67 mocking

11. *Fatigue-Sleepiness*
    .82 sluggish
    .81 fatigued
    −.72 awake

[a] Data from 1968 freshman testing ($N = 622$).

A slightly modified list of 72 5-point emotion-adjective scales (a revised DES) was administered to the next entering freshmen class (Fall, 1969, N = 1182). The factor analysis of the revised DES closely paralleled and confirmed the results shown in Table 5-3. The eight factors of interest, enjoyment, surprise, disgust–(mixed), anger–disgust–contempt, guilt, shyness, and fatigue emerged with very similar content. However, most of the fear and distress words mixed on a single (fear–distress) factor.

Three words were added for the fatigue factor in the 72-item DES, and all three had high primary loadings on the intended factor. The term fatigue was chosen in preference to arousal or activation to avoid the confusion that might arise from the surplus and erroneous connotations sometimes associated with the latter terms. On the whole, the similarity of factor structure on the two occasions was quite substantial.

A third factor analysis was computed from data on 163 black college students who were participating in a study to be described in more detail later. In this study the students were asked to say how they felt in three emotion-eliciting situations—two real and one hypothetical. Again, the factor structure was substantially similar to those obtained in the two previous analyses, but there were some minor differences.

I suspect that some degree of variation in factor structure might reasonably be expected when a state measure is given on different occasions to different samples. In situations or conditions where one or two emotions may be prominent and two or three notably absent, discrimination among the remaining emotions may not be as fine. In establishing the psychometric properties of state measures, current concepts of reliability and validity may have to be further delineated or complemented by some new concepts.

B. DES ANALYSES OF ANXIETY-ELICITING SITUATIONS

Izard, Chappell, and Weaver (1970) gave the 72-item DES to black college students. They were asked to describe the emotions characterizing the experience of being the recipient of race prejudice in one hypothetical (imagined) and two actual (remembered) situations. The order of presentation of the three situations was balanced so that the effect of order could be evaluated. Pilot interviews with several black college students revealed that their first clear memory of prejudice occurred somewhere around age 5 to 7. Most of the incidents designated as recent were likely to have occurred during the past few months.

We expected that the first instance of prejudice and the most recent instance would be characterized by different emotions and thus yield different emotion factor scores. Since the first instance usually occurs during the more vulnerable childhood years and probably in an adult–child relationship, and since prejudice can be both threatening and accusatory, we expected the black students' mean scores for this situation to be elevated in factors representing fear, distress, guilt, and shyness, a combination of emotions which may be considered as one of the anxiety patterns that follows from differential emotion theory. We also thought that the child's naïveté with respect to prejudice and his lack of expectation of racial discrimination would cause the scores on the surprise factor to be higher than for the other situations.

We expected that the most recent and the hypothetical situations, occurring during the college years when the subjects have greater understanding of prejudice and civil rights, would produce higher scores on the anger–disgust–contempt factor. We thought the hypothetical situation would be more like the most recent experience with prejudice than like the first encounter. Scoring was based on the factors of the 72-item DES, which contained seven identifiable emotion factors.

A separate analysis of variance was computed for each emotion factor, with situation and order as the main effects. Order was significant in only one instance—the enjoyment factor. As was expected, the variance in emotion-factor scores due to situation was significant. For four emotion factors—fear–distress, guilt, shyness, anger–disgust–contempt—p was less than .001. For interest, p was .004 and for enjoyment, .036. Also as expected, the situation of the first encounter with prejudice elicited higher scores on fear–distress, guilt, shyness, and surprise. The hypothetical situation elicited a higher score on anger–disgust–contempt than either of the other two situations, and the most recent encounter elicited a considerably higher score on this factor than did the first encounter. These results generally confirmed differential emotion theory predictions regarding patterns of emotions in anxiety and furnished evidence of one kind of validity for the DES.

Simpson (1971) used the DES to study a situation which is typically considered to be anxiety provoking. He had 59 college students complete a revised 33-item version of the DES while contemplating the certainty of their own death. This DES has three items for each of 11 a priori factors—one for each of the eight fundamental emotions of enjoyment, interest, surprise, distress, anger, disgust, contempt, and fear; two for shame (shyness and guilt); and one nonemotion factor (fatigue). Simpson based his analysis on scores derived from a priori factors as defined by differential emotion theory, since numerous factor analyses of this form have shown excellent correspondence between a priori and statistically derived factors (Izard & Dougherty, in preparation).

As expected, subjects contemplating the certainty of their own death had their highest mean on the fear factor. Their second highest mean was interest-excitement, an emotion which often oscillates in relation to fear in an anxiety pattern. The elevation of the interest mean may have been due in part to the fact that the students, in contemplating their own death, were engaged in a relatively novel experience. Their third highest mean was distress, a factor defined by the terms sad, discouraged, downhearted. The fear-interest-distress combination may be viewed as one of the possible anxiety patterns that follow from differential emotion theory.

Simpson divided his subjects by sex and religious status (religious, nonreligious) and compared these groups on each emotion factor by analysis of variance. Males tended to report more contempt ($p = .060$) than females. Nonreligious students experienced more interest than religious subjects ($p = .015$) and tended to experience less shyness ($p = .084$). Also, religious subjects reported more guilt, but the difference was not statistically significant ($p = .136$).

C. EMOTIONAL CONNOTATION OF DES "ANXIETY" ITEMS

In studying the factor analyses of the DES for possible indications of the hypothesized nature of anxiety, I discovered that several items (concepts) that are frequently included on anxiety scales had factor loadings that tended to be consonant with my conception of anxiety. These DES items and their factor loadings are presented in Table 5-4.

Interestingly, the term anxious had its primary loading on fear, but it had fairly substantial loadings on shyness, distress, and surprise. Most of the other terms which are typically considered to be anxiety terms also have their primary loadings on fear, with their next highest loadings on distress, guilt, and shyness. These data tend to confirm my conceptual analysis of anxiety.

90

TABLE 5-4

Factor Loadings for "Anxiety" Words on DES Emotion Factors[a]

Emotion factors	"Anxiety" words			
	Anxious	Jittery	Shaky	Inadequate
1. Interest-Excitement	.24	.13	.15	.12
2. Enjoyment-Joy	.42	.18	.10	.10
3. Surprise-Startle	.38²	.29	.24	.32
4. Distress-Anguish	.35³	.53²	.51²	.47³
5. Disgust-(Mixed)	—.01	.03	.19	.08
6. Anger-Disgust-Contempt	.01	.10	.11	—.03
7a. (Shame)-Guilt	.19	.42⁴	.41³	.37⁴
7b. (Shame)-Shyness	.33⁴	.49³	.37⁴	.49²
8. Fear-Terror	.52¹	.78¹	.66¹	.52¹
9. Contempt-Scorn	.17	.07	.01	.08
10. Fatigue-Sleepiness	.01	.14	.24	.19

[a] Condition: Freshman testing ($N = 622$). Superscript numbers on italic entries indicate the 1st, 2nd, 3rd, and 4th highest loadings.

III. COMBINING THE DES AND AN ANXIETY SCALE

The next step in the analysis of anxiety in terms of fundamental emotions was to combine the DES with a standard anxiety scale. In order for the combined instrument to be of reasonable length, the 33-item DES was used. The three words or terms representing each of the 10 emotion factors and the three representing the nonemotion factor of fatigue were selected on the basis of a priori factor definitions and factor loadings determined by previous analyses.

The state form of the Spielberger–Gorsuch–Lushene (1970) State Trait Anxiety Inventory (STAI) was chosen as the anxiety scale for combining with the DES. The STAI is brief (only 20 items); its scale format is similar to the DES; it has good psychometric properties; and it correlates very well with other well-accepted anxiety measures. For example, correlations between STAI and the Taylor Manifest Anxiety Scale have ranged from .79 to .83.

The STAI items were condensed to match the form of the DES items. This was easily done since each STAI item refers to only one feeling (concept), usually represented by a single word. The conversion of STAI items to DES-type items is shown in Table 5-5. Items 7 and 17 both seemed to be represented reasonably well by the term worried, and the term joyful is identical to one of the DES

TABLE 5-5
*Conversion of Spielberger-Gorsuch-Lushene STAI
Items to DES-Type Items*

STAI Item	DES+A Item
1. I feel calm	calm
2. I feel secure	secure
3. I am tense	tense
4. I am regretful	regretful
5. I feel at ease	at ease
6. I feel upset	upset
7. I am presently worrying over possible misfortunes	worried
8. I feel rested	rested
9. I feel anxious	anxious
10. I feel comfortable	comfortable
11. I feel self-confident	confident
12. I feel nervous	nervous
13. I am jittery	jittery
14. I feel "high strung"	"high strung"
15. I am relaxed	relaxed
16. I feel content	content
17. I am worried	worried
18. I feel overexcited and rattled	overexcited and rattled
19. I feel joyful	joyful
20. I feel pleasant.	pleasant

items. Thus, 18 independent STAI items were added to the 33-item DES to form the 51-item DES+A.

The DES+A represents 10 emotion concepts, one nonemotion concept, and an anxiety scale. The DES+A will be used in all subsequent studies reported in this chapter.

IV. DES+A AS A TOOL FOR ANALYZING THE EXPERIENCE OF ANXIETY

As the first phase of the empirical analysis of experiential anxiety, the DES+A was administered to five classes of introductory psychology students ($N = 339$). On the first occasion the subjects were asked to visualize a situation which made them anxious and, while recalling that experience, to fill out the DES+A. The specific instructions for the administration of the DES+A in the anxiety situation and the items of the DES+A are presented in Table 5-6.

The factor analysis of the DES+A is presented in Table 5-7. The items marked with an asterisk are the anxiety terms from the STAI.

IV. Analyzing Anxiety

TABLE 5-6
Instructions for the Anxiety Situation and the DES+A

Our era has been called the Age of Anxiety. Whether or not this is the best name for our era, all of us experience anxiety from time to time. Each of us has our own idea as to the meaning of anxiety and the feelings that go with it. We would like for you to use the scales below to describe your personal experience—your own feelings—when you are anxious.

Please try to recall a time or situation in which you felt anxious. Without revealing any names or personal information you do not wish to disclose, identify below the situation or type of situation you are recalling.

Situation:_____

Now, keeping the anxiety situation in mind, complete the scales below, circling the appropriate scale number to indicate the degree to which each word describes your feelings while you are experiencing anxiety.

1	2	3	4	5
very slightly or not at all	slightly	moderately	considerably	very strongly

1. comfortable	1 2 3 4 5	27. relaxed	1 2 3 4 5
2. repentant	1 2 3 4 5	28. angry	1 2 3 4 5
3. calm	1 2 3 4 5	29. sad	1 2 3 4 5
4. delighted	1 2 3 4 5	30. guilty	1 2 3 4 5
5. "high strung"	1 2 3 4 5	31. anxious	1 2 3 4 5
6. feeling of distaste	1 2 3 4 5	32. bashful	1 2 3 4 5
		33. nervous	1 2 3 4 5
7. downhearted	1 2 3 4 5	34. disgusted	1 2 3 4 5
8. surprised	1 2 3 4 5	35. joyful	1 2 3 4 5
9. confident	1 2 3 4 5	36. feeling of revulsion	1 2 3 4 5
10. fatigued	1 2 3 4 5	37. overexcited and rattled	1 2 3 4 5
11. contemptuous	1 2 3 4 5		
12. sheepish	1 2 3 4 5	38. disdainful	1 2 3 4 5
13. jittery	1 2 3 4 5	39. upset	1 2 3 4 5
14. attentive	1 2 3 4 5	40. blameworthy	1 2 3 4 5
15. scared	1 2 3 4 5	41. tense	1 2 3 4 5
16. secure	1 2 3 4 5	42. astonished	1 2 3 4 5
17. enraged	1 2 3 4 5	43. alert	1 2 3 4 5
18. happy	1 2 3 4 5	44. worried	1 2 3 4 5
19. scornful	1 2 3 4 5	45. mad	1 2 3 4 5
20. pleasant	1 2 3 4 5	46. rested	1 2 3 4 5
21. concentrating	1 2 3 4 5	47. discouraged	1 2 3 4 5
22. content	1 2 3 4 5	48. shy	1 2 3 4 5
23. amazed	1 2 3 4 5	49. regretful	1 2 3 4 5
24. fearful	1 2 3 4 5	50. sleepy	1 2 3 4 5
25. at ease	1 2 3 4 5	51. afraid	1 2 3 4 5
26. sluggish	1 2 3 4 5		

5. An Empirical Analysis of Anxiety

TABLE 5-7
Factor Analysis of DES+A (DES-33 + STAI Items)[a]

1. *Interest*	5. *Anger-Disgust-Contempt*
.75 alert	.86 mad
.75 attentive	.85 angry
.72 concentrating	.83 disgusted
	.82 enraged
2. *Enjoyment + "Negative*	.81 scornful
of Anxiety"	.80 contemptuous
.83 happy	.80 feeling of revulsion
*.81 pleasant	.77 disdainful
*.79 joyful	.74 feeling of distaste
*.78 content	
.78 delighted	6. *(Shame)-Shyness*
*.71 secure	.84 shy
*.68 confident	.82 bashful
*.67 relaxed	.64 sheepish
*.66 at ease	
*.60 rested	7. *Fear + "Anxiety"*
*.43 comfortable	*.83 nervous
	*.82 tense
3. *Surprise*	*.81 jittery
.85 amazed	.80 fearful
.84 astonished	.78 afraid
.79 surprised	*.77 worried
	.77 scared
4. *Distress-Guilt + "Anxiety"*	*.65 overexcited
*.84 regretful	and rattled
.84 blameworthy	*.60 anxious
.84 guilty	*.54 "high strung"
.71 repentant	
.71 downhearted	8. *Fatigue*
*.71 upset	.71 sleepy
.70 sad	.68 fatigued
.65 discouraged	.63 sluggish
	9. *Chance Factor*
	*—.55 calm

[a]Subjects were visualizing an anxiety situation
of their own choosing (N = 297).
*STAI items.

As can be seen, the factor structure and factor content of
the DES+A as administered in the anxiety situation are quite similar
to those obtained for the 67-item DES (Table 5-3) as administered
during freshman testing. The obtained factor structures correspond
rather well with the aprioristically defined fundamental emotions.
Without the STAI items, the contents of the statistically derived

94

factors and the contents of the aprioristically defined emotions are perfectly matched for interest, enjoyment, surprise, shyness, and fear. All the a priori terms for distress and all those for guilt combined into a single factor in this study. Similar combinations have occurred in previous studies. In the factor analysis of the data from the 1969 freshman testing study, distress combined with fear, and for the black students in the prejudice study, shyness combined with fear. Such combinations of fundamental emotions into single first-order statistical factors may reflect an instability of factor structure that would characterize any state measure; or, some of them may be seen as relatively good descriptions of anxiety as defined by one or more of the theorists discussed in this chapter. Viewed in this way, we have another illustration of the instability and variability of anxiety as a concept.

All the a priori terms for the three emotions of anger, disgust, and contempt combined into a single first-order factor. These emotions have combined in this way in several of the DES factor analytic studies, though occasionally some disgust terms emerge as a separate factor, as do some contempt terms. Other studies using other research approaches and measurement techniques have presented strong evidence as to the existence of anger, disgust, and contempt as discrete emotions. The strongest such evidence has come from cross-cultural and developmental studies of the recognition and labeling of facial expressions of emotions (Ekman, Sorenson, & Friesen, 1969; Izard, 1971). The DES's greater dependence on cognitive report of the phenomenological or experiential component of emotion may help explain the frequent emergence of anger–disgust–contempt as a single DES factor. It is likely that these three emotions are not always clearly differentiated experientially or semantically, at least in some situations or conditions. I consider anger, disgust, and contempt as the principal emotions involved in hostility.

Considering both the DES and STAI items, the factor content shown in Table 5-7 gives some support for my formulation of anxiety as a combination of certain fundamental emotions. The DES fear factor (represented by the words fearful, afraid, and scared) was the factor on which most of the negative items of the STAI loaded. This is quite as expected, since Spielberger emphasizes the emotion of fear in his substantive definition of anxiety.

In the present factor analysis, distress (aprioristically defined by the terms downhearted, sad, discouraged) and guilt (aprioristically defined by the terms blameworthy, guilty, and repentant) came together in a single statistical factor. Two of the STAI items loaded on this distress–guilt factor. One of the items of the STAI (calm) emerged as a separate factor, probably a chance factor.

All other STAI items loaded on the enjoyment factor of the DES. Using negatively weighted enjoyment items is not in keeping with the differential emotion theory of anxiety, but it is apparently not inconsistent with Spielberger's theorizing. In selecting these terms for the STAI scale, Spielberger was hypothesizing that the absence of security, confidence, comfort, relaxation, joy, etc., was in effect an indication of anxiety.

In summary, various STAI items had primary loadings on factors representing three of the fundamental emotions hypothesized as components of anxiety—fear, distress, and guilt. The failure of any STAI items to load on the shyness factor was probably due to the way the STAI defines anxiety. The loadings of anxiety terms on the DES factor representing enjoyment–joy may also be more a function of the particular substantive qualities of the STAI than of anxiety measures in general. Also, the fact that no STAI items loaded on the DES factors of anger and interest is apparently due to the lack of STAI content relating to these emotions.

V. DES+A APPLIED TO THE EMOTIONS THAT CONSTITUTE ANXIETY

The next step in the empirical analysis of experiential anxiety was to use the DES+A as a tool to study each of the fundamental emotions that I have hypothesized as a possible component of anxiety. The same psychology classes that visualized an anxiety situation and took the DES+A were used as subjects. The five classes were subdivided randomly into seven groups. The first subgroup was asked to visualize a fear situation, the second a guilt situation, the third a distress situation, the fourth an anger situation, the fifth a shyness situation, and the sixth an interest situation. The seventh group, also asked to visualize an interest situation, served as a check on the repeatability of the effects of the imaging procedure. In the first six groups, the anxiety situation and one of the emotion situations were stapled together and administered in the same session, making it possible to compare a given group of subjects' DES+A scores derived from the anxiety situation with their scores derived from a particular fundamental emotion situation. All subjects remained anonymous, having been told at the beginning of the session that they need not put their names on the test forms.

Instructions for visualizing or imagining the fear situation and for the subsequent completion of the DES+A are presented as Table 5-8. (To simplify things for the subjects, the instructions referred to the DES+A as the DES.) Corresponding instructions were used for the distress situation, the guilt situation, the anger situation, the shyness situation, and the interest situation.

As a check on the effectiveness of the imaging condition for increasing scores on anxiety-related emotion scales, the emotion scale scores in the imagined situation were compared with those in the freshman testing situation which furnished the data for the factor analysis of the DES-67 (see Table 5-9). As expected, all the emotions hypothesized as components of anxiety had higher mean scale scores in the imagined anxiety situation than they did in the freshman testing situation.

The overall analysis of variance for the anxiety scores of the six groups (emotion situations) is presented in Table 5-10. The variance due to emotion situations was highly significant (p = .0000). Inspection of the means (see Table 5-14) suggested that this significant variance was due primarily to the relatively low anxiety means in the shyness and interest situations. Since most STAI items loaded on the DES factors representing fear, guilt, and distress, it is quite reasonable that these three emotion situations yielded higher anxiety scores

TABLE 5-8
Instructions for Visualizing the Fear Situation and
Subsequent Completion of the DES+A

Emotions in Life Situations

All individuals experience fear in certain situations. Different individuals experience fear in different kinds of situations. We would like you to describe below a situation or condition that you have been in (or may be in again) and in which you have experienced fear. Please be careful to indicate a situation in which *fear*, not some other negative feeling, is the dominant emotion.

Fear Situation: _____

Now use the attached Differential Emotion Scale (DES) to describe your feelings in that situation. We would like your responses to be as true as possible to the real-life situation you have indicated above. Visualize the situation again, or recall it as vividly as you can, while you complete the attached DES.

97

TABLE 5-9
A Priori and Empirical Emotion Factor Profiles for an Imagined Anxiety Situation and a Control Situation

| | | Imagined anxiety situation (from DES-33 + A) | | | Control situation (freshman testing) (from DES-72) | |
| | A priori factors | | Empirical factors | | Empirical factors | |
Emotion	Scale $\bar{x}$	Factor	Scale $\bar{x}$		Factor	Scale $\bar{x}$
Fear	3.4	Fear + A	3.7		Fatigue	2.9
Interest	3.4	Interest	3.5		Interest	2.6
Distress	2.5	Distress–Guilt + A	2.4		Joy	2.2
Disgust	2.0	Shyness	2.0		Fear-Distress	1.7
Guilt	2.0					
Surprise	2.0					
Shyness	1.9					

than did shyness and interest. Also as expected, the mean anxiety scores in the five negative emotion situations were all substantially higher than the anxiety score from the one positive emotion situation, interest. The rank order of the mean anxiety scores (see Table 5-14) speaks well for the efficacy of the experimental procedure of imagining or visualizing emotion-eliciting situations.

TABLE 5-10

Analysis of Variance of Anxiety Scores Considering All Emotion Situations at Once (Fear, Distress, Guilt, Shyness, Anger, and Interest)

Source	df	MS	F	p
Between emotion situations	5	6427.770	38.2614	.0000
Within emotion situations	229	167.996		
Total	234	301.752		

Follow-up analyses of variance were then computed for each of the six groups separately, comparing the DES+A anxiety scores from the anxiety situation with DES+A anxiety scores from the particular emotion situation that the group visualized. Thus, for the group that imagined a fear situation, it was possible to compare DES+A anxiety scores based on the recall of their experience in an anxiety situation with DES+A anxiety scores based on their recall of their experience in a fear situation. The anxiety scores were based on the 19 items of DES+A which were derived from the STAI. Since there were 19 5-point scales, the minimum anxiety score would be 19 and the maximum anxiety score 95. (The corresponding minimum and maximum scores for the 20 4-point items of the STAI are 20 and 80.)

To illustrate these follow-up analyses, consider the group that completed the DES+A while imagining an anxiety situation and then later completed the DES+A while imagining a fear situation. The A X S (situations X subjects) analysis of variance of the anxiety scores from the anxiety and fear situations is presented in Table 5-11.

The significant F due to subjects is as expected, simply reflecting intersubject variability in anxiety scores. The term of most importance is the variance due to situations, which was far from statistically significant. Thus, anxiety as measured by the STAI items on the DES+A did not differ in the fear situation and the anxiety situation.

Similar analyses were performed for each of the other five emotion groups. As in the comparison of the anxiety and fear

99

TABLE 5-11
*Analysis of Variance of DES+A Anxiety Scores
from the Anxiety Situation and the Fear Situation*

Source	df	MS	F	p
Situations (anxiety versus fear)	1	62.6250	.6880	.5828
Subjects	37	227.6419	2.5009	.0035
Situations × Subjects	37	91.0236		

situations (Table 5-11), the variance in anxiety scores due to situations was not significant for the comparisons of the anxiety situation with the distress, guilt, and anger situations.

It was also desirable to see if anxiety scores differed between these four fundamental emotion situations. The anxiety scores from the fear, guilt, distress, and anger groups (situations) were compared by analysis of variance for random groups. As shown in Table 5-12, the variance due to emotion situations was not significant.

TABLE 5-12
*Analysis of Variance of Anxiety Scores for the Fear,
Guilt, Distress, and Anger Situations*

Source	df	MS	F	p
Between emotion situations	3	130.668	.8225	.4862
Within emotion situations	149	158.864		
Total	152	158.308		

These analyses demonstrate rather conclusively that a general index of anxiety such as the STAI can not differentiate between the subjective experience associated with the concept of anxiety, and the experiences of fear, distress, guilt, and anger. Nor did the anxiety measure differentiate among four of the fundamental emotions related to anxiety. Since the STAI correlates highly with the Taylor MAS, these results suggest that broad-gauge unidimensional measures of anxiety fail to distinguish between experiences that have importantly different motivational properties.

The difference in mean anxiety scores between the anxiety situation and each of the five negative emotion situations was significant only for the shyness situation. The analysis of variance for this comparison is presented in Table 5-13. Inspection of the means, presented in Table 5-14, revealed that the average DES+A anxiety score from the shyness situation was significantly lower than the anxiety score from the anxiety situation. Thus, the experience of shyness as imagined by these subjects did not produce as much anxiety as measured by the STAI items of the DES+A as did the imagined experience of the anxiety situation or any of the other negative emotion situations—fear, distress, guilt, anger—all of which produced approximately equal mean anxiety scores. There are two possibilities as to why the shyness experience produced the lowest anxiety score of all the negative situations. First, since the shyness concept is not represented on the STAI, the DES emotion items for shyness could not contribute to the anxiety score. More fundamentally, shyness is considered the least important contributor to the pattern of negative fundamental emotions in anxiety. Judging from the magnitude of the mean anxiety scores in the different emotion situations (Table 5-14), the order of importance is as follows: fear, distress, guilt, anger, shyness, interest. This order may be different with a different index of anxiety, but it matches rather closely what is predicted by differential emotion theory. This order for mean scores certainly does not preclude wide differences in order of importance among individuals.

TABLE 5-13

Analysis of Variance of DES+A Anxiety Scores
from the Anxiety Situation and the Shyness Situation

Source	df	MS	F	p
Situations (anxiety versus shyness)	1	776.8750	8.9669	.0050
Subjects	37	189.0777	2.1824	.0100
Situations × Subjects	37	86.6385		

Some other characteristics of shyness probably affect its role in anxiety. As will be shown in Chapter Six (Table 6-3), shyness occupies a kind of middle position between the traditionally positive and negative emotions. In particular, it was rated as significantly more pleasant than fear, guilt, distress, or anger.

The analysis of variance comparing the anxiety scores in the anxiety situation and the interest situation showed the anxiety mean to be significantly lower in the interest situation. As already suggested, the role of interest in the anxiety experience is important primarily because it may oscillate with fear to produce a facilitative effect, especially with respect to the focusing of attention and effort.

TABLE 5-14

Anxiety Score Means and SDs of the Six Groups in the Different Emotion Situations and in the Anxiety Situation

Situations	$\bar{x}$	SD
Group 1		
Anxiety	76.32	12.07
Fear	78.13	12.83
Group 2		
Anxiety	78.28	12.74
Distress	76.62	12.36
Group 3		
Anxiety	77.42	10.11
Guilt	75.67	12.46
Group 4		
Anxiety	73.75	11.96
Anger	73.64	12.08
Group 5		
Anxiety	75.77	11.39
Interest	45.57	14.31

Since interest is a positive emotion it was expected that the anxiety means in the anxiety and interest situations would differ significantly, and this was the case.

Although the mean anxiety score in the shyness situation was significantly lower than that in the anxiety situation, the shyness situation was by no means anxiety free. Remember, the minimum mean anxiety score would be 19.00, whereas that obtained in the shyness situation was 68.89. This corresponds to a mean scale score of 3.62 on a 5-point scale. The corresponding mean scale score derived from the state form of STAI taken under instructions to assume a calm state was 1.75 on a 4-point scale (Spielberger, Gorsuch, & Lushene, 1970). The difference in level of anxiety in the shyness and calm situations, measured by the DES+A STAI items, is quite substantial.

Of the six fundamental emotions hypothesized as components of anxiety, only the positive emotion of interest failed to show a markedly elevated anxiety score. This exception for interest is due partly to its positive nature and partly to its special role in the pattern of emotions in the anxiety experience.

The foregoing analyses generally support the hypothesis that anxiety is a combination of fundamental emotions. Subjects describing their experience in imagined emotion situations of fear, guilt, distress, and anger produced anxiety scores equally as high as subjects describing their experience while imagining or visualizing an anxiety situation. The mean anxiety scores in the fear, guilt, distress, anger, and anxiety situations were significantly higher than the mean anxiety score for shyness, which was higher than the mean for interest. Yet, even in the shyness situation, the anxiety scores were well above the minimum obtainable and substantially higher than those reported for subjects asked to describe their feelings (on the STAI) in a calm state.

Put another way, the foregoing empirical analyses suggest that anxiety as a concept and anxiety scales as measurement techniques do not constitute an adequate means for the study of discrete human emotions. The STAI is a carefully developed instrument with well above average psychometric properties; yet, as used in the DES+A, it failed to differentiate between a visualized anxiety situation and a fear, distress, guilt, or anger situation. This may be considered a reasonable and expected outcome rather than a failure in discriminatory power if we view the STAI as a measure of a complex concept that has certain fundamental, discrete emotion concepts as constituent elements.

In the interest of refining instruments for use in planning treatment and intervention programs, it would be well for STAI and all other anxiety scales to specify the extent to which they measure fear, distress, guilt, anger, or other discrete emotions. The assumption that the different fundamental emotions have different antecedents, different existential and motivational properties, and different consequences is rapidly achieving the status in science that it has long enjoyed in folk wisdom.

VI. PATTERNS OF EMOTIONS

Most theorists who deal with discrete emotions have suggested that existence of a pure emotion, such as pure fear or pure guilt, is probably fairly rare in day-to-day living and virtually impossible to obtain in the laboratory or in any other research setting. I share this position, particularly if the dimension of time is considered. I believe we experience pure emotion from time to time, but since any emotion is one of the principal activators of other emotions, the pure emotion or one of the constantly changing elements of the perceptual–experiential field quickly elicits a second or third emotion. The original pure emotion may dominate the scene for a while, but very soon there are other emotions alternating, interacting, or combining in some sort of pattern. There was evidence from the present studies that this kind of patterning obtained as the subjects visualized or imagined the six different emotion situations.

The purpose of the following section is to present and discuss the patterns of emotions that occurred in the imagined emotion situations. The evidence strongly supports the premise that emotions typically occur in patterns or combinations that have some degree of stability or relatedness. That is, a particular fundamental emotion, though dominant in a given experience, tends to occur with a set of related emotions. The patterns of empirical (statistically derived) factors will be dealt with first, followed by the patterns for the a priori scales.

VII. PATTERNING OF EMOTIONS AS REPRESENTED BY THE EMPIRICAL FACTORS

The first question to be answered is whether or not the patterns or profiles of empirical factor scores vary significantly among the imagined or visualized situations. This question was answered by a series of analyses of variance. Using the factor structure derived from the data of the 297 subjects visualizing the anxiety situation, I obtained for each individual in each situation eight factor scores, seven factors representing emotions and one representing fatigue. (Raw scores were converted to T scores so that factors containing different numbers of items would be comparable.) The mean factor scores for the different emotion situations are presented in Table 5-15.

First, a separate analysis of variance compared the profile of emotions in each of the emotion situations with that of the anxiety situation. One of these analyses, the one comparing the anxiety situation with the fear situation, is presented in Table 5-16. The main effects in this and all subsequent similar analyses are of little interest or importance. The significant variance due to emotions simply indicates that the mean emotion factor scores, with means based on both situations, vary significantly. The situation variance is based on the sum of scores across emotions (or factors) and hence provides no information regarding differences between emotion factor scores in the two situations. In the present analysis the variance for situations was attenuated since all factor means from the anxiety

104

TABLE 5-15

DES+A Empirical Factor Means for Each Emotion Situation Imagined by the Subjects[a]

DES+A emotion factors	Imagined emotion situations					
	Fear (N=36)	Guilt (N=40)	Distress (N=39)	Anger (N=36)	Shyness (N=38)	Interest (N=44)
Interest	52.13	43.41	45.89	48.13	44.43	59.19
Enjoyment + "Negative of Anxiety"	47.45	48.25	47.28	48.30	52.73	72.26
Surprise	55.33	50.63	56.70	57.19	52.07	57.94
Anger-Disgust-Contempt	52.70	56.40	60.24	72.01	52.02	42.97
Distress-Guilt + "Anxiety"	48.64	61.50	61.62	50.58	53.32	39.43
Shyness	48.66	56.44	51.35	42.99	63.72	45.31
Fear + "Anxiety"	54.28	46.66	46.33	41.73	42.75	30.56
Fatigue	47.31	50.44	54.62	47.64	49.36	45.04

[a]Means are reported in terms of T scores, with the factor means and standard deviations for the total sample in the anxiety condition arbitrarily fixed at 50 and 10, respectively. Since the T scores were based on the data from the anxiety situation in which negative emotions were elevated, we would expect those emotions most predominantly involved in anxiety to show relatively less elevation than others. Remembering how STAI defines anxiety, we can see that this is rather precisely what happened. According to STAI, fear is the predominant negative emotion in anxiety, followed by distress and guilt, with anger and shyness not represented. Consistent with this reasoning, the mean Fear + Anxiety score in the fear situation is the lowest of the five negative mean emotion factor scores in their respective emotion situations. The means for the Distress-Guilt + Anxiety factor in the distress situation and guilt situation are in the middle, and the mean Anger-Disgust-Contempt factor score in the anger situation is highest.

TABLE 5-16
Subjects × *DES+A Empirical Factor Scores* × *Situations Analysis of
Variance: Anxiety Situation versus Fear Situation*

Source	df	MS	F	p
Subjects (*Ss*)	37	392.4863		
Factors (*A*)	7	242.7143	2.3434	.0243
Situations (*B*)	1	334.0000	3.6846	.0596
Factors × situations	7	237.2857	3.6134	.0013
A × *Ss*	259	103.5753		
B × *Ss*	37	90.6486		
A × *B* × *Ss*	259	65.6680		
Total	607	107.7496		

situation tended to approach 50, the *T* score value assigned the factor
means of the total sample in the anxiety situation.

The term of greatest importance, the interaction of emo-
tion factors × situations, was highly significant. This *F* ratio indicates
that the profile or pattern of scores on the several emotion factors
was quite different for the fear situation and for the anxiety situation. The emotion factors × situations interaction was significant in
every comparison between the anxiety situation and a discrete emotion situation. Remember, when the anxiety scores based on the
STAI items of the DES+A were compared for the anxiety situation
and the fear, guilt, distress, and anger situations, there were no
significant differences. There was a significant difference for anxiety
scores only between the anxiety situation and the shyness situation.
However, the comparisons of the patterns of emotion factor scores
from the anxiety situation and each of the emotion situations,
yielded consistent and highly significant differences in every instance.

The next step was an overall (Lindquist Type I) analysis of
variance comparing the empirical emotion factor profiles, considering
all six fundamental-emotion situations at once. This analysis is presented in Table 5-17. As expected the variance due to situations
approached significance at the .01 level, and the variance due to
factors was highly significant.

The term of importance in Table 5-17, the interaction of
situations × emotion factors, was also highly significant. This significant interaction indicates that the groups in the different emotion
situations responded differentially to the several factors of the

TABLE 5-17

Analysis of Variance of DES+A Empirical Factor Scores Considering All Emotion Situations at Once

Source	df	MS	F	p
Subjects	234	196.129		
Situations	5	542.637	2.8777	.0153
Between error	229	188.564		
Within subjects	1645	143.549		
Factors	7	3647.862	46.9550	.0000
Situations × factors	35	2459.108	31.6535	.0000
Within error	1603	77.688		
Total	1879	150.097		

DES+A profile. Thus as predicted, emotion factor means varied significantly from situation to situation.

Typically, a given pattern of emotions has one emotion that is experienced more strongly and/or more frequently than the others. This emotion is the key or dominant emotion of the pattern. In the present study, it was expected that the key emotion would be the one corresponding to the kind of emotion situation the subjects were asked to visualize. For the empirical factors, this was the case in four of the five negative emotion situations (see Table 5-15). That distress should be the key emotion in the imagined distress situation could be said to follow from the demand characteristics of the experiment. However, the demand characteristics do not call for any particular hierarchy of means among the other emotions experienced in the distress situation. Thus, the occurrence of logically and dynamically related patterns support differential emotion theory. When students were asked to imagine a distress situation their scores on the factor representing distress were elevated, but so were their scores on the factor representing anger–disgust–contempt and on the factor representing surprise. The picture was similar for the other emotion situations. (It is interesting to note, as shown in Table 5-15, that the nonemotion factor representing fatigue had its highest mean in the distress situation. Clinically, sad or bereaved clients often appear fatigued, and there is a similar loss of muscle tone in some depressions and in fatigue.)

The patterns were clearer in the case of the a priori scales, but definite patterning occurred with the empirical factors even though several of them represented more than one fundamental

107

emotion. Two of the clearer examples of patterning occurred in the shyness and guilt situation. In the shyness situation, the shyness factor had by far the highest mean. The next highest mean was for the factor of distress –guilt. If we look at the guilt situation, column 2 of Table 5-15, we find a parallel and consistent pattern. In the guilt situation, the highest mean was on the distress–guilt factor, with shyness having the second highest score. In this situation the mean factor score for anger–disgust–contempt was virtually the same as that for shyness, but this too makes sense in terms of emotion dynamics. Psychoanalytic theory posits a relationship between guilt and hostility in explaining the dynamics of grief (Janis, 1969); and Tomkins (1962) maintains that distress (an emotion component of grief) and anger are activated by a similar condition of neural activation—a relatively high and steady level of neural stimulation.

In the fear situation the mean for the factor representing the functionally related emotion of surprise was slightly higher than the mean for the fear factor. However, in the fear situation, the fear factor mean may be artificially low and the range of mean factor scores restricted because fear is a prominent component of anxiety; and the T scores used to compute the means in Table 5-15 were based on the means and standard deviations derived from the data of the anxiety situation in which fear was elevated. That is, it was a fairly high raw score mean for fear that was converted to the T score mean of 50. Within the restricted range of means for the fear situation, it is still possible to find a pattern that fits reasonably well with our hypothesis with respect to the activation of a dynamically related cluster or pattern of emotions. Three of the four highest factor means were those representing fear, surprise, and interest, long thought to be functionally and dynamically related (Darwin, 1872; Izard, 1971; Tomkins, 1962).

The case for patterning around the key emotion was not quite as clear for the interest situation. Here, the interest factor had the second highest mean, enjoyment the highest. However, even in this case, the factor scores for the positive emotions and for surprise are clearly higher than all of the factors representing negative emotions. Furthermore, shyness—the least unpleasant of the negative emotions—had the fourth highest mean.

VIII. CAN ANXIETY BE CONSIDERED A SECOND-ORDER FACTOR?

One way of viewing the results of the analysis of the substantive components of the concept of anxiety as presented in the first section of the chapter is to assume that the various theorists and investigators have tacitly accepted the fact that emotion has a number of different elements or components. Some theorists have attempted to put this into more rigorous mathematical or statistical language. As we have already noted, Cattell has argued that anxiety is a second-order factor and has specified certain primary factors as its constituents.

If I were to follow the form of Cattell's argument, I would say that anxiety is a second-order factor in which the discrete fundamental emotions are the primary factors. To test the reasonableness of this formulation, I computed the second-order factors for the data obtained on the 297 subjects who took the 51-item DES+A while imagining an anxiety situation. The second-order factors and the primary factors composing them are shown in row 1 of Table 5-18. It is evident that there is no second-order factor which contains all of the hypothesized emotions of anxiety. However, second-order factor II contains primary factors representing all of them except shyness and interest.

In all, we have looked at the second-order factors from four different investigations involving the DES. The factors shown in row 2 of Table 5-18 were derived from the data obtained by means of a summer mailout of the 72-item DES to incoming Vanderbilt freshmen. The mailout included a letter which, in effect, told them that their previous letter of acceptance to Vanderbilt was a mistake and that they actually could not be admitted to the university. The instructions told them that the "delayed rejection" letter was a hoax, but they were to respond to it as though it were true, using the DES to describe their emotions. As can be seen in row 2, the second-order factors do not correspond precisely with those in row 1, but there is some consistency. Again, there is no single second-order factor which contains all of the emotions hypothesized as components of anxiety, but factor II contains three of them.

Row 3 of Table 5-18 shows the second-order factors for the 72-item DES which was administered to freshmen during the on-campus placement and personality testing of orientation week. The second-order factors in this case are quite similar to those for the DES+A as shown in row 1, and factor II contains four of the five negative emotions of anxiety.

The second-order factors shown in row 4 were obtained during the placement and personality testing session for entering freshmen in 1968. Again, second-order factor II contains separate

TABLE 5-18

Second-Order Factors for the DES+A and Other Forms of the DES

Study (Row)	Factor I	Factor II	Factor III
1. DES+A (51 items) 1970; $N = 297$	.62 Interest —.58 Enjoyment	.61 Fear + Anxiety .72 Fatigue .69 Anger-Disgust-Contempt .77 Distress-Guilt + Anxiety .54 Surprise	.58 Shyness
2. DES (72 items) 1969; $N = 823$	.50 Interest .79 Contempt .64 Anger-Disgust-Contempt	.78 Fear .49 Disgust .79 Distress .62 Surprise	.67 Shyness .68 Guilt .66 Enjoyment .51 Fatigue (a) .48 Fatigue (b)
3. DES (72 items) 1969; $N = 1189$	.61 Interest .77 Enjoyment	.74 Fear-Distress .75 Guilt .63 Anger-Disgust-Contempt .58 Surprise	.58 Shyness .57 Fatigue .75 Mixed
4. DES (67 items) 1968; $N = 622$	—.77 Interest —.76 Enjoyment .64 Fatigue .52 Mixed	.83 Fear .64 Guilt .79 Distress .76 Shyness	.79 Contempt .77 Anger-Disgust-Contempt .58 Surprise

primary factors for four of the negative emotions hypothesized as components of anxiety.

The data in Table 5-18 suggest that anxiety cannot be considered as a second-order factor with fixed and stable primary factors as its component first-order factors. However, in each of the four factor analytic investigations, there was a second-order factor that contained factors representing the key emotion of fear and two or more of the other emotions hypothesized as components of anxiety. These results are generally consistent with my formulation of anxiety as a *variable* pattern of fundamental emotions and their interactions.

110

IX. RELATIONSHIPS AMONG FREE-RESPONSE DESCRIPTIONS
OF THE ANXIETY SITUATION AND THE DISCRETE
EMOTION SITUATIONS

On the occasions when the subjects were asked to visualize the anxiety situation and the different fundamental emotion situations they were also asked to give a brief description of the scene they were visualizing or imagining. I was highly impressed by the apparent candidness of the subjects. The situations that they listed had a great deal of face validity for the type of situation they were asked to visualize.

The chief use made of these data was to determine the degree to which the content of the free-response descriptions of the anxiety situation overlapped with the content of the free-response descriptions of the various discrete emotion situations. Two judges independently determined the number of anxiety situation descriptions that were identical to descriptions of one or more of the five discrete emotion situations. These data, summarized in Table 5-19, offer some of the strongest support for my conception of anxiety. The subjects gave free-response descriptions of what they considered to be a fear situation, a distress situation, a guilt situation, an anger situation, a shyness situation, and an interest situation. As my conception of anxiety would predict, we have a rather substantial overlap in these free-response descriptions between anxiety situations and each of the fundamental emotion situations.

TABLE 5-19
*Percentage of Free Responses in Each Fundamental
Emotion Situation Identical or Equivalent to Free
Responses in the Anxiety Situation*

Situation	Percentage of responses identical or equivalent to anxiety responses
Fear	55
Distress	59
Guilt	38
Shyness	47
Anger	47
Interest	23

In summarizing the data presented in Table 5-19, it is clear that the population of events and situations that people see as causes of anxiety overlap considerably with what they see as causes of fear, distress, guilt, anger, shyness, and interest–excitement. This overlap in perceived causes furnishes another kind of evidence that anxiety is not a unitary concept but a pattern or combination of fundamental emotions.

X. PATTERNING OF EMOTIONS AS REPRESENTED BY THE A PRIORI SCALES

On the a priori scales, each of the fundamental emotions is represented by three items. Although this is a small number of items per scale, the factor reliabilities for the a priori scales are quite satisfactory, as reflected by alpha coefficients that average about .75. Since each a priori scale represents only one fundamental emotion, the patterns should be even clearer than those for the empirical factors, which sometimes represented more than one emotion.

A. THE ANXIETY PATTERN

The overall profile of fundamental emotion means for anxiety is presented in Table 5-20. The anxiety pattern is fairly consistent with the hypothesized component structure of anxiety. The means for five of the six emotions hypothesized as components

TABLE 5-20
*Rank Order of DES a Priori
Means in the Anxiety Situation*

Emotion	$\bar{x}$
Interest	10.34
Fear	10.10
Distress	7.63
Disgust	6.14
Guilt	6.03
Surprise	6.00
Shyness	5.81
Fatigue	5.76
Anger	5.32
Contempt	5.23
Enjoyment	4.98

of anxiety are above 5.50, an arbitrarily adopted level for indicating the existence of the emotion in the pattern. The mean for anger was slightly below this level.

The key emotion of fear has the highest mean among the negative emotions in anxiety. The fact that interest has a slightly higher mean than fear does not detract substantially from the hypothesis. DES interest is measured by the terms alert, attending, concentrating. Mild to moderate anxiety (or fear) would be expected to increase alertness and to focus attention. Thus the interest score can be interpreted as consistent with the general pattern.

The presence of disgust among the elevated means is very likely a function of the dynamic relationship between anger and disgust, and the two taken together might be considered as the hostility component in anxiety. The hostility component, though present, is of relatively low intensity in comparison with the fear component, and this is quite in keeping with differential emotion theory's conception of the nature of anxiety. The slightly elevated mean for surprise is probably due to the dynamic relationship between surprise and the emotion of fear. As detailed elsewhere (Izard, 1971), a number of theorists have postulated neurophysiological and psychological relationships among the emotions of fear, surprise, and interest.

In summary, the key and dominant emotion in anxiety is fear, and the intensity of this emotion is elevated well above that of other negative emotions in the average profile for a large group. In the average profile, other negative emotions of distress, guilt, shyness, and disgust and anger are moderately to slightly elevated.

It should be emphasized that Table 5-20 presents an average profile for a large group. The anxiety pattern for individuals, particularly individuals with psychological problems, may vary considerably. For some individuals guilt may be almost as intense as fear while for others fear may oscillate with the anger–disgust (hostility) component.

Table 5-21 presents an emotion profile of a client who experienced frequent and intense anxiety associated with homosexuality. As part of the psychotherapeutic program the client was asked to complete the 33-item Differential Emotion Scale as soon as possible after experiencing a situation that elicited a high degree of anxiety. The pattern shown in Table 5-21 was fairly typical for this client when he had to confront typical male authority figures in his profession. At this point in therapy, the client was having sexual relations with both men and woman. In situations such as the one

113

TABLE 5-21
Anxiety Associated with Homosexuality

Situation: 8:00 a.m. rounds with resident

Client's description of situation: I do not know exactly why I was so anxious this morning. I do know I had trouble sleeping—went to bed late, woke up early, and had difficulty getting back to sleep (restless). Then I didn't want to get up, but preferred to lay in bed as though I could prevent 8:00 a.m. from arriving. I think my feeling is based on fear of showing ignorance (which is a very real occurrence) and thereby not being able to relate to the guys in this profession. It works another way, too, in that I hate to sit down and read for fear of not being settled down enough to comprehend (which also happens, but when I'm calm I do comprehend).

DES Factors	Scores[a]
Fear	15.0
Shyness	12.0
Interest	9.0
Distress	9.0
Fatigue	9.0
Disgust	6.0
Anger	6.0
Guilt	6.0
Contempt	6.0

[a]Scores range from a minimum possible of 3 to a maximum possible of 15.

described in Table 5-21, he expressed his anxiety in terms of fear of being "put down" or "shown up for what he is." While these phrases could well refer to his expressed fear of being proven intellectually inferior, they probably also symbolized his fear of being exposed as a homosexual.

It can be seen that the anxiety pattern of this psychotherapy client is rather similar to the hypothesized anxiety pattern and to the empirical pattern obtained from a large group of normal subjects visualizing an anxiety situation. The relatively high magnitude and rank of the shyness mean may be related to the clients' homosexuality.

B. PATTERNS OF EMOTIONS IN THE
FUNDAMENTAL EMOTION SITUATIONS

The profiles of a priori scale means for the different emotion situations are presented in Table 5-22. Means greater than 7.5 are above the middle of the DES intensity scale. Emotions

TABLE 5-22
Profiles (or Patterns) of Emotions in Imagined Situations Characterized by an "Anxiety-Related" Fundamental Emotion[a]

Fear situation (N = 38)		Distress situation (N = 39)		Guilt situation (N = 40)		Shyness situation (N = 38)		Anger situation (N = 36)		Interest situation (N = 44)	
Emotion	$\bar{x}$	Emotion	$\bar{x}$	Emotion	$\bar{x}$	Emotion	$\bar{x}$	Emotion	$\bar{x}$	Emotion	$\bar{x}$
Fear	11.71	Distress	11.67	Guilt	10.85	Shyness	8.82	Anger	13.19	Interest	12.80
Interest	9.90	Fear	8.33	Fear	8.60	Interest	7.55	Disgust	11.69	Enjoyment	10.52
Surprise	6.55	Disgust	8.28	Distress	8.52	Fear	7.34	Contempt	10.42	Surprise	8.59
Disgust	5.90	Interest	8.03	Disgust	8.08	Distress	7.18	Interest	10.03		
		Anger	7.49	Interest	7.30	Guilt	6.63	Surprise	8.44		
		Guilt	7.46	Shyness	6.70	Disgust	6.05	Distress	8.31		
		Surprise	7.10	Anger	5.80	Surprise	5.58	Fear	6.36		
		Contempt	6.46								
		Fatigue	5.95								

[a] A priori factors: minimum score 3, maximum score 15; $\bar{x} \div 3 = \bar{x}$ scale score.

115

experienced at this intensity would certainly be expected to influence organismic processes, including thought and action. Such influence may be direct, or by way of the particular emotion's influence on other emotions in the pattern, or both. Emotions may have some influence even at lower intensities. Of course, means that differ little from 3.00 indicate that the emotion was experienced very slightly or not at all, since 3.00 is the minimum a priori factor score.

The next question to be answered is whether the emotion profiles presented in Table 5-22 differ significantly among themselves. Before considering the comparisons of pairs of emotion profiles, an overall (Lindquist Type I) analysis of variance was computed, considering all six profiles at once. This analysis is presented in Table 5-23. As already noted, the variance due to situations and emotions (a priori factors) is of no interest. The important term is the situations × emotions interaction, which is highly significant. This significant interaction shows that the differences between some emotion means from situation to situation are greater than are the corresponding differences between others. A similar analysis was computed considering the three most prominent negative emotions related to anxiety—fear, distress, guilt. The results were essentially the same.

The next step in the study of emotion patterns was the comparison of all possible pairs of emotion situations. First, I shall make some observations based on inspection of the six emotion situation profiles of Table 5-22, followed by statistical comparisons of the profiles.

Before I begin, it should be noted that the pattern or profile of emotions obtained in a *situation* in which the individual is imagining conditions that elicit a particular fundamental emotion is not to be thought of as defining the *experience* of that fundamental emotion. For example, there is the fundamental emotion of fear, which has been defined aprioristically on the DES, and the a priori definition is very like the empirical definition of fear obtained in numerous factor-analytic investigations. Thus we have a definition of the fundamental emotion of fear.

On the other hand, the fear situation should be distinguished from the experience of the fundamental emotion of fear. When a person visualizes a fear situation and fills out the DES, a pattern of emotions emerges, with fear as the key factor but with other emotions elevated. As already indicated, this merely confirms the differential emotion principle that human experience is not to be conceived as a sequence of pure emotions experienced in tandem.

X. Patterning as Represented by a Priori Scales

TABLE 5-23

Analysis of Variance of the a Priori Profiles from the Six Emotion Situations

Source	df	MS	F	p
Subjects	234	72.214		
Situations	5	235.687	3.4334	.0055
Between error	229	68.640		
Within subjects	2350	13.378		
Emotions	10	450.385	63.5704	.0000
Situations × emotions	50	214.185	30.2316	.0000
Within error	2290	7.085		
Total	2584	18.706		

Typically, life is characterized by a pattern or combination of interacting emotions. There may often be a key emotion that is most important and that remains dominant for a period of time for a given situation, but there are almost always other emotions that serve to attenuate, amplify, or modulate both the key emotion and its effects upon cognition and action.

When we look at the pattern of emotions in anxiety and see fear, distress, and guilt, it is not necessary to conceive of anxiety as a pattern of emotions for a fear situation plus the pattern of emotions for a distress situation, etc. In an anxiety situation, the fundamental emotions interact as components, just as they do in the fundamental emotion situations. The differences in the pattern for the anxiety situation and for a fundamental emotion situation may result from differences in the complexity of the situation and the person–situation interactions. Situations or conditions that elicit anxiety may be fearlike situations which are less well defined than an ordinary fear situation but which may be able to elicit, in addition to fear, the emotions of distress, guilt, shyness, or anger and possibly interest.

Table 5-22 shows that the number of emotions with factor means above 5.50, the arbitrary minimum intensity level for including an emotion in the profile, varies considerably among the different fundamental emotion situations. The number of emotions in the profile or pattern is considered as one criterion of complexity.

C. THE PATTERN OF EMOTIONS IN THE INTEREST SITUATION

With the number of elevated emotion means as the criterion of complexity, the simplest emotion situation was that of interest. In this case there are elevated means only on the two positive emotions of interest and enjoyment and on the channel-clearing emotion of surprise. None of the negative emotions had scale means above 5.50. Thus, this pattern is considered to be character-ized by harmonious and smoothly interacting motivational tenden-cies and capable of sustaining efficient and constructive behavior.

D. THE PATTERN OF EMOTIONS IN THE FEAR SITUATION

The second simplest of the emotion patterns was that of the fear situation. The second and third highest means in the fear situation were those for interest and surprise which, as already indicated, are considered to be dynamically related to fear. It is interesting that the only other emotion in the fear situation whose mean exceeded the cutoff score was disgust. Fear and disgust have a common characteristic—they both motivate the individual to sepa-rate himself from the emotion-eliciting object. The elevated mean for interest in the fear situation may also be considered supportive of the motivational condition that would be most adaptive in a fear situa-tion. Interest is measured on the DES by the terms attentive, concen-trating, and alert. Certainly interest, as defined by these terms, would contribute to adaptive behavior in a fear situation. Thus, the fear situation may be considered a rather highly consistent set of motiva-tional tendencies.

There is one possible conflict inherent in the pattern for the fear situation. When interest is sufficiently high relative to fear and involves relating to or exploring the object that elicits the fear, some ambivalence or conflict may be experienced. This condition is more likely to occur in an interest situation in which interest is the key emotion or in a situation that does not elicit strong fear. When fear is high and dominant, the motivational forces in a fear situation are necessarily consistent in order to facilitate essential adaptive action. Of course, extreme fear can literally paralyze the individual. This highly toxic effect probably results only when extreme fear precludes all other emotions that ordinarily would interact with fear to produce a moderating effect.

E. THE PATTERN OF EMOTIONS IN THE DISTRESS SITUATION

Using number of emotions involved as a criterion, the most complex pattern of emotions was that of the distress situation. Eight of the ten a priori emotion factor means were elevated. All of these factor means were above 7.00 except for contempt, which was 6.46.

The complexity of the pattern in the distress situation is further increased by its being the only one of the anxiety-related fundamental emotion situations in which the fatigue factor was above the cutoff point of 5.50.

The pattern in the distress situation contains a number of potentially conflicting emotions or motivational tendencies. Fear and anger represent one set of opposing forces, disgust and interest another. The pattern for the distress situation is potentially quite debilitating. With these built-in conflicting forces, distress would be expected to render customary activities difficult, to decrease efficiency, and to have a general retarding effect.

F. THE PATTERN OF EMOTIONS IN THE GUILT SITUATION

In the guilt situation, the pattern of emotions is moderately complex. Again we have the potentially conflicting emotions of fear and anger, disgust and interest. It is quite reasonable that a guilt situation could lead to fear of the consequences of one's behavior. The fear might also be a function of the feeling of isolation and estrangement that is associated with guilt. Here the disgust, which also is elevated in the proximity of the fear and distress means, is very likely inner-directed, though some disgust may also be directed toward another person or object involved in the guilt situation. Shyness probably represents the person's feeling of embarrassment or desire for concealment—the need to get away from it all. The slight degree of anger present in the guilt situation is probably partly directed toward the self and partly outer-directed.

G. THE PATTERN OF EMOTIONS IN THE SHYNESS SITUATION

The pattern in the shyness situation is different from all other anxiety-related fundamental emotion situations in several unusual ways. First, the key emotion of shyness is only moderately elevated, not as high as the second-highest emotion in three of the other patterns. There are four means in the anger situation that are higher than the highest mean in the shyness situation. Furthermore, the gap between shyness and the positive emotion of interest, which is the second highest in the shyness pattern, is smaller than is the case for any of the patterns of the other negative emotions. The means for the other negative emotions represented in the shyness pattern are only slightly elevated. These characteristics are consistent with the fact, already noted, that shyness is the least unpleasant of the negative emotions. The proximity of shyness and the positive emotion of interest in the shyness pattern suggests that the emotion of shyness probably occurs in relatively nonthreatening situations and in situations where there is considerable likelihood of experiencing positive emotions.

Shyness is the emotion that motivates the individual to separate or conceal the self from others and move away from the situation either literally or psychologically. Virtually all the emotions in the shyness pattern are consistent with such behavior. There is a potential conflict between interest and fear and interest and disgust, but the elevation of disgust is so slight here that it probably does not represent a strong force. As already suggested, when fear and interest are elevated only moderately, the two may oscillate without being debilitating. Such conflict or oscillation may be present even in creative endeavors.

H. THE PATTERN OF EMOTIONS IN THE ANGER SITUATION

The pattern in the anger situation contrasts sharply with that of the shyness situation. The mean for the key emotion of anger is higher than that of any other key emotion in the situations for negative emotions. Further, the dynamically related emotions of disgust and contempt, which occupy the second and third places in the anger situation, are considerably more elevated than are any other emotions in comparable positions in other patterns. In keeping with evidence from neurophysiology and with common sense, the pattern of emotions in the anger situation presents a picture of a highly aroused, highly activated individual.

For the most part, the emotions with the highest means in the anger pattern interact harmoniously and sustain a high level of activity that is clearly focused and directed. Distress, which is moderately elevated, is the most difficult emotion to analyze as a part of the dynamics of the anger pattern. As I have already noted, anger and distress, according to Tomkins (1963), are activated by similar gradients of neural firing. This may help explain the presence of distress in the pattern, but not its role. The role of distress might be to moderate the intensity of anger and the related emotions of disgust and contempt. Should anger lead to aggression, distress could serve as a basis for empathy with the victim and thus serve as a sort of safety valve. It is also quite possible that as a result of social experience and learning, individuals may feel some distress (sadness, discouragement) in anger situations since anger is so seldom expressed in satisfying and rewarding ways in our society and since it often arises in the face of disappointment resulting from thwarting or postponement of goals. It should be noted that in the anger situation, fear is lower both in absolute value and in relative rank than it is in any other negative emotion situation. This follows from the fact that anger inhibits fear. The probable role of fear in the anger situation, like that of distress, is to exercise a moderating effect on the potentially dangerous hostility triad—anger, disgust, contempt.

I. COMMON COMPONENTS AND
INTERRELATIONSHIPS AMONG PATTERNS

Except for its role in the anger situation, fear occupies either second or third place in the patterns of other negative emotions related to anxiety. This may well point up the overriding characteristic of the set of fundamental emotions that I have termed anxiety-related.

Some emotions occur in more situations than do others. As already noted, fear is prominent in all these anxiety-related emotion situation patterns except the anger situation, where it still appears above the cutoff point. Disgust is present in all the negative emotion situations though, as already noted, it is probably inner-directed in some, outer-directed in others, and both inner- and outer-directed in still other emotion situations. Disgust was not hypothesized as a component of anxiety. It may be that its presence is explained in part by its dynamic relationship to anger, since anger frequently seems to play a significant role in the overall anxiety picture.

Distress is present in all the negative emotion situations except fear. The role of distress in the anxiety-related emotion patterns is apparently quite substantial.

Guilt is not as prominent in the separate emotion situations as one might have expected. It appears in only two situations other than the guilt situation, and in both cases its absolute mean and relative rank are fairly low. It is sixth in the distress situation and fifth in the shyness situation. Its position in other fundamental emotion situations does not necessarily preclude its playing an important role relative to other fundamental emotions in an anxiety pattern.

Shyness appears in only one emotion situation other than the shyness situation: It occupies the sixth rank in the guilt situation. Shyness may well be the least troublesome of the emotions in an anxiety pattern.

The positive emotion of interest was elevated from the lower middle to the upper middle range of intensity in all the anxiety-related fundamental emotion situations. This suggests that it may be a fairly essential part of all emotion situations. However, it is well worth noting that the magnitude of the means for interest varies considerably in the different emotion situations. The relative ranking of interest in the different patterns may indicate the degree to which the individual is motivated to respond directly to the situation. This notion is consistent with the fact that interest is highest in anger, second highest in fear, and is lowest and second lowest in guilt and shyness, respectively.

J. STATISTICAL COMPARISONS OF PATTERNS FROM FUNDAMENTAL EMOTION SITUATIONS

Since the overall analysis of variance (Table 5-23) comparing the a priori emotion profiles for the six emotion situations yielded a highly significant variance for the situations X emotions interaction, separate analyses comparing pairs of emotion situations were computed. A Lindquist Type I analysis of variance was used to compare the a priori profiles for each of the possible pairings among the six anxiety-related emotion situations. There were 15 such analyses.

For illustrative purposes, the analysis comparing the profiles in the fear and guilt situations is presented in Table 5-24. This analysis was typical. In each of the 15 analyses, the variance due to situations X emotions was highly significant. In every case p was less than .0000. Thus for each possible pair of emotion situations, the

TABLE 5-24
Analysis of Variance of the DES a Priori Factor Profiles in the Fear and Guilt Situations

Source	df	MS	F	p
Subjects	77	91.028		
Situations	1	166.551	1.8499	.1745
Between error	76	90.034		
Within subjects	780	11.954		
Emotions	10	322.679	51.7833	.0000
Situations X emotions	10	136.185	21.8549	.0000
Within error	760	6.231		
Total	857	19.059		

corresponding emotion means in the two profiles varied significantly. That is, the subjects in the different situations responded in a very different fashion to some of the emotion scales. The results of these analyses indicate that the DES is a highly discriminative instrument, sensitive to differences in subjective experiences associated with a wide variety of emotion-eliciting situations. The results also show that there is a wide variety of discriminable human experiences that can be distinguished in terms of their unique patterns of emotions— their experiential–motivational properties.

XI. PATTERNS OF EMOTIONS IN A HIGHLY THREATENING REAL-LIFE SITUATION

The study using the 72-item DES to analyze the emotions involved in black–white encounters characterized by race prejudice was extended to a predominantly black institution, Jackson State College, during a highly stressful and threatening time. (The original study, discussed on pages 88-89 was conducted in February, 1970, at predominantly black institutions, Fisk and Tennessee State Universities in Nashville, Tennessee, during a normal time.) The experiment was conducted in Jackson, Mississippi, on June 30, 1970, after the May 14th police–student encounter which resulted in the killing of two students and the injury of more than ten other students.

Some students were still very much concerned over the May 14th incident. Student rallies and rap sessions focusing on the event and how to deal with it were being held periodically. The content and atmosphere of these meetings and the material obtained in interviews with individual students suggested that mean scores would be elevated for certain emotions—the emotions associated with a highly threatening situation. In particular, I expected that the Jackson State students would have higher means on some of the DES factors representing the emotions related to the concept of anxiety— fear, distress, shame (including shyness and guilt), anger, and interest. I also expected that the recent tragedy on the Jackson State campus would result in significant cities X situations interactions for the emotions related to anxiety, with the Jackson State students' scores on the most recent situation yielding higher means than those of black college students in Nashville.

A two-way (cities X situations) analysis of variance was performed for each of the seven DES+A empirical factors and for the nonemotion factor of fatigue. An example of these eight analyses of variance—the fear–distress factor—is presented in Table 5-25.

TABLE 5-25

Two-Way Analysis of Variance (Cities × Situations) for the Fear-Distress Factor Scores

Source	df	MS	F	p
Subjects	270	158.821		
Cities	1	2843.188	19.1021	.0001
Between error	269	148.842		
Within subjects	542	52.584		
Situations	2	2610.312	62.1801	.0000
Cities × situations	2	347.447	8.2765	.0005
Within error	538	41.980		
Total	812	87.909		

The statistical analyses confirmed the expectation that some of the factors representing the emotions related to the concept of anxiety would be elevated. The means for the Jackson State students were higher than those for the Nashville students on all but one of the hypothesized emotions, that for shyness on which the two group means were about the same. Jackson students had a higher mean on interest, though the difference, considered separately, was not statistically significant ($p = .20$). The means of the Jackson State students were significantly higher on fear–distress ($p = .0001$), and on guilt ($p = .0048$). The Jackson State and Nashville students differed on only one other factor: Jackson State students were significantly higher on surprise ($p = .0039$), an emotion dynamically related to fear.

The high mean on the fear–distress factor is readily understood. Many students continued to fear for their lives; this was particularly true for a sizable number who, at the time the study was conducted, were participating in a boycott of white businesses on the main street of Jackson. Most students were afraid that anything they did that could be interpreted as a sign of disorder would result in another police invasion of the campus and more deaths. Of course, they were also distressed and saddened by the deaths of their fellow students. Many felt helpless to do anything about what they saw as unprovoked or needless killings.

The high mean on guilt may not appear so immediately understandable, but there are several reasonable explanations in terms of emotion–emotion interactions and the actual events. Some students reported in interviews with the author that they were ashamed of being scared. Many students might well have felt guilt about leaving the campus when the college closed officially immediately after the tragedy, though few could see a feasible alternative. Only about 10 students remained on campus and "on the case." Most of these became members of the Committee of Concerned Students, and in some of the rallies they made speeches which unequivocally placed blame on their fellow students for running scared and leaving the scene.

The analyses also tended to confirm the expectation of significant cities × situations interactions, with higher DES factor means for Jackson State students who responded to their most recent black–white prejudice encounter. These interactions were significant in the analyses for fear–distress, guilt, interest, and surprise. For each of these four analyses, the Duncan range test indicated that the Jackson State students had significantly higher means for the most recent situation than did the Nashville students. The meaningfulness of this finding is increased by the fact that in the free-response descriptions of the most recent prejudice encounter, approximately one-third of the Jackson State students described the tragic night of May 14th when white police fired upon them, killing two and seriously injuring several others.

There is the possibility that some of the differences between the Jackson State and Nashville black students for the most recent encounter could be attributed to regional sociocultural differences (deep south versus border state) or to time of testing (winter versus summer). If these possible sources of uncontrolled variance were responsible for the differences, there should be as many differences for the hypothetical situation as for the most recent encounter. The situations are comparable in that both involve experiences at the same age level: young adulthood. However, for the hypothetical (experimenter-defined) situation, there were no significant differences between the Jackson State and Nashville students. This does not mean that there are no important sociocultural differences for the regions represented by the two groups of students. There probably are differences, and it is reasonable to expect their influence to be greater in childhood than in adulthood and somewhat more repressive for Jackson State students, most of whom come from rural Mississippi or elsewhere in the deep South. The results confirmed this expectation. For the earliest encounter, Jackson State students had significantly higher mean scores on the factors representing fear–distress and guilt.

XII. SUMMARY

Differential emotion theory defines anxiety as a variable combination of two or more of the fundamental emotions of fear, distress, shame (including shyness and guilt), anger, and interest. In different persons and in different situations, anxiety may be any combination of these fundamental emotions in which fear is dominant, and the emotion components may exist and interact at different levels of intensity. Anxiety is always a complex of fundamental emotions and their interactions. It cannot be adequately conceptualized and understood or effectively assessed and treated when considered as a unitary concept.

The empirical studies reported in this chapter yielded additional support for the theory. "Anxiety words" loaded on emotion factors representing the fundamental emotions that constitute anxiety. A modified standard anxiety scale failed to differentiate between an anxiety situation and the emotion situations of fear, guilt, distress, and anger. In contrast, the patterns or profiles of emotions derived from the Differential Emotion Scale were significantly different for the anxiety situation and each of the emotion situations.

In addition, both the empirical and a priori emotion profiles derived from the six fundamental emotion situations varied significantly. In reviewing the analyses of these patterns of emotions, two important points emerge. In the first place, it appears from the data in Table 5-22 that when subjects visualize or imagine a situation that they perceive as most closely related to a particular fundamental emotion such as fear, they not only experience an elevation in the particular emotion of fear but in other emotions that are functionally or dynamically related to it and that frequently interact with it. Furthermore, as demonstrated by the analyses presented in Tables 5-23 and 5-24, the patterns of emotions vary significantly and in a logically consistent fashion from situation to situation. In short, each of the six fundamental emotions related to the concept of anxiety tends to occur as the key emotion in a unique pattern, distinct from all other patterns.

The 72-item Differential Emotion Scale was administered to Jackson State College students during a highly stressful and threatening time. The resulting pattern of emotions (DES profile) was quite close to what was expected under the prevailing conditions. Most of the factors related to the concept of anxiety had elevated means. These high means, particularly those for the fear–

distress and guilt factors, were quite consistent with independently reported experiences and with actual events.

A particular individual in a particular emotion-eliciting situation typically experiences more than one emotion, as well as interactions among emotions. To call such intrapersonal processes "anxiety" probably leads to more difficulties than solutions. This is particularly so if anxiety is viewed as a unitary concept and the operations used to measure the intrapersonal processes take on the nature of unidimensional measures. The scientific usefulness of the term anxiety has been rendered highly questionable. To use it intelligently, we need to have certain understandings about its complexities and its components. Each time the term is used, it should be accompanied by a series of subscripts or qualifications specifying the qualities and intensities and probable interactions of the constituent fundamental emotions.

Differential emotion theory and the supporting evidence presented in this chapter suggest that the development of the science of emotions would be facilitated by using the concept of patterns or profiles of emotions. This would mean viewing any significant social or person–environment interaction as one that is characterized by a pattern of emotions rather than by a single discrete emotion. The DES provides an effective means of defining patterns and of discriminating among them.

CHAPTER SIX

A Dimensional and Discrete Emotions Investigation of the Subjective Experience of Emotion*

I. INTRODUCTION

There are two approaches to the study of emotion as it relates to subjective experience: the dimensional approach and the typological or discrete emotions approach. A detailed analysis of the two approaches has been presented by Bartlett (1969) and Izard (1971). Here a summary of central concepts and major empirical findings will suffice.

The dimensional approach stipulates that emotion is not a special state in the organism. It holds that emotion is part of a more general process commonly termed activation or arousal.

The dimensional approach has roots in Spencer's concept of a pleasantness—unpleasantness (P-U) continuum and in his early enunciation of the concepts of activation and adaptation level (Spencer, 1890). In an extension of this line of thinking, Wundt (1896) proposed that emotional experience varied along the dimensions of pleasantness–unpleasantness, excitement–quiet, and tension–relief. Woodworth (1938) modified the meaning of these dimensions when he concluded that "pleasantness and unpleasantness correspond to the attitudes of acceptance and rejection, excitement and depression to the momentary level of muscular activity or

*This chapter was written in collaboration with Edmund S. Bartlett as first author.

readiness for activity, tension and relaxation to the degree of muscular tension [p. 241]." Although Woodworth used discrete emotion concepts like surprise, fear, and disgust, his work laid the foundation for contemporary dimensional theory and research. He represented the emotions as segments of a single continuous linear scale, the precursor of the concept of emotion as a part of an essentially unidimensional process (Duffy, 1962; Lindsley, 1951). He saw emotional experience as a function of attitudinal and neuromuscular processes, thus paving the way for the elimination of discrete emotion concepts and for thinking of the dimensions of subjective experience in nonemotional terms. It was an easy step to the conceptualization of subjective experience as functions of organismic processes which, according to the dimensionalists, could be described better by concepts such as activation and pleasantness than by discrete emotion labels. These concepts and a number of others specified by subsequent research have been variously thought of as dimensions of emotional expression, dimensions of emotion, and dimensions of behavior in general.

Duffy (1941, 1957, 1962) and Lindsley (1951, 1957) used a concept of neurophysiological activation in an attempt to explain behavior in general, including that which is commonly termed emotional behavior. Schlosberg (1941, 1952, 1954), Triandis and Lambert (1958), Frijda (1970), Frijda and Philipszoon (1963), and Abelson and Sermat (1962) delineated dimensions of facial expression and considered these as dimensions of emotion. Osgood (1966, 1969), Block (1957), Davitz (1970), and Nowlis (1970) developed dimensions of verbal expression and treated them as indices of emotion or emotional expression.

In the present study, dimensions such as pleasantness and activation are conceived as dimensions of subjective experience, the latter being viewed as a broader concept than emotional experience. They are considered as functions of organismic processes which are usually auxiliary to emotion but which can operate relatively independently of emotion. The dimensional approach will be represented operationally by the Dimensions Rating Scale (DRS), which has items corresponding to the dimensions derived in previous research and which will be described in detail in a later section.

The second approach stipulates that there are different types of emotions (e.g., joy, distress, fear, anger) which are qualitatively distinct. Each discrete emotion is thought to constitute a special state or process in the organism and to have particular motivational and experiential properties. The first systematic search

130

for fundamental emotions was initiated by Darwin (1872). Contemporary formulations of a discrete emotions approach have been presented in Tomkins (1962, 1963), Izard (1971), and this book.

Following Izard's differential emotion theory (1971), each emotion is considered as having a neurochemical, neuromuscular-expressive, and phenomenological level. The neurochemical and neuromuscular components of emotion proper are not identical with the neurophysiological substrates of the subjective or experiential dimensions as defined above.

The present study focuses on the phenomenological level, or subjective experience of emotion. The discrete emotions approach will be represented operationally by an abbreviated form of the Differential Emotion Scale.

The first aim of this study is to specify a set of descriptive and substantive dimensions (the DRS) that will differentiate among the subjective experiences associated with the fundamental emotions. The second aim will be to compare an imagined anxiety situation with a real (test) anxiety situation by means of (a) the DRS and (b) the DES. The third aim will be to compare the relative efficacy of DRS and DES in distinguishing between high- and low-anxiety groups.

II. BASIC DIMENSIONS OF EMOTION

Without exception, bipolar factors related to (a) pleasantness and (b) intensity or activation have appeared as the predominant explanatory factors in every study of the dimensions of experience. They have appeared in spite of variations among stimulus modes (facial expressions, emotion concepts, self-reports of mood, and self-reports of emotion-laden critical incidents), and response modes (a single P-U scale, a single scale rating the global similarity between two facial expressions, a set of diverse emotion terms, a set of semantic differential scales, an a priori set of a bipolar dimensions scales, and free responses). They also appeared in cross-cultural studies of Greek and American subjects, Dutch subjects, and different American populations.

A. ADDITIONAL DIMENSIONS OF EMOTION

The need for more than two dimensions has been the subject of much debate and very little agreement. When facial expressions were used as emotional stimuli, a major difficulty in defining

131

additional dimensions appeared to be "that the facial communication system is a noisy and unreliable one [Osgood, 1966, p. 13]," especially when the task for the subjects was to select emotion labels or make scale ratings in a context-free situation.

When Abelson and Sermat (1962) used only a global similarity rating and only 13 photographs, they got no additional dimensions. However, when Frijda (1970) used 40 substantive scales and 130 photographs, he found three additional dimensions.

Frijda (1970) adopted Schachter's (1964) view that a single behavior pattern may refer to a whole array of different emotions. The proposition of a one-to-many relationship between one particular facial expression and several qualitatively different emotions or subjective experiences brings up the question of how differentiated is emotional or expressive behavior when compared to the rich descriptive terminology of the person observing or experiencing an emotion or emotions. Frijda's dimensional scales may be accounting not only for the emotion component in facial expressions but also contextual dimensions (social, cultural, behavioral, intellectual) along which observers can, from their experience, arrange facial expressions of emotion.

These descriptive and substantive dimensions also can be derived when stimuli other than facial expressions are used. For example, Davitz (1970) derived his dimensions from a 556-item checklist of emotion terms used by subjects who were evaluating critical incidents in their lives. His relatedness dimension contained three clusters of items which he interpreted as moving toward, moving away, and moving against. This dimension has some definite similarities to Schlosberg's (1954) attention-rejection dimension, Frijda and Philipszoon's (1963) attention-disinterest dimension, and Nowlis' (1970) positive and negative social orientation dimension.

Another general dimension was initially defined by Osgood (1966) as control. One pole was defined by annoyance, disgust, contempt, scorn, and loathing, and the opposite pole by dismay bewilderment, surprise, and excitement. Frijda (1970) proposed an emotional intensity–emotional control or indifference dimension where control seemed to mean a visible effort to keep from expressing an emotion facially. Nowlis (1970) specified a control–loss-of-control dimension, where control was exemplified by the term concentration and loss-of-control by anxiety.

Finally, there has been some agreement that White's (1959) concept of competence might be another possible dimension. Davitz (1970) noted the similarity between White's concept and three clusters of the Davitz checklist items that reflect feelings of enhancement, incompetence or dissatisfaction, and inadequacy. Frijda (1970) described a somewhat similar dimension of self-assured–insecure.

B. CONSTRUCTION OF THE DRS

The assessment of subjective experience in specific emotion situations is considered a complex task in which the essential measurement technique, self-report, incorporates aspects of feeling, cognition, and behavior. For this reason, dimensions on the DRS were represented by three scales, one for each of these three levels of functioning. The instructions defined the feeling level as bodily cues, such as breathing, heart rate, perspiration, and muscle tension. The behavior level was defined as primarily facial–postural expression. The thought level permitted a subject to evaluate the way in which he was cognitively appraising (Arnold, 1960a, 1968) the emotion situation. The intention was to give additional specificity to the dimension as well as flexibility to the communicator. The DRS is presented on page 134.

Dimensions were selected on the basis of their apparent salience for assessing subjective experience in a specifically defined emotion situation. Pleasantness was unequivocally the first dimension to be chosen because of its wide empirical support and obvious salience for assessing the hedonic tone of subjective experience.

Activity and tension were chosen as dimensions to represent neurophysiological activation which has both theoretical and empirical support as a component or concomitant of emotion. The scales representing the activity dimension were expected to measure the tendency toward movement and verbal expression. The tension dimension was thought to relate to activation and to reflect phenomena such as increased muscle tone and inhibition in the expression of emotion semantically and behaviorally. The hedonic and activation dimensions were expected to be the necessary but not sufficient dimensions for distinguishing between discrete emotion experiences.

After pleasantness and activation, the next dimension to be chosen was control. As a salient dimension for assessing emotional experience, it represents an aspect of interaction primarily with people but also with objects and institutions. It enables a person to communicate the degree to which he considers his feelings, thoughts, or actions to be intentional or voluntary.

6. Subjective Experience of Emotion

Dimensions Rating Scale (DRS)

Directions: A number of questions are given below that ask people to describe themselves. As you recall and visualize the emotion situation, please try to answer each question by taking a moment to evaluate thought patterns, behavior (e.g., facial expressions) and inner bodily feelings (e.g., breathing, heart rate, perspiration, muscle tone, etc.). Give your answer by circling the appropriate number to the right of each question.

There are no right or wrong answers. Do not spend too much time on any one question.

		Not at all		Moderately			Extremely	
1								
	a. How active do you feel?	0	1	2	3	4	5	6
	b. How active are your thoughts?	0	1	2	3	4	5	6
	c. How active is your behavior?	0	1	2	3	4	5	6
2								
	a. How deliberate do you feel?	0	1	2	3	4	5	6
	b. How deliberate are your thoughts?	0	1	2	3	4	5	6
	c. How deliberate is your behavior?	0	1	2	3	4	5	6
3								
	a. How tense do you feel?	0	1	2	3	4	5	6
	b. How tense are your thoughts?	0	1	2	3	4	5	6
	c. How tense is your behavior?	0	1	2	3	4	5	6
4								
	a. How impulsive do you feel?	0	1	2	3	4	5	6
	b. How impulsive are your thoughts?	0	1	2	3	4	5	6
	c. How impulsive is your behavior?	0	1	2	3	4	5	6
5								
	a. How controlled do you feel?	0	1	2	3	4	5	6
	b. How controlled are your thoughts?	0	1	2	3	4	5	6
	c. How controlled is your behavior?	0	1	2	3	4	5	6
6								
	a. How self-assured do you feel?	0	1	2	3	4	5	6
	b. How self-assured are your thoughts?	0	1	2	3	4	5	6
	c. How self-assured is your behavior?	0	1	2	3	4	5	6
7								
	a. How extraverted do you feel?	0	1	2	3	4	5	6
	b. How extraverted are your thoughts?	0	1	2	3	4	5	6
	c. How extraverted is your behavior?	0	1	2	3	4	5	6
8								
	a. How pleasant do you feel?	0	1	2	3	4	5	6
	b. How pleasant are your thoughts?	0	1	2	3	4	5	6
	c. How pleasant is your behavior?	0	1	2	3	4	5	6

Following Osgood's (1966) suggestion, the bipolar dimension of deliberate–impulsive was selected but separated into two unipolar dimensions, since it was decided that all DRS scales should be unipolar. The scales representing the deliberateness dimension enable a person to communicate the degree to which he anticipates or is prepared for the given emotion-eliciting situation. The degree of reported impulsiveness, on the other hand, communicates a lack of preparedness or anticipation.

The impulsiveness scales also carry the connotation of spontaneity, which characterizes the suddenness with which an emotion is experienced. Spontaneity also implies a personal mode of expression. The extraversion scale was selected from the well-known extraversion–introversion dimension, which has some empirical validity as a salient dimension in the assessment of subjective experience. The extraversion dimension enables a person to communicate a feeling or social orientation (to be with people), socially oriented thought or attention, and a behavioral movement toward people.

The final dimension was the positive pole of Frijda's (1970) self-assured–insecure dimension. The self-assurance dimension enables a person to communicate feelings of competence and adequacy. On the cognitive level a person can report the degree to which he understands the dynamics of the emotion-eliciting situation. At the behavioral level he can report the degree to which he thinks his actions are appropriate for the emotion situation.

The enunciation of the DRS dimensions and their possible relationship to emotion is based on a series of loosely affiliated studies that vary widely in their conceptualization of emotion. Nevertheless, these studies do suggest that emotion can and should be studied not only as an independent subsystem of personality, but also in terms of its effect on physiological systems and on the cognitive and behavioral activity of the observer or of the person experiencing emotion.

C. DISCRETE EMOTIONS THEORY AND THE DIFFERENTIAL EMOTION SCALE

Differential emotion theory defines emotion as a "complex concept that has neurophysiological, neuromuscular, and phenomenological aspects. At the neurophysiological level, emotion is defined in terms of patterns of electrochemical activity in the nervous system and in the facial and trigeminal nerves. The cutaneous nerve supply in the face and the proprioceptors in the facial muscles also participate in emotion at the neurophysiological level. At the neuromuscular level, emotion is primarily facial activity (patterning) and secondarily body (postural-gestural, visceral, and sometimes vocal) responses. At the phenomenological level, emotion is essentially motivating experience and/or experience that has immediate meaning and significance for the person [Izard, 1971, p. 185]."

The theory specifies nine fundamental emotions (interest–excitement, enjoyment–joy, surprise–startle, distress–anguish, disgust–revulsion, anger–rage, shame–humiliation, fear–terror, contempt–scorn). For each emotion, there is a range of intensity that can be defined by semantic labels on a numerical scale.

Differential emotion theory led to the development of the Differential Emotion Scale. As shown in earlier chapters, factor analyses of DES data from several studies showed good matching of aprioristically defined emotion factors and statistically derived factors. In each study, there was a perfect theoretical–empirical matching for several emotions. The DES, as adapted for the present study, is presented on the next page.

D. OVERVIEW OF THE TWO STUDIES

Perhaps the most obvious study, suggested by the literature just reviewed, is to test the enunciated dimensions by having subjects view the well-standardized sets of facial expressions developed by Izard (1971) and analyze their ratings on each dimension as Frijda (1970) did. This procedure, however, leaves uncontrolled the meaning that each dimension has for the observers. In contrast to previous dimensional studies designed to analyze emotional expressions (typically photographs), the present study focused on the subjective experience of the observer himself.

The project was divided into two related experiments. In the first experiment, the emotion-imaging procedure was used (see Chapter Five). Each subject was asked to recall and visualize specific incidents or situations in which a specified fundamental emotion was dominant and intensely experienced. The subjects described each incident (or experience related to it) by means of both the DES and DRS. Although each incident occurred in their past, they were instructed to make, essentially, a "state" evaluation of it (Cattell & Scheier, 1961; Spielberger, Gorsuch, & Lushene, 1970).

In addition to imagining the fundamental emotion situations, subjects were asked to follow a similar procedure for an anxiety situation. While visualizing the anxiety situation the subjects

II. Basic Dimensions of Emotion

Differential Emotion Scale as Used in the Present Study

Directions: A number of emotion words that people have used to describe themselves are given below. Read each statement and then circle the appropriate number to the right of the emotion word to indicate how you feel right now; that is, in the emotion situation you have recalled and are now visualizing.

There are no right or wrong answers. Do not spend too much time on any one emotion word but give the answer that seems to best describe your feelings as you recall them.

		Not at all		Moderately		Extremely		
1.	repentant	0	1	2	3	4	5	6
2.	delighted	0	1	2	3	4	5	6
3.	downhearted	0	1	2	3	4	5	6
4.	surprised	0	1	2	3	4	5	6
5.	sheepish	0	1	2	3	4	5	6
6.	attentive	0	1	2	3	4	5	6
7.	scared	0	1	2	3	4	5	6
8.	enraged	0	1	2	3	4	5	6
9.	happy	0	1	2	3	4	5	6
10.	concentrating	0	1	2	3	4	5	6
11.	amazed	0	1	2	3	4	5	6
12.	fearful	0	1	2	3	4	5	6
13.	angry	0	1	2	3	4	5	6
14.	sad	0	1	2	3	4	5	6
15.	guilty	0	1	2	3	4	5	6
16.	bashful	0	1	2	3	4	5	6
17.	joyful	0	1	2	3	4	5	6
18.	blameworthy	0	1	2	3	4	5	6
19.	astonished	0	1	2	3	4	5	6
20.	alert	0	1	2	3	4	5	6
21.	mad	0	1	2	3	4	5	6
22.	discouraged	0	1	2	3	4	5	6
23.	shy	0	1	2	3	4	5	6
24.	afraid	0	1	2	3	4	5	6

completed the STAI as well as the DES and DRS. Although this task was presented to the subjects as part of the first experiment, it was analyzed as part of the second experiment.

In the second experiment a midterm exam was a common anxiety-inducing situation for all subjects. Immediately before the exam, the STAI, DES, and DRS were again administered. On the basis of STAI scores, subjects were assigned to high- or low-anxiety groups. An attempt was made to evaluate the relative efficacy of the DES and DRS for discriminating high- and low-anxiety subjects.

The imagined anxiety situation of experiment one and the real (test) anxiety situation of experiment two were compared by separate analyses of STAI, DRS, and DES data. The analysis of STAI scores for the imagined anxiety situation confirmed the procedure and the instructions for this task by being uniformly high and higher than the STAI scores in the real anxiety situation.

The DRS data were used to compare *(a)* the imagined and real anxiety situations, *(b)* the high- and low-anxiety groups, *(c)* the high-anxiety group in the real anxiety situation and in the imagined anxiety situation, and *(d)* the low-anxiety group in the real and imagined situations. A parallel set of comparisons was made with the DES data of experiments one and two.

E. HYPOTHESES FOR EXPERIMENT ONE

1a. The DRS dimension of pleasantness will be the best single dimension for distinguishing among the fundamental emotions. At least one other dimension will be necessary to distinguish between all pairs of fundamental emotions. This dimension will either reflect the subject's evaluation of *(a)* his relationship to his environment (e.g., dimensions of self-assurance or control) or *(b)* body cues (e.g., dimensions of tension or activity).

1b. The DES profile or pattern of emotions will differ among emotion situations.

1c. Each emotion situation will have highest ratings on the items that aprioristically define that fundamental emotion, with next highest ratings on the scales of dynamically related emotions. For example, the a priori defining items for surprise–startle and interest–excitement usually receive elevated ratings in a fear situation (see Chapter Five).

138

F. HYPOTHESES FOR EXPERIMENT TWO

2a. In the real anxiety situation, the high- and low-anxiety groups will be significantly different on their ratings of pleasantness and self-assurance.

2b. In the real anxiety situation, the high-anxiety group will be distinguished from the low-anxiety group by higher mean ratings on the DES scales for fear, distress, shyness, guilt, and anger. The high-anxiety group also may have a higher mean on interest, although the fact that the measure will be given in a course-examination situation may tend to equalize groups on this factor.

2c. The DRS profiles of the low-anxiety group in the real and imagined situations will differ more than the corresponding DRS profiles of the high-anxiety group. The low-anxiety group will consist of subjects relatively unthreatened by the midterm exam (real anxiety situation); consequently, they will have a low level of anxiety and ratings that will differ from their ratings in the imaging condition in which, according to instructions, they imagined situations that make them highly anxious. Conversely, the high-anxiety group, relatively more threatened by the test (reality) condition, will have similar ratings in the real and imagined situations.

2d. The DES profiles of the low-anxiety group in the real and imagined situations will differ more than the corresponding DES profiles of the high-anxiety group. The justification proposed for hypothesis 2c applies equally to hypothesis 2d.

III. METHOD

A. SUBJECTS

Two hundred twenty-nine subjects participated in this project. They were volunteers from the Vanderbilt University classes in general psychology. Each subject received 2 hours of credit toward his 4-hour minimum requirement for research participation. This population of subjects had approximately the same socioeconomic status, intelligence, and level of academic achievement.

B. MATERIALS

The DES contained 24 emotion terms representing eight fundamental emotions. The emotions of disgust and contempt were omitted to simplify the study and to equalize the number of emotion scales and dimensions. Each DES item (emotion term) was put in the form of a rating scale of 0 through 6, instead of the usual 5-point scale, to conform with the style chosen for the DRS scales. The DRS consisted of eight dimensions that were discussed in the introduction as being dynamically related to emotion. Each dimension was represented by three separate questions, each having a numerical rating scale of 0 through 6. The three questions referred to feeling, thought, and behavior. The addition of the thought and behavior levels provided greater flexibility for the subject to evaluate his subjective experience on a particular dimension. Also, the sum across levels was thought to be a better estimate than a single score on the feeling level.

The conventional anxiety measure, the state form of the STAI, was discussed in Chapter Five. The STAI items are shown in Table 5-5, page 92

IV. PROCEDURE

A. EXPERIMENT ONE

Each subject received a packet containing a statement of purpose, formal instructions, and eight sets of DES and DRS (stapled together), one for each of eight discrete emotion situations. In addition they received one set of scales with the STAI preceding the DES and DRS.

The present study followed the procedure detailed in Chapter Five.

(a) The subjects were given the name of a fundamental emotion and were asked to recall a situation or event in their lives in which that emotion was strongly experienced.

(b) They were asked to give a brief description of the event.

(c) They were asked to recall and visualize or imagine the event as vividly as possible while filling out the DES and DRS scales. In this experiment, the order of presenting the DES and DRS was randomized for each emotion situation.

For the imagined anxiety situation, subjects always completed the STAI first. Although the DES and DRS took only 3 to 4 min each, subjects were instructed to visualize or recall the emotion situation again before rating the next set of scales.

The order in which the nine emotion situations were evaluated was left to each subject's preference. However, since the completion of two or more situations at one sitting might attenuate the intensity with which the latter situations were recalled or experienced, subjects were asked to visualize and rate only one situation per day. They were requested to average at least three a week.

B. EXPERIMENT TWO

All the students in the general psychology class from which the subjects for experiment one were drawn participated in the second experiment. The first exam after the data for experiment one had been collected served as the common emotion-eliciting event for all subjects.

When the subjects entered the classroom, they were given a booklet of materials with the STAI placed in the first position, followed by the DES and DRS in random sequence. The instructions explained *(a)* that each set of scales was to be used to describe their present subjective experience ("right now!"), and *(b)* that each set of scales was directed at different aspects of their experience and should be treated as an independent task.

V. RESULTS

Both the DRS and DES were used in the assessment of emotional experiences, nine imagined situations and one real (test) anxiety situation. The kinds of emotion-eliciting situations described by the subjects varied greatly.

The DRS and DES assessed the subjective experience within and between these emotion situations. The two tests were similar in that they have an equal number of scales representing eight dimensions (DRS) and eight fundamental emotions (DES). The numerical score for either the DRS or DES scale is the sum of ratings over three defining items. The fact that the DRS and DES differ in content precludes any statistical comparison of a dimension and a

141

fundamental emotion. Thus the hypotheses were tested separately for the DRS and DES in experiments one and two.

The pattern of analysis for testing each hypothesis was an analysis of variance followed by a Duncan Range Test of ordered means when the appropriate interaction was significant. In order to reduce chance effects from repeated measures and a large subject population, the criterion for significance for all analyses was $p < .01$.

A. EXPERIMENT ONE

1. *DRS and the Differentiation of Fundamental Emotion Situations.* A total of 113 males and 116 females were considered in the analyses. Table 6-1 presents the primary analysis, a 2 (sexes) × 8 (emotion situations) × 8 (DRS dimensions) analysis of variance (Lindquist, 1953, pp. 292–297). As expected, the main effects for dimensions (A) and emotion situations (B) were highly significant.

The highly significant AB interaction indicated that the subjects responded differently to the several dimensions in the different emotion situations. The comparison of individual means by the Duncan Range Test (Duncan, 1955) summarized in Table 6-2 did not confirm the prediction that the DRS dimension of pleasantness would be the best single dimension for distinguishing between the eight fundamental emotion situations. The pleasantness dimension

TABLE 6-1
Analysis of Variance of DRS and Fundamental Emotion Situations

Source	df	MS	F	p
Subjects (Ss)	228	82.382		
Sex (male–female) (C)	1	467.394	5.793	.0160
Between error	227	80.685		
Within subjects error	4427	27.381		
Dimensions (A)	7	4377.453	176.441	.0000
AC	7	49.948	2.013	.0497
Emotion situations (B)	7	6528.362	249.504	.0000
BC	7	64.994	2.484	.0154
AB	49	2073.317	172.306	.0000
ABC	49	29.480	2.450	.0000
Within error	4301	15.023		
Within error 1	1589	24.810		
Within error 2	1589	26.165		
Within error 3	1123	12.033		
Total	4655	28.236		

TABLE 6-2

Duncan Range Test of Emotion Situation Means for Each DRS Scale[a]

DRS scale	DRS scale means in different emotion situations[b]							
Activity	Jo 15.1	An 14.5	Su 13.7	In 12.9	Fe 12.7	Sh 9.2	Gu 8.9	Di 6.9
Deliberateness	In 12.2	An 11.9	Jo 10.4	Fe 9.8	Su 9.4	Gu 9.3	Sh 8.5	Di 7.5
Tension	Fe 16.0	An 14.1	Sh 14.0	Gu 13.4	Di 10.7	Su 8.6	In 8.4	Jo 6.2
Impulsiveness	An 13.5	Jo 12.7	Su 11.6	Fe 10.4	In 8.7	Gu 8.1	Sh 7.7	Di 7.4
Control	In 10.8	Sh 9.4	Gu 8.8	Di 8.0	Su 7.7	Fe 7.6	Jo 7.5	An 7.3
Self-assurance	Jo 13.7	In 11.5	Su 10.4	An 9.3	Di 5.4	Sh 4.9	Gu 4.9	Fe 4.2
Extraversion	Jo 13.9	Su 11.7	In 11.1	An 9.6	Fe 5.7	Sh 5.2	Gu 4.7	Di 4.6
Pleasantness	Jo 16.7	Su 13.7	In 13.3	Sh 7.3	Gu 3.2	Di 3.0	Fe 2.7	An 2.6

[a]The emotion situations indicated in the body of the table are abbreviated: interest (In), joy (Jo), surprise (Su), distress (Di), anger (An), guilt (Gu), shyness (Sh), and fear (Fe).

[b]Means that do not have common underscoring differ significantly, $p < .01$.

was not the best discriminator because subjects gave uniformly low pleasantness ratings in four of the eight emotion situations—the guilt, distress, fear, and anger situations.

When the eight emotion situations were compared on the basis of DRS means for the pleasantness dimension, the mean differences were significant for 21 of the 28 possible comparisons of any two emotion situations. However, six of the eight other dimensions did as well or better. The DRS means for tension and for impulsiveness were significantly different in 24 of 28 comparisons. The DRS means for activity, self-assurance, and extraversion were significantly different in 23 to 28 comparisons.

Although principal interest was in dimensions (A) and situations (B), it should be noted that the main effect for sex (C) and the situations × sex (BC) interaction approached significance (p = .016 and .015, respectively), and the dimensions × situations × sex (ABC) interaction was highly significant (p = .0000). This combination of results suggests that sex is of some importance in these data, the effect being most substantial in the triple interaction. Triple interactions are often difficult to interpret and, while more than one interpretation is possible here, it appears that the situations × sex (BC) interaction varied among the different dimensions.

It was of interest to see how many dimensions were necessary to distinguish between all emotion situations. This analysis was based on *(a)* the mean profile of emotion situations for each dimension represented in the DRS (Table 6-2), and *(b)* the profile of the DRS means for each emotion situation (Table 6-3). The pleasantness dimension, for instance, was a necessary choice because it was the only dimension to have a significant mean difference in the comparison of the shyness and guilt situations. The procedure, then, was to select other dimensions whose situation means distinguished between the pairs of emotion situations that were not differentiated by the comparison of situation means for the pleasantness dimension. The impulsiveness dimension satisfied this requirement. Thus the subjects' ratings on the pleasantness and impulsiveness dimensions were sufficient to distinguish between all paired comparisons of emotion situations.

Other combinations of dimensions also were sufficient to distinguish between all paired comparisons of emotion situations. One such combination was pleasantness, tension, and deliberateness. Another combination was pleasantness with the activity and deliberateness dimensions. However, the profiles of mean ratings on the pleasantness, tension, and self-assurance dimension gave the most

TABLE 6-3

Duncan Range Test of DRS Scale Means for Each Emotion Situation[a]

Situation	DRS scale means[b]							
Interest	Pl 13.3	Ac 12.9	De 12.2	Sa 11.5	Ex 11.1	Co 10.8	Im 8.6	Te 8.4
Joy	Pl 16.7	Ac 15.0	Ex 13.9	Sa 13.7	Im 12.6	De 10.4	Co 7.5	Te 6.2
Surprise	Ac 13.7	Pl 13.7	Ex 11.7	Im 11.5	Sa 11.4	De 9.4	Te 8.6	Co 7.7
Distress	Te 10.7	Co 8.0	De 7.5	Im 7.3	Ac 6.9	Sa 5.7	Ex 4.6	Pl 3.0
Shyness	Te 14.0	Co 9.4	Ac 9.2	De 8.5	Im 7.7	Pl 7.3	Ex 5.1	Sa 4.9
Guilt	Te 13.4	De 9.3	Ac 8.9	Co 8.8	Im 8.1	Sa 4.9	Ex 4.7	Pl 3.2
Anger	Ac 14.4	Te 14.0	Im 13.5	De 12.0	Ex 9.6	Sa 9.2	Co 7.3	Pl 2.6
Fear	Te 16.0	Ac 12.6	Im 10.4	De 9.8	Co 7.5	Ex 5.7	Sa 4.2	Pl 2.7

[a]The DRS dimensions are abbreviated: activity (Ac), deliberateness (De), tension (Te), impulsiveness (Im), control (Co), self-assurance (Sa), extraversion (Ex), and pleasantness (Pl).
[b]Means that do not have common underscoring differ significantly, $p < .01$.

convincing differentiation that could be made between the eight fundamental emotion situations. This is shown graphically in Figure 6-1.

Figure 6-1 shows that the profile of situation means for the pleasantness dimension was quite different from the profile of emotion situations on the tension dimension. Both dimensions clearly distinguished the joy situation from all other situations, with low ratings on the tension dimension and high ratings on the pleasantness dimension. Similarly, the fear and anger situations received high tension ratings and low pleasantness ratings.

The pleasantness, tension, and self-assurance dimensions had significant mean differences for all comparisons involving the joy or surprise situations. The self-assurance dimension was necessary for distinguishing between interest and surprise situations and between guilt and anger situations.

The pleasantness dimension was the only one that distinguished shyness from all other emotions and that separated the shyness and guilt situations. Only the tension dimension differen-

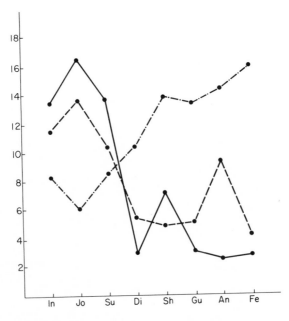

Fig. 6-1. *Profiles of situation means for dimensions of pleasantness* (———), *tension* (—·—), *and self-assurance* (— — —).

tiated the distress and guilt situations. For all other comparisons of emotion situations, at least two of these three dimensions showed a significant mean difference.

No single dimension emerged as dominant. The self-assurance dimension was salient in the interest, joy, surprise, and anger situations because it distinguished these situations from all comparisons made with them. The tension dimension was particularly salient for comparisons involving the distress, fear, or joy situations. The pleasantness dimension was the only one that distinguished shyness from the other emotion situations. The impulsiveness dimension was sufficient for comparisons involving either the surprise or fear situations.

No one dimension was sufficient to make all distinctions between the guilt situation and the other emotion situations. The deliberateness and activity dimensions were discriminating dimensions only in comparisons involving the distress situation. Control was the least salient of the eight dimensions, although it distinguished the interest situation from the other emotion situations.

With regard to hypothesis 1a, one may conclude that pleasantness, while not necessarily the most important dimension, was essential in any combination of dimensions that could make distinctions between all comparisons of the eight fundamental emotions. Although all emotion situations can be distinguished on the basis of ratings on the pleasantness and impulsiveness dimensions, the tension and self-assurance dimensions in combination with pleasantness made the most convincing demonstration of differences between emotion situations.

2. *DES and the Differentiation of Fundamental Emotion Situations.* As in the DRS analysis, Table 6-4 shows that the main effects for the DES (A) and emotion situations (B) were highly significant. The AB interaction was also significant, indicating that subjects responded to the DES differently in some emotion situations.

Again, the principal interest was in the DES (emotion scales) and the situations (B), but the role of sex (C) is noteworthy. Unlike the analysis of the DRS data, in the case of the DES, neither the main effect of sex (C) nor the BC interaction approached significance. However, the AC and the ABC interactions were highly significant. The AC interaction shows that men and women responded differentially to some of the scales of the DES. The triple interaction suggests that the DES × sex interaction varied significantly from situation to situation.

147

TABLE 6-4

Analysis of Variance of DES and Fundamental Emotion Situations

Source	df	MS	F	p
Subjects (Ss)	228	131.887		
Sex (male-female) (C)	1	17.531	.1324	.7173
Between error	227	132.391		
Within subjects error	4427	37.657		
DES (emotion scales) (A)	7	8656.991	413.7717	.0000
AC	7	83.935	4.0118	.0004
Emotion situations (B)	7	2080.865	130.0315	.0000
BC	7	11.616	.7259	.6520
AB	49	5774.379	514.6978	.0000
ABC	49	21.102	1.8810	.0003
Within error	4301	12.829		
Within error 1	1589	20.922		
Within error 2	1589	16.003		
Within error 3	1123	11.219		
Total	4655	39.123		

As shown in Table 6-5, the comparison of individual means by the Duncan Range Test clearly indicated that the DES profile (pattern of scale means) differed among emotion situations. Each situation had, as its significantly highest mean, the DES scale corresponding to the emotion category that was used to define that situation. Even if the highest means were excluded, each emotion situation had a distinctly different pattern of DES means. In cases where the rank order of DES means was quite similar, such as for the joy and surprise situations and for the anger and fear situations, the pattern of mean differences was still clearly different. These results provide strong confirmation for the findings in Chapter Five, where analyses of variance distinguished between the DES profiles of all possible pairs of emotion situations.

This confirmation of hypotheses 1b and 1c showed that the DES, like the DRS, can distinguish between the fundamental emotion situations. Thus the procedure used to specify the necessary and sufficient DRS dimensions for distinguishing between emotion situations was applied to the DES scales.

Table 6-6 presents the profile of situation means for each fundamental emotion scale represented in the DES. The mean ratings for each scale resulted in clearly different profiles of situation means. The highest mean in each profile was the one for the emotion situation in which subjects had been instructed to experience that

TABLE 6-5

Duncan Range Test of DES Scale Means for Each Emotion Situation[a]

Situation	DES scale means[b]							
Interest	In 16.0	Jo 11.3	Su 7.9	Fe 3.2	Sh 2.7	Di 1.9	Gu 1.2	An .95
Joy	Jo 17.3	In 11.2	Su 9.4	Sh 2.6	Fe 2.1	Gu 1.0	Di .41	An .22
Surprise	Su 16.2	Jo 13.4	In 11.3	Sh 4.5	Fe 3.5	Gu 1.9	Di 1.8	An 1.3
Distress	Di 14.9	In 7.5	Su 7.2	Fe 7.1	An 5.6	Gu 5.3	Sh 4.8	Jo .38
Shyness	Sh 15.5	In 10.7	Fe 10.1	Di 7.0	Jo 5.3	Su 5.1	Gu 3.6	An 2.4
Guilt	Gu 15.6	Di 11.5	Fe 10.7	In 9.1	Sh 8.8	An 5.8	Su 5.3	Jo 1.4
Anger	An 16.9	In 10.7	Su 8.9	Di 8.3	Fe 5.1	Gu 2.7	Sh 2.2	Jo .87
Fear	Fe 17.1	In 13.3	Su 9.5	Di 7.4	An 5.9	Gu 5.7	Sh 4.9	Jo .88

[a] The emotion (DES) scales are abbreviated: interest (In), joy (Jo), surprise (Su), distress (Di), anger (An), guilt (Gu), shyness (Sh), and fear (Fe).

[b] Means that do not have common underscoring differ significantly, $p < .01$.

TABLE 6-6

Duncan Range Test of Emotion Situation Means for Each DES Scale[a]

DES scale	DES scale means in different emotion situations[b]							
Interest	In 16.0	Fe 13.3	Su 11.3	Jo 11.2	Sh 10.7	An 10.6	Gu 9.1	Di 7.5
Joy	Jo 17.3	Su 13.4	In 11.3	Sh 5.3	Gu 1.4	Fe .88	An .87	Di .38
Surprise	Su 16.2	Fe 9.5	Jo 9.4	An 8.9	In 7.9	Di 7.2	Gu 5.3	Sh 5.1
Distress	Di 14.9	Gu 11.5	An 8.3	Fe 7.4	Sh 7.0	In 1.8	Su 1.8	Jo .41
Shyness	Sh 15.5	Gu 8.7	Fe 4.9	Di 4.8	Su 4.5	In 2.7	An 2.2	
Guilt	Gu 15.6	Fe 5.7	Di 5.3	Sh 3.6	An 2.7	Su 1.8	In 1.2	Jo 1.0
Anger	An 16.9	Fe 5.9	Gu 5.8	Di 5.6	Sh 2.4	Su 1.3	In .95	Jo .22
Fear	Fe 17.1	Gu 10.6	Sh 10.1	Di 7.1	An 5.1	Su 3.5	In 3.1	Jo 2.1

[a] The emotion situations indicated in the body of the table are abbreviated: interest (In), joy (Jo), surprise (Su), distress (Di), anger (An), guilt (Gu), shyness (Sh), and fear (Fe).

[b] Means that do not have common underscoring differ significantly, $p < .01$.

fundamental emotion most intensely. This mean rating was always significantly higher than the mean ratings for the same scale in the other emotion situations.

Mean ratings on no one scale distinguished between all comparisons of emotion situations. However, mean ratings on any one scale made at least 22 of 28 possible distinctions. The DES mean ratings for the fear and distress scales distinguished between 26 of 28 possible pairs of emotion situations.

When the number of distinctions between emotion situations made by one DES scale were added to those made by another DES scale, eleven different pairs of DES scales distinguished between each possible pair of emotion situations. In no case were more than two DES scales necessary to make all the distinctions. The effective pairs were: joy with interest or with distress, guilt or fear; surprise with distress or with guilt or anger; interest with distress or fear; distress with shyness; and shyness with fear.

The mean DES ratings for joy in combination with the mean ratings for fear and sadness, presented in Figure 6-2, gave the clearest demonstration of differences between the eight fundamental

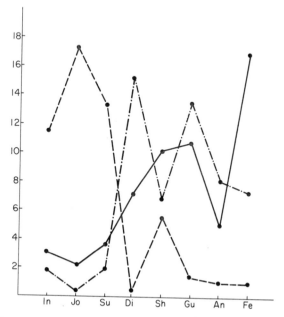

Fig. 6-2. *Profiles of means across situations for the emotion scales of joy (- - -), fear (——), and distress (-·-·).*

151

emotion situations. Each of these DES scales had a distinctly different profile of means across emotion situations. Only in the shyness situation were the DES means for joy, fear and distress somewhat similar.

B. EXPERIMENT TWO

1. STAI and the Comparison of Anxiety Situations. The subjects for these analyses and those in two subsequent sections were 80 males and 80 females. All had completed the STAI, DRS, and DES for an imagined anxiety situation as well as for the real (test) anxiety situation. The STAI scores from the real anxiety situation were used to divide subjects into high- and low-anxiety groups. There were 40 males and 40 females in each group, with no subject in the high-anxiety group having the same STAI score as a subject in the low-anxiety group. The subjects retained their high or low labels in the DRS and DES analyses.

Table 6-7 presents the 2 (anxiety levels) × 2 (sexes) × 2 (situations) analysis of variance (Lindquist, 1953, pp. 220-254) of STAI scores indicating that the high- and low-anxiety groups responded to the STAI differently. Neither the main effect for sex nor the anxiety × sex interaction was significant.

The main effect for imagined versus real situations was significant, and, as expected, the higher means were in the imagined

TABLE 6-7

Analysis of Variance of STAI Scores from the
Real and Imagined Anxiety Situations

Source	df	MS	F	p
Subjects (Ss)	159	156.204		
Anxiety (high-low) (B)	1	12363.781	159.7833	.0000
Sex (male-female) (C)	1	399.181	5.1588	.0230
BC	1	2.500	.0323	.8518
Between error	156	77.378		
Within subjects error	160	199.422		
Conditions (imagined-real) (A)	1	16893.481	296.5457	.0000
AB	1	5736.675	100.7008	.0000
AC	1	146.250	2.5673	.1071
ABC	1	244.156	4.2859	.0376
Within error	156	56.968		
Total	319	177.881		

152

situation. The situations $\times$ anxiety interaction was also significant, indicating that the high- and low-anxiety subjects responded to the STAI differently in the imagined and real anxiety situations. High-anxiety subjects had relatively high scores in both conditions, while low-anxiety subjects had significantly higher scores in the imagined situation than in the test anxiety situation.

2. *DRS and the Comparison of Anxiety Situations.* Table 6-8 presents the 2 (anxiety levels) $\times$ 2 (sexes) $\times$ 2 (situations) $\times$ 8 (dimensions) analysis of variance (Lindquist, 1953, p. 305). The main effect for anxiety was significant, but males and females did not respond differently to the DRS nor were the real and imagined situations different. However, the separate dimensions were treated differently, and their interactions with anxiety, with situations, and with the combination of situations and anxiety were also significant. These results indicate that some of the DRS dimension means vary

TABLE 6-8
*Analysis of Variance of DRS and the Experience of
Anxiety Under Real and Imagined Conditions*

Source	df	MS	F	p
Subjects (Ss)	159	47.338		
Anxiety (high-low) (C)	1	370.602	8.2073	.0050
Sex (male-female) (D)	1	2.281	.0505	.8172
CD	1	109.702	2.4292	.1170
Between error	156	45.155		
Within subjects error	2400	22.208		
Dimensions (A)	7	1980.088	131.7167	.0000
AC	7	338.819	22.5384	.0000
AD	7	25.686	1.7086	.1025
ACD	7	25.110	1.6703	.1118
Conditions (imagined-real) (B)	1	86.314	3.2808	.0684
BC	1	46.200	1.7561	.1838
BD	1	8.302	.3155	.5821
BCD	1	50.650	1.9252	.1636
AB	7	494.469	48.7675	.0000
ABC	7	180.487	17.8007	.0000
ABD	7	6.397	.6309	.7326
ABCD	7	22.542	2.2232	.0299
Within error	2340	13.501		
Within error 1	1092	15.033		
Within error 2	156	26.309		
Within error 3	1092	10.139		
Total	2559	23.769		

TABLE 6-9
Duncan Range Test of DRS Scale Means for Anxiety Groups

Group[a]	DRS scale means[b,c]							
HR	Te 14.1	Ac 10.0	De 8.9	Im 8.8	Co 8.5	Ex 6.4	Sa 5.9	Pl 4.8
LR	Co 11.2	De 10.8	Ac 10.6	Sa 10.0	Pl 9.6	Ex 8.4	Te 8.1	Im 7.2
HI	Te 15.9	Ac 10.4	Im 9.7	De 8.8	Co 7.4	Ex 6.0	Pl 4.4	Sa 4.2
LI	Te 14.8	Ac 12.3	De 9.8	Im 9.4	Co 8.3	Ex 6.3	Sa 5.4	Pl 4.5

[a] The abbreviations for the groups are: HR = high-anxiety group in real anxiety situation; LR = low-anxiety group in real anxiety situation; HI = high-anxiety group in imagined anxiety situation; LI = low-anxiety group in imagined anxiety situation.

[b] Means that do not have common underscoring differ significantly, $p < .01$.

[c] The DRS dimensions are abbreviated: activity (Ac), deliberateness (De), tension (Te), impulsiveness (Im), control (Co), self-assurance (Sa), extraversion (Ex), and pleasantness (Pl).

154

not only in the different anxiety situations but also with different levels of anxiety.

The comparison of DRS means by the Duncan Range Test, presented in Table 6-9, supported hypothesis 2a that high- and low-anxiety subjects in the real anxiety situation differed in their ratings on the dimensions of pleasantness and self-assurance. (This hypothesis is further confirmed by the data in Table 6-10.) The high- and low-anxiety subjects also differed on their ratings in all other dimensions except activity. Figure 6-3 shows that the DRS means for deliberateness, control, self-assurance, extraversion, and pleasantness were significantly higher for the low-anxiety subjects, whereas the tension and impulsiveness dimensions had significantly higher means for the high-anxiety subjects.

The significant situations × anxiety × dimensions interaction also permitted a comparison of real and imagined anxiety situation means for high- and low-anxiety subjects. The Duncan Range Test, presented in Table 6-10, confirmed hypothesis 2c that the DRS means of the low-anxiety group in the real and imagined situations had significantly larger mean differences than did the corresponding DRS means for the high-anxiety group. On seven of eight DRS dimensions, the means for the low-anxiety subjects differed for the real and imagined situations. With the largest possible mean

TABLE 6-10
Duncan Range Test of Anxiety Group Means for Each DRS Scale

DRS scale	Means for anxiety groups[a,b]			
Activity	LI 12.3	LR 10.6	HI 10.4	HR 10.0
Deliberateness	LR 10.8	LI 9.8	HR 8.9	HI 8.8
Tension	HI 15.9	LI 14.8	HR 14.1	LR 8.1
Impulsiveness	HI 9.7	LI 9.4	HR 8.8	LR 7.2
Control	LR 11.2	HR 8.5	LI 8.3	HI 7.4
Self-assurance	LR 10.0	HR 5.9	LI 5.4	HI 4.2
Extraversion	LR 8.4	HR 6.4	LI 6.2	HI 6.0
Pleasantness	LR 9.6	HR 4.8	LI 4.5	HI 4.4

[a] Abbreviations are the same as in Table 6-9.
[b] Means that do not have common underscoring differ significantly, $p < .01$.

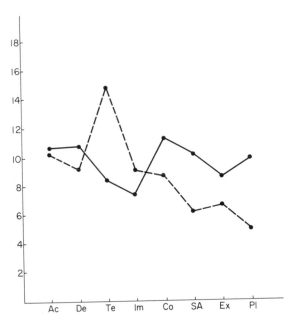

Fig. 6-3. *Profiles of DRS means for high-anxiety (— — —) and low-anxiety (——) subjects under a real anxiety condition.*

difference being 18.0, the average mean difference for the seven DRS dimensions was 3.601, with a range of 1.675 (activity) to 6.675 (tension). The means for the real and imagined situations differed for high-anxiety subjects on only one dimension—self-assurance— where the mean difference was 1.700.

The rank order of DRS means for the high-anxiety subjects (Table 6-9) was quite similar in the real and imagined situations, with the tension dimension as the highest mean and with self-assurance and pleasantness as the lowest means. As predicted, the rank order of DRS means for the low-anxiety subjects was noticeably different in the real and imagined situations. In the real situation, the DRS mean for control was the highest and the mean for impulsiveness the lowest; whereas in the imagined situation these dimensions were ranked fifth and fourth respectively and were not different from each other. Also, as predicted, in the imagined situation, the highest and lowest means for low-anxiety subjects were the same as for high-anxiety subjects.

3. *DES and the Comparison of Anxiety Situations.* The DES was taken under the same circumstances as the DRS, but

subjects were told that the DES measured different aspects of their subjective experience and should be treated as an independent task. Table 6-11 presents the 2 (anxiety levels) X 2 (sexes) X 2 (situations) X 8 (DES scales) analysis of variance. Sex was the only nonsignificant main effect. The anxiety X situations X DES scales interaction was significant, indicating that high- and low-anxiety subjects responded to the DES differently in the real and imagined anxiety situations.

The comparison of DES means by the Duncan Range Test presented in Table 6-12 confirmed hypothesis 2b that high-anxiety subjects differed from low-anxiety subjects in the real anxiety situation by having higher DES means for fear, distress, shyness, guilt, and anger (see Figure 6-4). The DES means for interest and surprise did not distinguish between high- and low-anxiety groups. As would be expected, the DES means for joy was higher for the low-anxiety group.

TABLE 6-11

Analysis of Variance of DES and the Experience of Anxiety Under Real and Imagined Conditions

Source	df	MS	F	p
Subjects (Ss)	159	68.486		
Anxiety (high-low) (C)	1	1035.320	16.4061	.0002
Sex (male-female) (D)	1	2.514	.0398	.8364
CD	1	7.000	.1109	.7390
Between error	156	63.106		
Within subjects error	2400	27.979		
DES (emotion scales) (A)	7	3345.337	218.9188	.0000
AC	7	290.654	19.0204	.0000
AD	7	30.562	2.0000	.0517
ACD	7	13.761	.9005	.5061
Conditions (imagined-real) (B)	1	3031.966	140.4457	.0000
BC	1	198.011	9.1722	.0032
BD	1	16.242	.7524	.6088
BCD	1	13.528	.6266	.5643
AB	7	634.085	56.4572	.0000
ABC	7	155.157	13.8148	.0000
ABD	7	28.871	2.5706	.0125
ABCD	7	11.598	1.0326	.4065
Within error	2340	13.812		
Within error 1	1092	15.281		
Within error 2	156	21.588		
Within error 3	1092	11.231		
Total	2559	30.496		

157

6. Subjective Experience of Emotion

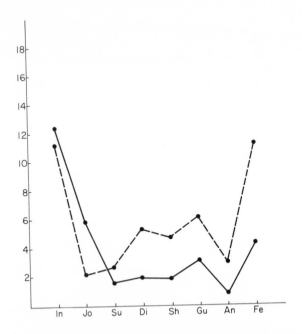

Fig. 6-4. *Profiles of DES means for high-anxiety (- - -) and low-anxiety (——) subjects under a real anxiety condition.*

TABLE 6-12
Duncan Range Test of Anxiety Groups for Each DES Scale

DES scale	Means for anxiety group[a]			
Interest	LR 12.7	LI 11.7	HR 11.2	HI 10.4
Joy	LR 5.8	HR 2.4	LI 2.1	HI 2.0
Surprise	HI 5.5	LI 4.3	HR 2.7	LR 1.5
Distress	HI 11.1	LI 9.4	HR 5.3	LR 2.0
Shyness	HI 5.7	HR 4.7	LI 4.6	LR 1.9
Guilt	HI 6.3	HR 6.2	LI 5.8	LR 3.2
Anger	HI 5.9	LI 4.1	HR 3.0	LR .82
Fear	HI 12.8	LI 12.2	HR 11.3	LR 4.3

[a] Abbreviations are the same as in Table 6-9, page 154.

158

Table 6-12 presents the comparison of individual means for high- and low-anxiety groups for both the real and imagined situations. The DES means for the low-anxiety group in the real and imagined situations differed more than the corresponding DES means for the high-anxiety group, confirming hypothesis 2d. On six of eight DES scales, the means for low-anxiety subjects were significantly lower in the real than in the imagined situation. With the largest possible mean difference being 18.0, the average mean difference for the six DES emotions was 4.321 with a range of 2.600 (guilt) to 7.925 (fear). For the high-anxiety subjects, there were significant mean differences between the real and imagined situations for only four of the eight DES emotions (surprise, distress, anger, and fear). The average mean difference for these four DES emotions was 3.261 with a range of a 1.525 (fear) to 5.837 (distress).

The rank order of DES means, presented in Table 6-13, for the high-anxiety subjects, was quite similar in the real and imagined situations with fear as the highest mean and joy the lowest mean. The rank order of DES means for the low-anxiety subjects was noticeably different in the real and imagined situations. The DES mean for joy was the lowest mean for low-anxiety subjects in the imagined anxiety situation but the next to highest in the real anxiety situation.

VI. DISCUSSION

The DRS results from experiment one showed that ratings on substantive dimensions could differentiate between the subjective experiences associated with the different fundamental emotions. The profile of dimension means for each emotion or emotion situation was clearly different, indicating that each emotion was accompanied by a qualitatively distinct subjective experience. Not all dimensions were necessary to make these differentiations, but ratings on any one dimension were sufficient to distinguish at least one emotion experience from all others. A major focus in this discussion section will be the relationship between the DRS dimensions and the subjective experience of emotion.

The DES results in experiment one clearly demonstrated that subjects did treat each emotion situation as a qualitatively different emotional experience. These results support the use of an imaging technique as a means of studying emotional experiences. This technique circumvents the problem of inducing equivalent emotion in all subjects via a standard stimulus. The profile of DES means

TABLE 6-13
Duncan Range Test of DES Scale Means for Anxiety Groups

Group	DES scale means							
HR	Fe 11.3	In 11.2	Gu 6.2	Di 5.3	Sh 4.7	An 3.0	Su 2.7	Jo 2.4
LR	In 12.7	Jo 5.8	Fe 4.3	Gu 3.2	Di 2.0	Sh 1.9	Su 1.5	An .82
HI	Fe 12.8	Di 11.1	In 10.4	Gu 6.3	An 5.9	Sh 5.7	Su 5.5	Jo 2.0
LI	Fe 12.2	In 11.7	Di 9.4	Gu 5.8	Sh 4.6	Su 4.3	An 4.1	Jo 2.1

for each emotion situation provided a confirmation of the effectiveness of the instructions to subjects and some additional information on relationships among the fundamental emotions.

The appropriateness of the imaging technique and the applicability of the dimensional and discrete emotion approaches to the study of complex emotional experiences will be discussed with respect to the comparisons of real and imagined anxiety. A relevant issue in this discussion is the application of these approaches and techniques in a clinical setting.

A. VALIDATION OF EMOTION SITUATIONS AS QUALITATIVELY DIFFERENT EMOTION EXPERIENCES

The DES results clearly established that the emotion situations represented different subjective experiences. As expected, the subjects recalled and visualized situations that apparently were relevant to the fundamental emotions. For each situation, the highest DES mean was the one corresponding to the emotion specified by the instructions. The most parsimonious interpretation of this result is that it is a function of a demand characteristic of the experiment. That is, when subjects were asked to use the DES to describe their emotions in, say, a fear situation, the instructions essentially demanded that the DES fear items (fearful, afraid, scared) be given the highest ratings.

However, subjects also reported the subjective experience of other emotions in each situation which Tomkins (1962, 1963) and Izard (1971) have shown to have a dynamic relationship to the dominant fundamental emotion. This result, which was not a function of the demand characteristics of the experiment, provided another convincing demonstration of the characteristic pattern of emotions that results in a situation in which a particular fundamental emotion is dominant. Essentially the same patterns were evident in the data discussed in Chapter Five.

These patterns of emotions for the different emotion situations in this study are quite comparable to those reported in Chapter Five, even though the DES in this experiment represented fewer fundamental emotions than does the standard DES and used a 6-point rather than a 5-point rating scale. For example, the interest scale had a relatively high mean in the fear situation and a low one in the distress situation. The interest and joy scales were positively related when joy ratings were high, but interest ratings remained elevated in experiences in which the joy ratings were low. The shy-

161

ness and guilt ratings were quite similar and generally low for all emotion experiences except in the shyness and guilt situations. In the shyness situation, the guilt component was quite low, but in the guilt situation, the shyness ratings were comparatively high.

In the distress situation, no DES scale means were nearly as high as the mean for the distress scale. Apparently, subjects were able to experience distress with very little of the subjective experience of other emotions. In contrast, the guilt situation had strong fear and distress components and also an element of interest and shyness.

In each emotion situation, there was a pattern of DES means that could be explained by the differential emotion theory presented in the foregoing chapters. It seems clear that the imaging technique provided reliable information about the subjective experience of emotion. There were no patterns of DES means that suggested that subjects simply rated scales without being guided by a previously experienced emotion situation that they were vividly imagining or recalling.

The DES scales proved to be more than a set of experimental control variables. In fact, there were eleven different pairs of DES scales that provided sufficient information for distinguishing between all possible comparisons of emotion situations. Table 6-6, however, showed that these distinctions were most clearly made by ratings on the joy, distress, and fear scales.

B. RELATIONSHIP OF THE DRS AND THE SUBJECTIVE EXPERIENCE OF EMOTION

The subjects reported their emotional experience as ratings on eight sets of dimensional scales. These ratings provided information about the relative intensity or salience of each dimension for a given emotion situation, and information as to how the emotion situations compared with each other when ratings on only one dimension at a time were considered. In a clinical setting, a DRS profile might be used to infer what emotions are being experienced by a client who is unable to describe his feelings with the labels that represent discrete emotions.

The dimensions of pleasantness, tension, self-assurance, and impulsiveness were the most discriminating dimensions. These dimensions would be of most value in clinical work and in clinical research, since they provide a means of delineating the discrete

162

emotions of subjective experience. The other dimensions provided no unique predictive information.

The pleasantness dimension clearly separated the emotion situations into two groups: the joy, interest, and surprise situations, characterized by high-pleasantness ratings, and the guilt, distress, fear, and anger situations, characterized by low-pleasantness ratings. The shyness situation was not easily classifiable because it had a moderately pleasant quality.

Among high-pleasantness emotions, the joy situation had the highest ratings, but interest and surprise were indistinguishable. Among the low-pleasantness emotions, the pleasantness scale separated shyness from all others, but no other distinctions between "negative" emotion situations could be made. In light of the fact that shyness and guilt situations were indistinguishable on other dimensions, pleasantness must be considered a necessary dimension for the DRS.

The tension dimension complemented the pleasantness dimension by rank-ordering emotion situations very differently. Here, the high-pleasantness emotion situations received low ratings and the low-pleasantness emotion situations received high ratings. Although both the pleasantness and tension dimensions made numerous overlapping discriminations, ratings on the tension dimension, unlike those on the pleasantness dimension, distinguished between some of the low-pleasantness emotion situations. Tension ratings were very high for the fear experience and might be confused only with anger in a psychodiagnostic study. The tension rating for distress was significantly lower than the tension ratings for the other low-pleasantness emotion situations but clearly higher than the tension ratings for the high-pleasantness emotion situations. The only emotion situations that were still indistinguishable were the low-pleasantness emotions of anger and guilt and the high-pleasantness emotions of interest and surprise.

Ratings on either the impulsiveness or the self-assurance dimensions made the remaining distinctions among emotion situations, and both were needed for making the distinction between interest and surprise. The interest situation received significantly higher ratings on the self-assurance dimension, but surprise received significantly higher ratings on the impulsiveness dimension.

The difference between the anger and guilt situations was most clearly demonstrated on the impulsiveness dimension where anger received a much higher rating. The same distinction was made by the self-assurance dimension, but the ratings were considerably lower than those on impulsiveness.

From the subjects' view, the emotion situations differed mainly in terms of pleasantness, tension, and self-assurance ratings. For the interest, joy, and surprise situations, the rank order of scale means was pleasantness, self-assurance, and tension. For the distress, guilt, anger, and fear situations, the rank order was reversed. Once again, interest, joy, and surprise were seen as high-pleasantness emotions while distress, guilt, anger, and fear were seen as low-pleasantness emotions.

Within the high-pleasantness and low-pleasantness emotions, however, the mean ratings on the deliberateness and impulsiveness dimensions were important. The interest and surprise situations were not essentially different with respect to pleasantness, self-assurance, and tension ratings, but the interest situation had significantly higher mean ratings on the deliberateness scale than on the impulsiveness scale. The reverse was true in the surprise situation. The joy situation had the strongest impulsiveness rating, but it also was distinguishable from interest and surprise situations with significantly higher ratings on the pleasantness and self-assurance dimensions and a lower mean rating on the tension dimension.

For the low-pleasantness emotions, the pleasantness ratings were uniformly low, but the tension and self-assurance ratings varied significantly. For example. the fear situation had extremely high tension ratings in contrast to the distress situation. The guilt and anger situations shared equivalent tension ratings, but in the anger situation, subjects had significantly higher ratings on the self-assurance dimension. The guilt and anger situations differed from both the fear and distress situations on the tension dimension.

Unlike the case for high-pleasantness emotion situations, the ratings on the impulsiveness and deliberateness scales added very little information for differentiating the low-pleasantness emotion situations. Each emotion shared fairly uniform ratings on these two dimensions.

The shyness situation was similar to the low-pleasantness emotion situation, except that it had a significantly higher rating on the pleasantness dimension. To some extent, the DRS profile of the shyness situation was similar to those of the distress and guilt situations.

In principle, then, the DRS can provide the clinician with a set of hypotheses which, if confirmed by other diagnostic or therapeutic procedures, would detail a well-delineated picture of the client's emotional experience. The convergence of quantitative evidence from the DRS and clinical evidence from observations in psychotherapy would justify a high level of confidence in the emotion analysis (see Izard, 1971, Chap. 15).

VII. COMPARISON OF DRS AND DES IN THE ASSESSMENT OF THE ANXIETY EXPERIENCE

The subjective experience of anxiety was defined by the inducing situations (real and imagined) and by the classification of subjects into high- and low-anxiety groups (STAI scores in real situation). The DRS and DES ratings can not be compared directly, but some comparisons can be made, since each was used to distinguish between the anxiety experience of high-anxiety subjects in the real and imagined situations and that of low-anxiety subjects in the same situations. Some of these comparisons will also permit a closer evaluation of the imaging (recall and visualization) condition as compared to emotion induction by a reality (test anxiety) condition.

A. DRS AND THE ASSESSMENT OF ANXIETY EXPERIENCE

Figure 6-5 is a graphic representation of Table 6-9. The graph clearly demonstrates that the shape of the DRS profile for low-anxiety subjects in the reality condition differed from the profiles for all other groups. The only qualitative differences between the high-anxiety subjects in the reality and imaging conditions and the low-anxiety subjects in the imaging condition were slightly higher means on the activity dimension for the low-anxiety subjects. Also, the high-anxiety subjects in the imaging condition had higher means on the tension dimension and lower means on the self-assurance dimension than the subjects in the other groups.

The low-anxiety subjects in the reality condition had significantly higher means on the control, self-assurance, extraversion, and pleasantness dimensions, and significantly lower means on the tension and impulsivity dimensions than any other group. Figure 6-6 shows that this profile of mean ratings bears a close resemblance to the DRS profile for the interest situation. As suggested in Chapter Four, interest may oscillate with fear in certain emotion-eliciting situations, and when interest is the stronger, the often-observed facilitative effect of "anxiety" may occur.

Figure 6-7 shows that the DRS profiles for the high-anxiety subjects in the imaging and reality conditions and low-anxiety subjects

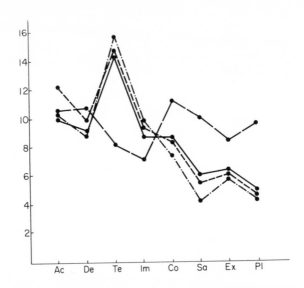

Fig. 6-5. *Profiles of DRS means for high-anxiety subjects under real* (——) *and imagined* (-·-·) *conditions and low-anxiety subjects under real* (— —) *and imagined* (— — —) *conditions.*

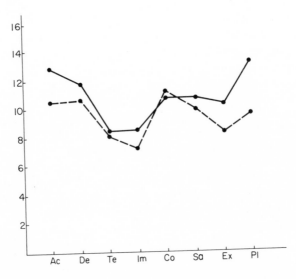

Fig. 6-6. *Comparison of DRS mean profiles for low-anxiety sub-jects under a real anxiety condition* (— — —) *and in the imagined interest situation* (——).

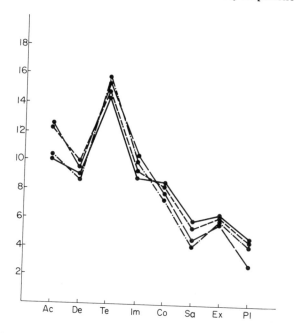

Fig. 6-7. *Comparison of DRS mean profiles for high-anxiety subjects in the reality (———) and imaging (—·—·) condition and low-anxiety subjects in the imaging condition (— — —) and all subjects in the fear condition (— —).*

in the imaging condition closely resembled the DRS profile for the fear situation. This is also consistent with the differential emotion theory definition of anxiety as a combination of fundamental emotions, with fear as the dominant emotion. The profile for the fear situation had slightly higher ratings on all scales except deliberateness and control, but these differences were negligible.

B. DES AND THE ASSESSMENT OF ANXIETY EXPERIENCE

Figure 6-8 is a graphic representation of Table 6-13. The graph clearly demonstrates that the DES profile of the anxiety experience for the low-anxiety subjects in the reality condition differed greatly from those of other anxiety groups in intensity of DES ratings and slightly in profile (shape of line connecting the means in Figure 6-8). The low-anxiety subjects in the reality condition described themselves primarily as being interested, with a moderate DES rating on both the joy and fear scales. Otherwise, the pattern of means suggested that the other scales were not particularly relevant.

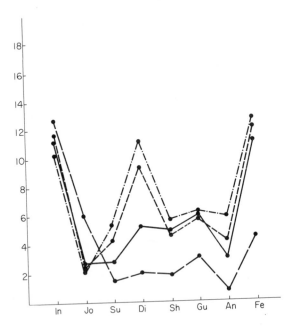

Fig. 6-8. *Profiles of DES means for high-anxiety subjects under real* (——) *and imagined* (-·-·) *conditions and for low-anxiety subjects under real* (— —) *and imagined* (— — —) *conditions.*

In contrast, the other anxiety groups had a dominant fear–interest experience. The high- and low-anxiety subjects in the imagining condition also had significantly elevated means on the distress scale. The three groups shared equally low means on the joy scale.

Unlike the DRS, the DES, as shown in Table 6-12, differentiated among the anxiety experiences of the high-anxiety subjects in the reality and imaging conditions and the low-anxiety subjects in the imaging condition. In particular, the ratings on the distress scale differentiated between all three conditions. Ratings on the anger and fear scales differentiated the anxiety experiences of high-anxiety subjects in the reality and imaging conditions, but neither was significantly different from the anxiety experience of low-anxiety subjects in the imaging condition. On the surprise scale, only the means of high-anxiety subjects in the reality conditon were significantly different.

In general, the subjective experience of anxiety in the imaging condition consisted primarily of fear, interest, and distress with some elevation of means for guilt, shyness, anger, and surprise. In the reality condition, the anxiety experience consisted primarily of fear and interest for high-anxiety subjects, but only interest for the low-anxiety subjects. In addition, the high-anxiety subjects in the reality condition experienced some guilt, distress, and shyness. Low-anxiety subjects in the reality condition experienced a degree of joy and fear. These results rather strongly suggest that some subjects were not threatened or made to feel anxious by the midterm exam. The subjects who felt threatened and anxious in the reality condition presumably had similar feelings in the imaging condition.

C. COMPARISON OF DRS AND DES

Ratings on seven of the eight DRS dimensions and six of the eight DES scales distinguished between the anxiety experience in the reality condition for subjects whose STAI scores were in the high-anxiety range and those whose STAI scores were in the low-anxiety range. While the average mean differences between high- and low-anxiety subjects in the reality condition were comparable for DRS and DES ratings, the DRS scales had considerably larger mean differences. The principal differentiating scale on the DES was fear (mean difference of 7.06), but the DRS had mean differences of 6.01 on the tension dimension, 4.83 on the pleasantness dimension, and 4.06 on the self-assurance dimension. Since ratings on the DRS were generally higher than on the DES, it was concluded that dimensions were somewhat more salient than fundamental emotions for distinguishing between subjects who were experiencing high levels of anxiety and subjects who were not. However, the DES ratings specified that certain emotions present in the high-anxiety experience were clearly absent in the low-anxiety experience.

The DRS and DES can also be compared for their relative efficacy in distinguishing between a real (test) anxiety experience and an imagined or remembered anxiety experience. The high-anxiety subjects in the reality and imaging conditions were the most appropriate for these comparisons, since the same subjects were in both conditions and their STAI scores in both conditions indicated that they were highly anxious.

However, the anxiety experienced by these subjects in the reality and imaging conditions differed in two ways. In the imaging condition, the subjects were free to recall and visualize any anxiety situation, but in the reality condition, the midterm course exam was the standard stimulus for all. Also, the mean STAI score for these

169

subjects was higher (70.800) in the imaging condition than in the reality condition (66.837). The DRS was relatively insensitive to the differences between anxiety-inducing conditions. The only DRS rating that distinguished between these two anxiety experiences was on the self-assurance scale. The subjects in the reality condition rated themselves as more self-assured.

On the DES, the high-anxiety subjects rated their experience as characterized more by distress, surprise, anger, and fear in the imaging condition than in the reality condition. These mean differences ranged from 5.84 (distress) to 1.53 (fear). Anxiety experienced in the imaging condition was clearly different in intensity from anxiety experienced in the reality condition. Thus, the DES was sensitive to differences between anxiety experiences in the reality and imaging conditions, but the DRS was not. The DES results suggest that the imaging condition elicited a wider range of emotions.

VIII. RELATIONSHIP OF DIMENSIONAL AND DISCRETE EMOTION APPROACHES TO THE STUDY OF EMOTIONAL EXPERIENCE

In contrast to studies focusing on the behavioral–expressive and physiological components of emotion, this investigation of subjective experience through self-reported emotions brings the apparently antithetical dimensional and differential emotion approaches into harmony. The subjects' reports were not restricted only to the evaluation of emotion words, facial–postural expressions, or physiological activity. The subjects were specifically asked on the DRS to evaluate all feelings, thoughts, and behavior characterizing different emotion experiences. As a result, the three dimensions that emerged as prominent shared a direct relationship to these types of human functioning. While the ratings on the DRS scales were not as sensitive to nuances of emotional experience as the DES scales, they nevertheless could distinguish among emotion experiences and between real and imagined experiences of anxiety. The empirical evidence from the present research project suggests some changes in the current view of the dimensional approach.

A. MODIFICATION OF THE DIMENSIONAL APPROACH

The Face of Emotion (Izard, 1971) presented theory and evidence to support the notion that emotion is distinct from activation, arousal, and other systems of the organism. Nevertheless, those other systems can be importantly related to the emotion process and still retain functions that are independent. Previous dimensional research measured aspects of those systems and incorrectly concluded that the emotion process was being studied directly.

The present program of research assumed that the dimensions represented systems of the organism that function independently of the emotion process but interact with it, sometimes with a reciprocally amplifying or attenuating effect. The relationships between the emotion process and these other systems were studied by having subjects report aspects of their feelings, thoughts, and behavior when a specific emotion was experienced. A relationship among dimensions was seen as the patterning of systems of the organism, indicating that a specific emotion was being experienced. In certain clinical settings, working with repressed or nonfluent populations, these patterns may be the only information available for the clinician to confirm his hypotheses regarding a client's emotion experiences.

Specifically, the scales representing the dimensions of pleasantness, tension, and self-assurance emerged as the major dimensions of the DRS. The pleasantness scales are thought to represent a dimension of feeling or preference based on hedonic tone. In previous studies, this dimension has usually had the closest relationship to emotion and has been considered the dominant dimension of emotion in the dimensional literature. In this study, no dimension was dominant, but ratings on the pleasantness scales did divide the fundamental emotion situations into high- and low-pleasantness emotion situations and successfully distinguished between shyness and guilt situations.

The tension scales apparently represented a dimension of arousal or activation. No emotion situation was without some tension, but the higher ratings were associated with the low-pleasantness emotion situations. This dimension was particularly important for making DRS distinctions between shyness and distress situations and guilt and fear situations.

The self-assurance dimension represented an attitude toward self, a kind of personal or ego assessment dimension. It was particularly important for making DRS distinctions between surprise and interest situations and guilt and anger situations. Except for the anger situation, elevated self-assurance ratings suggested that the pleasant emotions were being experienced.

The dimensions of pleasantness (hedonic tone), tension (arousal), and self-assurance (attitude toward the self) were systematically affected by a set of qualitatively different emotion experiences. The fact that ratings on these and some of the other dimensions can identify the quality of a felt emotion does not necessarily imply that they are dimensions of emotion.

Emotion is only part of the total phenomenology of subjective experience. The two sets of scales (DRS and DES) may be measuring different aspects of subjective experience. Discrete emotion scales represent aspects of the emotion process, while dimensional scales represent aspects of organismic processes that can be measured in the absence of reported emotion. The assumption underlying the present study was that there are organismic processes that can, under emotional conditions, reflect changes in the emotion process but also retain functions independent of the emotion process.

This study suggests that dimensional research should be directed toward the specification and measurement of systems of feeling, thought, and behavior as they are affected by the emotion process. In the full assessment of complex subjective experiences, dimensions such as pleasantness, tension, and self-assurance could be combined with a set of discrete emotion terms that specify the fundamental emotions.

IX. SUMMARY

Traditionally, there have been two distinct and apparently antithetical approaches to the study of the subjective experience of emotion—one concerned mainly with descriptive dimensions, the other with discrete emotions. The research reported in this chapter applied both approaches concurrently and attempted to resolve some of the differences between them.

A set of eight dimensions were abstracted from previous dimensional research and adapted into a self-report rating scale (DRS). A set of discrete emotion terms representing eight fundamental emotions (Izard, 1971; Izard & Tomkins, 1966; Tomkins, 1962) were selected and also adapted into a self-report rating scale (DES). The ratings on the DES confirmed the effectiveness of the instructions to subjects that they recall and vividly imagine situations in which a particular fundamental emotion was the dominant emotional experience. Ratings on the DRS then established that a subset of dimensions could distinguish between all possible comparisons of these emotion situations.

In the second experiment, anxiety was induced by having subjects recall and vividly imagine a specific occasion when anxiety was dominant. In addition, anxiety in a real situation was induced by the anticipation of a midterm exam. Prior to the exam, the STAI was given to provide a means of separating subjects into high- and low-anxiety groups. The DRS and DES ratings were compared for relative efficacy in distinguishing between anxiety experienced by low- and high-anxiety subjects in the real situation and the same high-anxiety subjects in an imagined situation.

The pattern of DRS ratings clearly distinguished between the anxiety experiences for high- and low-anxiety subjects in the reality condition, but did not distinguish between anxiety experiences for high-anxiety subjects in the reality and imaging conditions. In contrast, the pattern of DES ratings clearly distinguished between anxiety experiences for high-anxiety subjects in the reality and imaging conditions. In the reality conditions, low-anxiety subjects described their experience as high in interest and low in all other emotions. These results suggested that the DRS and DES had measured some different aspects of anxiety.

A modification of the dimensional approach was proposed that reduced the apparent antithesis between approaches. Dimensions were seen as representing systems within the organism that function independently of the emotion process but could, under specific circumstances, either affect or be affected by the emotions. A pattern of DRS ratings may be primarily a complex indicator of the type and intensity of the felt experience but may not directly represent the emotion process.

The DES, on the other hand, is a semantic code that directly represents the discrete emotions. Its usefulness is dependent on a person's verbal facility and previous experience in associating discrete emotion terms to specific changes in the operation of the emotion process. In the clinical setting, clients often do not have the verbal facility to reflect the quality of emotional experience in discrete emotion terms. In these circumstances, the dimensions may be more salient and also may provide the clinician with valuable information about the discrete emotions of human experience and their facilitating or debilitating influences on human activities.

CHAPTER SEVEN

Neurophysiological and Biochemical Factors in Depression

I have taken the position that neurophysiology and biochemistry can contribute to our understanding of the emotions and emotion processes. These disciplines may tell us more about *how* emotion processes work than *why* they occur. But the *how* of the emotion process has immediate implications for the management of emotions and behavior.

The evidence reviewed in Chapter One indicated that distress (sadness, dejection), the most prominent fundamental emotion in depression, was accompanied primarily by parasympathetic activity rather than by sympathetic activity. If distress were the only emotion involved in depression, its neurophysiological and biochemical study would be greatly simplified. As we shall see, depression involves other emotions. It involves anger, which apparently is accompanied by both parasympathetic and sympathetic activity. If there are emotion-specific neurophysiological and biochemical patterns, the biological study of depression is obviously highly complex.

Most of the physiologically oriented studies in this area have been inspired by clinical problems and conducted by clinically oriented investigators. As a consequence, the studies have focused on the clinical syndrome or unitary concept of depression, rather than on discrete fundamental emotions. This has created some confusion and difficulty and may well have contributed to the fairly frequent contradictory or unreplicated findings in this field.

I. NEUROPHYSIOLOGICAL CONSIDERATIONS

The neurophysiology of depression is highly complex because it involves a number of fundamental emotions and their interactions. In view of the complex nature of depression, it is necessary to approach the search for consistency in neurophysiological functioning with caution. Since it is generally agreed that distress, defined as sadness and dejection, is the most important single emotion in depression, I shall also draw on information relative to this discrete emotion.

One point on which there is some agreement is that the parasympathetic nervous system predominates in states of sadness, dejection, and defeat (Gellhorn & Loofbourrow, 1963; Stanley-Jones, 1970). Weeping, although its relationship to distress and depression is not simple or linear, is also generally considered a parasympathetic function (Gellhorn, 1964). These observations seem consistent with a major conclusion of the biochemical studies to be discussed in the next section; namely, that increase in the amount of functionally active norepinephrine, the chemical transmitter of the sympathetic nervous system and a facilitator of sympathetic activity, usually decreases depression. Because of the reciprocal relations between the parasympathetic and sympathetic systems, the increase in norepinephrine at sympathetic synapses and the consequent increase in sympathetic activity would be expected to inhibit or counteract the parasympathetic functions that subserve distress.

The role of the parasympathetic system in distress (sadness, dejection) may be better understood after we review some of the characteristics and functions of this system. It will be recalled that parasympathetic activity dilates the blood vessels that subserve alimentation, increases the secretory and motor activity of the gastrointestinal tract, and accompanies the pleasurable sensations associated with eating. There is definite evidence that stimulation of the parasympathetic vagus nerve increases insulin and lowers the level of blood sugar (Gellhorn & Loofbourrow, 1963, p. 70). All of these parasympathetically influenced processes are consistent with the fact that parasympathetic activity leads to decreased tone and responsiveness of the striate muscles and accompanies periods of relaxation and quiescence. Normal depression and some psychopathological depressions are characterized by some of these parasympathetically influenced phenomena—loss of muscle tone, general inactivity, and decrease in heart rate and blood pressure.

176

Interestingly, parasympathetic dominance is associated with many functions other than distress. Gellhorn and Loofbourrow (1963) have noted that parasympathetic activity is dominant in sexual functions such as the erection of the penis and increased blood flow to the vagina. These authors have also noted some interesting species differences in reactivity of the autonomic system, noting that the sympathetic system may be relatively more prominent in cats and dogs while the parasympathetic system may be relatively more prominent in the rabbit. According to Stanley-Jones (1970), lust is mediated by the parasympathetic system, mainly by the nerves of genital erection. The parasympathetic system, the vagus nerve in particular, mediates the decrease in heart rate and blood pressure and the dilation of the arterioles that accompany sexual arousal.

Gellhorn (1970) has described two more general neurophysiological systems—the ergotropic and trophotropic—that underlie emotion processes (see Chapter One, pp. 20-22). Much of what has been said about the parasympathetic system and its role in distress would hold for the trophotropic system. The dominance of the trophotropic system in distress is evident from the several parasympathetic effects already noted, plus sleeplike EEG potentials and cortical synchronization.

It is appropriate at this point to say a word about grief, the normal reaction to loss of a loved one. Grief has some characteristics in common with distress and depression but is not identical to either. Distress is a single fundamental emotion; grief, like depression, is a pattern of emotions and emotional attitudes. In both grief and depression, distress is typically the most prominent emotion, but other emotions, particularly, anger, disgust, contempt, and guilt are often involved.

Averill (1968) has recently published a very informative paper on grief. He made a number of useful observations, but his concept of grief as analogous to injury or disease has all the weaknesses of Lazarus' theory of emotion as a disease syndrome (see Chapter Four). Equally as vulnerable is Averill's case for sympathetic nervous system dominance in grief. He drew his arguments mainly from the controversial literature on clinical depression. We have already presented the problems involved in assaying the neurophysiological literature on depression. To recapitulate, depression involves a number of emotions, some being ergotropic (and sympathetic) and others being trophotropic (and parasympathetic). Furthermore, as

Averill acknowledges, grief, too, involves a number of different emotions, and grief and depression are not identical.

Averill (1969) has obtained data that he has interpreted as evidence of heightened sympathetic nervous system activity during sadness. He also found that subjects in the sadness condition had significantly higher ratings on a self-report anger scale than did controls or subjects in a mirth condition. Furthermore, anger ratings were correlated .51 ($p < .05$) with self-report sadness ratings. Although Averill did not acknowledge it, the presence of anger in any appreciable degree could have accounted for the observed sympathetic reactions of the subjects in the sadness condition.

Increasing knowledge of the neurophysiology of depression awaits two developments. First, we need a clearer understanding of the neurophysiology of the discrete fundamental emotions. Second, we must have more precise information as to the pattern of emotions involved in depression. Furthermore, it may well prove necessary to delineate different types of depression, each involving a somewhat different pattern of emotions.

II. BIOCHEMICAL CONSIDERATIONS

For the most part, biochemical studies have implicitly or explicitly assumed that distress (sadness–dejection) is the only discrete emotion in depression. It is easy to understand how this conclusion was developed. First, distress is probably the most important emotion in depression. Second, depressives look and act distressed—sad, dejected, defeated. More depressives exhibit this clinically observable picture more often than they do any other.

Since distress appears as the dominant emotion, biopsychiatrists and psychopharmacologists have typically assumed that the parasympathetic system is dominant and hyperactive in depression. The search has been for drugs that would decrease parasympathetic activity, either directly or by increasing sympathetic dominance.

Differential emotion theory holds that depression involves a pattern of emotions. In addition to distress, the depressive pattern includes inner-directed and outer-directed anger and other emotions. The presence of anger, perhaps the second most important emotion in depression, and the fact that it may be both inner- and outer-directed seriously complicate the biochemistry of depression. This means that depression cannot be treated simply as a function of the parasympathetic (cholinergic) system. Anticholinergic drugs or drugs

178

that stimulate the sympathetic system (adrenergic drugs) may lead to increased hostility with consequent aggression and guilt and a recycling of the depression.

Differential emotion theory has not yet influenced biological psychiatry and psychopharmacology. Hence, the search is still for the "right" anticholinergic drug (parasympathetic inhibitor) or adrenergic (sympathomimetic or sympathetic facilitator) drug. Currently, the main effort has been focused on adrenergic or, more frequently, noradrenergic drugs which affect the metabolism and utilization of the catecholamine, norepinephrine. Another catecholamine, dopamine, has also received attention recently. However, by far the most widely used antidepressant drugs are those which in one way or another increase the norepinephrine level in the nervous system and hence facilitate sympathetic activity.

In their excellent review entitled "Biochemistry of Depressions," Schildkraut, Davis, and Klerman (1968) noted that 20 years ago a reviewer of this area concluded that biochemistry had little to contribute to an understanding of the mechanisms underlying depression. Schildkraut, Davis, and Klerman were more optimistic and had eight pages of references to bolster their attitude.

Schildkraut, Davis, and Klerman addressed themselves mainly to nonnormal (psychopathological) depressions, and most particularly to "endogenous" depressions. The latter were said to be "characterized by the autonomy of the depression once it is established, and by the lack of reactivity of the symptoms to day-to-day alterations in the patient's environment or to interpersonal treatment modalities [p. 626]." Endogenous depressions include manic-depressive and involutional depressions and are distinguished from schizoaffective, characterological, situational, and normal depressions.

The reviewers examined the literature dealing with the three broad classes of chemicals—biogenic amines, steroids, and electrolytes—and concluded that biogenic amine metabolism held the most promise for the biochemical study of the depressions.

A. THE BIOGENIC AMINES AND DEPRESSION

In its simplest form, the biogenic amine hypothesis holds that depression is associated with low levels of amines in the brain, and mania with high levels. Kety (1970) observed that since practically every drug that alters affective states in man also affects the catecholamines in the brain, it is reasonable to hypothesize that

179

amines are involved in the mediation of depression and mania and in the action of the drugs that influence them.

There are several subhypotheses regarding the relationships between the amines and depression. Some evidence suggests that a deficit in the indoleamine, serotonin, leads to depression. Currently, however, considerably more evidence indicates that norepinephrine deficiency in the brain and sympathetic nervous system is even more critical in the biochemistry of depression (Davis, 1970).

However, contradictory or seemingly inexplicable findings continue to emerge. Cohn, Dunner, and Axelrod (1970) have recently found that catechol-o-methyltransferase (COMT), believed to be one of the enzymes involved in the metabolism of catecholamines, was significantly reduced in depressed females but not in depressed males. But more recently Paul, Cramer, and Bunney (1971) found marked elevations of urinary adenosine $3',5'$-monophosphate (cyclic AMP) on the day of a rapid switch from a depressed to manic phase in manic-depressive patients. They suggested that "this increase might serve as a trigger function for the process by which catecholamines are elevated during the manic phase of the illness [p. 300]." (The evidence relating specifically to cyclic AMP will be reviewed in Section C.)

Thus, it is generally believed that the efficacy of the most popular antidepressant drugs is a function of their influence on the biogenic amines, most particularly the monoamine, norepinephrine. Current evidence indicates that norepinephrine is synthesized within the nerve cell from the amino acid tyrosine, the final step being the conversion of dopamine into norepinephrine. The role of norepinephrine and other biogenic amines in central neural processes has not been definitely established, but it is generally assumed that norepinephrine functions as a chemical transmitter in the peripheral sympathetic nervous system. Thus, increases in norepinephrine would lead to increased sympathetic activity and potentially to sympathetic dominance.

The final step of the biosynthesis (dopamine → norepinephrine tend to act as euphoriants or antidepressants (Kety, thought that the norepinephrine is present at various sites throughout the cell. Norepinephrine is released from the nerve endings to find its way to a receptor site on another nerve cell. In this way, norepinephrine functions as a neurotransmitter. Once norepinephrine has activated the receptor, it is inactivated, primarily by an active reuptake process in the presynaptic nerve terminal. Once inside the nerve ending again, the norepinephrine may either be stored in the granules or inactivated through oxidative deamination catalyzed by monoamine oxidase. In both of these chemical processes the norepinephrine is metabolized into compounds that are not neurotransmitters. (For more detailed information on the synthesis and metabolism of the biogenic amines, see Davis, 1970.)

There is some direct and indirect evidence for the hypothesis that drugs which increase the norepinephrine level act as antidepressants. The hypothesis has two aspects—drugs that decrease norepinephrine at the synapse and thereby inhibit adrenergic transmission (e.g., the drug reserpine) are associated with depressive phenomena, while drugs that have the opposite effect on norepinephrine tend to act as a euphoriant or antidepressant (Kety, 1970). Reserpine apparently depletes norepinephrine by disrupting the process by which it is stored in the neuron, and large doses of reserpine produce severe depression in some patients. Reserpine produces a syndrome in animals that has been considered an analog to depression in human beings. Its effects in animals have been shown to be associated with decreased brain levels of the catecholamines, norepinephrine and dopamine, and the indoleamine, serotonin.

Although there are some inconsistencies in the clinical and experimental findings, there is considerable evidence which supports the general hypothesis that the synthesis and metabolism of the biogenic amines is importantly related to depression and mania. Some investigators have suggested that norepinephrine and the other amines are related to motivational systems. The location of the amines in the brain supports this possibility.

McGeer (1971) has noted that the cells of the brain involved in emotion, awareness, and cognition differ from all other living cells. Though the sources of their special properties are unknown, some of them may well relate to the complex of hormones, neurohumors, and enzymes involved in their functioning. McGeer concluded that the amines are important in setting the level of activity and the goal-directed tasks of brain cells.

In his recent and thorough review of the biochemistry of depression, Davis (1970) summed up the case for the amine hypothesis.

> Since depression and mania are disease states characterized by alterations in affect and drive and associated with marked sleep disturbances, and since amines are localized in and appear to function in [brain] areas related to drive, emotion, and sleep, additional supportive evidence is provided for the hypothesis that a relationship does exist between amines and these two disease states [p. 149].

181

However, the tentativeness of this conclusion must be kept in mind, for it is frequently called into question by clinical and experimental findings. For example, Goodwin, Murphy, Brodie, and Bunney (1970) found L-dopa, a catecholamine percursor, clearly lacking in therapeutic effectiveness with depressives. They thought their study offered some evidence against the biogenic amine hypothesis, but they qualified their conclusion on the grounds that norepinephrine in the brain may not be increased by L-dopa.

B. STEROIDS, ELECTROLYTES, AND DEPRESSION

Schildkraut, Davis, and Klerman (1968) and Davis (1970) have presented comprehensive reviews of the studies relating the adrenocortical hormones (steroids) and electrolytes to depression. The research in this area has shown some consistent relationships at a very general level, but much work remains before the evidence can have specific implications for the diagnosis and treatment of depression.

1. Steroids. The steroids were linked to emotions and moods when it was observed that patients suffering from Addison's disease, one due to deficiency of adrenocortical hormones, experienced depression, apathy, inability to concentrate, irritability, apprehension, and sleep distrubance. Of special interest to the hypothesis that the striate muscle system is involved as a component of the emotion process is the fact that extreme muscle weakness is one of the symptoms of Addison's disease. This raises the possibility that some of the changes in emotions and moods associated with this disease are secondary, or symptom-induced.

A number of clinical investigators have shown that the steroids are associated with depression and mania. Depression as an emotional disturbance may well precede and determine steroid changes. However, some recent studies point to a possible etiological role for the steroids.

Most of the evidence points to an increase in patients' plasma steroid levels and steroid excretion during periods of depression. The increase is relative to levels observed in these individuals during phases of mania or normalcy. There is some evidence that, as a group, patients who suffer depressions have an adrenal dysfunction.

Among the adrenal corticosteroids implicated in depression are the 17-hydroxycorticosteroids (17-OH-CS). Bunney and Fawcett (1965) found that 17-OH-CS levels were elevated in de-

182

pressed patients. Fluctuation in 17-OH-CS levels often correlated with behavioral ratings of depression.

While there is an increase of plasma steroids in depression, there may be a relative insufficiency in the central nervous system. Davis (1970) cited evidence that "pretreatment with dexamethasone shortens the lag period before the therapeutic response to MAO inhibitors or tricyclic drugs [p. 165]." This finding is generally supported by a recent study of Maas and Mednieks (1971) that showed that hydrocortisone mediated an increase in norepinephrine uptakes in slices of the cerebral cortex of adult rats. Since the uptake of norepinephrine is the principal way in which the released amine is inactivated, the net effect of the observed hydrocortisone–norepinephrine interaction was a lowered level of free and active amines in the brain, as observed in depression. Their study supported the earlier conjecture of Ramey and Goldstein (1957, cited in Maas and Mednieks, 1971) that epinephrine and norepinephrine function as a physiological unit with cortisol.

Brady (1970) has studied extensively 17-OH-CS and its relation to other hormones and to emotion and emotional behavior. His work has focused on anxiety, without any consideration of depression. He induced anxiety in monkeys by superimposing punishment (electric shock) on a recently acquired lever-pressing response that delivered a food reward. During periods of "conditioned anxiety," the monkeys showed marked elevations in 17-OH-CS. Of special interest for the biochemistry of depression was his finding of an elevated norepinephrine level and no change in epinephrine level. This is consistent with the concept, previously mentioned, that the steroids and catecholamines may act as a physiological unit or have a common control mechanism. Brady's work is also relevant in terms of differential emotion theory, which defines anxiety and depression as overlapping combinations of fundamental emotions. A notion analogous to this differential emotion theory concept has also appeared in the thinking of biochemical investigators. Bunney, Mason, and Hamburg (1965) surmised that abnormal levels of 17-OH-CS reflect an increase in "psychic pain" or distress, a factor they thought might be common to anxiety and depression.

2. *Electrolytes.* The role of water and electrolyte balance in depression continues to be considered, but very few consistent findings have emerged from the research in this area. Some studies have found decreased extracellular or total body water during depression, relative to level after recovery, and an increase during the manic phase. Davis (1970) pointed out that measurement problems becloud

many of the findings from these studies. He also cited evidence which suggests that phenomena such as sodium retention may be a function of the elevated cortisol observed in depression. Thus, there is the possibility that the amines, steroids, and electrolytes function as a physiological unit in mediating emotional changes, particularly depression and mania. At least, all three types of substance may interact in influencing emotion processes.

C. ADENOSINE 3',5'-MONOPHOSPHATE (CYCLIC AMP) AND DEPRESSION

The evidence linking the biogenic amines, steroids, and electrolytes to depression tends to implicate adenosine 3',5'-mono-phosphate (cyclic AMP), since cyclic AMP mediates some of the effects of the aforementioned substances. Indeed, Sutherland's discovery of cyclic AMP came partially as a result of experiments analyzing the relationships between epinephrine and blood sugar level (Sutherland, 1970b).

1. *The Basic Functions of Cyclic AMP.* Sutherland (1970a) and Sutherland, Robison, and Butcher (1968) have concluded that cyclic AMP mediates the effects of numerous hormones and enzymes, including the catecholamines. They view hormones as primary messengers that transfer information from one set of cells to another. Cyclic AMP is considered to be a second messenger that operates within the cell, signaling or initiating specific cellular activities such as increasing the quantity of enzymes, altering membrane permeability, and synthesizing specific intracellular chemicals (Williams, 1968). Cyclic AMP is derived from ATP (adenosine triphosphate) through a process catalyzed by adenyl cyclase, a substance presumably located in the cell membrane. The latter is differentially affected by different hormones and thus serves to screen signals from the messengers (hormones) in the cellular environment and to generate signals for intracellular action. Cyclic AMP is the only well-established second (intracellular) messenger at present, though other nucleotides (e.g., cyclic GMP, dibutyryl cyclic AMP) are thought to have this function.

In fine, many hormones exert at least some of their effects by stimulating adenyl cyclase, which in turn catalyzes the formation of cyclic AMP and alters its level within the cell. Of particular significance for the biochemistry of emotion is the evidence amassed by Sutherland and his associates that cyclic AMP translates and amplifies the signals carried by the catecholamines. The evidence for the relationship between deficiency of the latter hormones and depression was reviewed in the foregoing sections of this chapter. Furthermore, Sutherland and his associates hypothesize that adrenergic beta receptors may be an integral part of the adenyl cyclase system. This would be consistent with the notion that increased adrenergic—sympathetic activity, paralleling increased intracellular levels of cyclic AMP, is contraindicative of depression.

   2. *Cyclic AMP and Studies of Clinical Depression.* The investigation of the role of cyclic AMP in depression began only very recently, and the findings, though sometimes highly suggestive, are not always consistent.

   The cyclic AMP hypothesis is similar to the amine hypothesis. The amines acting as first (extracellular) messengers and cyclic AMP acting as a second (intracellular) messenger influence specific cells to perform their respective autonomic and somatic functions. Both are suspected to be deficient in depression and superabundant in mania.

   Paul, Ditzion, Pauk, and Janowsky (1970) studied 37 psychiatric in-patients diagnosed as having "affective psychoses." Ten normal females served as controls. Subjects were divided into four diagnostic groups: *(a)* psychotic depressives, *(b)* neurotic depressives, *(c)* manic patients, and *(d)* normals. Urine samples for 24-hour periods were collected over an average of 3 weeks. Psychotic depressives yielded significantly smaller amounts of urinary cyclic AMP metabolites than neurotic depressives ($p < .05$). Amounts for normals and neurotic depressives were comparable. Manic subjects yielded significantly more cyclic AMP than normals and neurotic depressives ($p < .01$ for both).

   Abdulla and Hamadah (1970) studied urinary cyclic AMP metabolites in 26 depressive and manic-depressive female in-patients. Two samples of 24-hour urine were collected, one on admission, and one on discharge or "switch" from depression to mania or vice versa. The two groups of samples were significantly different in the predicted manner ($p < .01$)—the depressive samples showed much lower amounts of cyclic AMP metabolites than manic samples. The authors noted that cyclic AMP deficiency is also associated with muscular fatigue, loss of libido, low gastric acidity, low salivary secretion, and constipation—common somatic symptoms of depression. They suggested that the cyclic AMP hypothesis also explains the efficacy of antidepressant drugs (via inhibition of cyclic AMP degradation) and the ability of cyclic AMP to reverse reserpine-induced ptosis (an animal analogue of depression).

Paul, Cramer, and Bunney (1971) also studied changes in urinary cyclic AMP metabolites during the manic-depressive "switch." They collected two 24-hour urine samples from six manic-depressive patients, at admission and following the "switch." Cyclic AMP levels were strikingly higher during manic phases than during depressive phases.

At least two studies have cautioned against premature attribution of importance to the role of cyclic AMP in depression. Eccleston, Loose, Pullar, and Sugden (1970) investigated urinary levels of cyclic AMP metabolites following various forms of physical activity and inactivity. They found much higher cyclic AMP levels in subjects who had just completed vigorous physical exercise than in subjects who had been inactive. The differences were comparable to those found by other authors in depressive versus manic phases. They cautioned that the greater physical activity of manic patients may act to spuriously inflate their cyclic AMP level while the relatively inactive depressive patients might show below normal levels.

Robison, Coppen, Whybrow, and Prange (1970) investigated the relative quantities of cyclic AMP in the cerebrospinal fluid of four groups of patients (*N* not stated): *(a)* severe depressives, *(b)* manic patients, *(c)* hypochondriacal patients, and *(d)* epileptics. In contrast to other findings, the level of cyclic AMP was lowest in manic patients and highest in epileptics. None of the differences were judged to be significant.

Robison *et al.* (1970) pointed out that measurement of urinary cyclic AMP, as done in most of the studies of depressives, is difficult to interpret. For one thing, the kidney itself produces about 40% of the cyclic AMP found in the urine. Robison *et al.* considered levels of cyclic AMP in cerebrospinal fluid (CSF) to be more directly related to the central nervous system and hence to emotions, moods, and behavior. Although their study failed to support a relationship between affective disorder and cyclic AMP, they qualified their results. They pointed out that the relationship between levels of urinary or CSF cyclic AMP and the level of cyclic AMP in any given brain area is unknown, as is the distribution of cyclic AMP between CSF and blood. They concluded: "It seems quite possible to us that subtle changes in the level of cyclic AMP in certain neurons within the central nervous system do have an important influence on mood and behavior, and that larger changes may be involved in the symptomatology of affective disorders [p. 1029]."

D. ANTIDEPRESSANT DRUGS

The use of antidepressant drugs has been justified in part on the basis of research on the role of the biogenic amines. Recent research, however, has produced evidence linking or relating the amines, steroids, electrolytes, and cyclic AMP. All of these may be related by common processes.

1. Monoamine Oxidase Inhibitors. One class of antidepressant drugs is the monoamine oxidase inhibitor (MAOI). The MAOI drugs have the ability to block the catabolism (oxidative deamination) of the naturally occurring amines (such as norepinephrine). The MAOIs form stable, irreversible complexes with the MAOs, and the result is inactive degradative enzymes. Since one of the pathways for the breakdown of norepinephrine is blocked, there is an increase in the level of norepinephrine. Depressions characterized by depletions of norepinephrine are sometimes reversed by the administration of MAOIs. "However, the relationship between MAO inhibitors and the therapeutic action of these (MAOI) drugs is not firmly established [Goodman & Gilman, 1970, p. 183]." This is in part due to the fact that the MAOIs interfere not only with MAO but also with other enzymes.

One of the undesirable side effects of MAOI drugs is a prolonging and intensification of the effects of other drugs. There is some evidence that the action of the sympathomimetic amines (such as the amphetamines) are potentiated following the use of MAOI. This is due to the fact that the sympathomimetic drugs act by releasing catecholamines in nerve endings; since the level of amines is also raised by MAOI, greatly increased sympathetic effects are expected and found.

MAO inhibitors may also interfere with the body's degradation and deactivation mechanisms for other drugs. The effects of barbiturates, alcohol, analgesics, and anticholinergic agents and other antidepressant drugs are prolonged and intensified. Administration of MAOI drugs must be carefully considered if the patient is taking any other medication. MAOI drugs may not only prolong the effects of certain drugs, but they may also produce unexpected and even fatal results.

Many foods, when taken in conjunction with MAOI drugs, produce undesirable side effects (Kline, 1969, p. 37). Among the foods and beverages not to be taken when one is on MAOI drugs are beer, cheeses, wine, pickled herring, chicken liver, yeast, coffee, broad bean pods, and canned figs. The result of the interaction of these foods and MAOI drugs is known as a hypertensive crisis. It is certainly the most serious side effect of the MAOI drugs. The symptoms are a steep rise in blood pressure and other cardiovascular changes. In some cases, intracranial bleeding has occurred with death following. Headaches and fever frequently accompany a hypertensive episode. Treatment is generally directed at lowering the blood pressure and fever and removing the food causing the toxic interaction from the diet.

The most useful action of the MAO inhibitors is to elevate the mood of depressed patients. Measurement of elevation in mood is dependent on self-report of subjective processes, and it is made more difficult by the fact that several weeks are required to obtain any discernible results in depressed patients. The elevation in mood is not generally dramatic. Occasionally, however, a patient will react with hyperactivity or extreme talkativeness. It is not always clear if this is a result of the drug treatment or due to the course of the depression.

Work on the MAOI drugs indicates that they are successful only in certain cases, and it is still not clear how they produce their effects. The effectiveness is generally felt to be slight and the dangers considerable. For these reasons, such drugs are used mainly for patients who are resistant to other types of treatment.

2. *Tricyclic Drugs.* A second type of antidepressants are the tricyclic drugs. Two specific drugs in this family are imipramine and amitriptyline; these are the most widely used drugs for the treatment of depression. They are generally felt to be the most effective pharmacological agents for combatting severe depressions.

The antidepressant action of imipramine was discovered clinically, for it was first thought to be an antipsychotic drug. However, it was found that the drug potentiated sympathetic responses which antipsychotic drugs (such as chlorpromazine) did not. At first it was not seen how imipramine fit into the norepinephrine hypothesis outlined above, for it is neither a MAOI nor a COMT inhibitor. Work done in the past few years elucidated its mode of action: Imipramine decreases the physiological reuptake and rebinding of norepinephrine done by the membrane of the presynpatic nerve terminal. This process increases the amount of free norepinephrine that can act at the receptor site. Such an increase in the level of norepinephrine supposedly accounts for the reversal of the

188

depression. Amitriptyline is structurally related to imipramine and acts in a very similar manner.

Although the tricyclic drugs are used only for their effects on the central nervous system, they also have numerous side effects. In normal human beings the drug produces not euphoria but fatigue, dryness of mouth, palpitations, and blurred vision. Depressed patients are helped by the drug, although they suffer from the same side effects. Continued administration accentuates these unpleasant reactions. Patients taking the drug do not generally experience euphoric stimulation; their general reaction is one of relief from their depressed mood.

Imipramine also has some other very serious complications associated with its use. Occasionally a patient will experience manic excitation. More serious, however, are the reported incidents of myocardial infarctions, cardiac arrhythmias, and tachycardia. Negative inotropic effects (less efficient pumping by the heart) are sometimes seen in patients under treatment. For these reasons, cardiac patients must be carefully monitored when using imipramine or any similar drug.

There seems to be a plethora of data on the effects of these two types of antidepressant drugs, particularly the tricyclic variety. Nothing really conclusive is evident, however. Some studies indicate quite noticeable and desirable effects in the treatment of severe depressions. Other studies suggest that these drugs are little more effective than placebos. The lack of clearcut results is a function of many factors. Paramount among these are the heterogeneous types and severities of mental depressions. The terminology used to describe depressions is by no means agreed upon or interpreted in the same way by all psychiatrists and psychologists. Treatments vary in like manner.

It is to be remembered that drug therapy is rarely the only means used in the treatment of a depression. There are also the methods of psychotherapy and behavior modification. These methods may be used at various times throughout the course of a depression, or they may be used simultaneously. It is sometimes impossible to determine which is the most effective treatment. One must also keep in mind the toxic side effects of some of the antidepressant drugs. MAOI drugs are used only in refractory patients because of the real dangers present in inadvertent combination with other drugs or foods.

The question of whether to use the antidepressant drugs is cautiously answered yes. The same statement can be made for their effectiveness. Sometimes desirable results are obtained; often they are not. "The antidepressants are clinically neither specific nor highly effective. They do benefit patients to a degree greater than placebo, but fail to help, or help only partially a great many patients [Davis, 1970, p. 166]." Use of antidepressants requires an extensive knowledge of their effects, the past history of the patient, and knowledge of the particular type of depression being treated. At present, there are good grounds for continuing neurophysiological, biochemical, and psychological studies of depression and for working toward more sophisticated and more comprehensive treatment approaches.

III. THE NEED FOR A NEW CONCEPT OF DEPRESSION

Schildkraut, Davis, and Klerman (1968) and Davis (1970) have presented thorough and critical reviews of the hypotheses and the clinical and experimental evidence on the biochemistry of depression and mania. They tend to support the biogenic amine hypothesis, yet they concluded that the evidence is indirect and indefinite. These investigators, as well as a number of others, suggested that the problems in the neurophysiology and biochemistry of depression may be due in part to "the possibility that depression is not a single diagnostic entity [Davis, 1970, p. 166]."

In addition to the biogenic amines, water and electrolyte (e.g., sodium, potassium) balance, and the steroids are implicated in depression. As Davis (1970) pointed out, there are many possible interrelationships between the various chemical changes allegedly related to depression, and though there are promising leads, the biochemistry of depression is far from settled.

In addition to these factors, which complicate biochemical research on depression, Kline (1969) indicated that depressions are often misdiagnosed as anxiety states or schizophrenia. The latter misdiagnosis occurs when clinicians forget that in cases of psychosis, delusions and hallucinations may be part of a depression syndrome. These misclassifications of patients may result in serious errors in treatment. For example, tranquilizers may relieve anxiety symptoms but increase an underlying depression. Finally, Kety (1970) and others have suggested that depression involves important cognitive factors, a topic which will be treated in Chapter Nine.

Grossman (1970), using intracranial microinjection techniques, has also emphasized the complexity of drug-behavior relationships. He found that microinjections of epinephrine in certain loci of the mesencephalon produced behavioral and EEG signs of arousal, while injections of a similar agent (acetylcholine) at the same sites induced behavioral depression and EEG patterns characteristic of rapid eye movement (REM) sleep.

Discovering that depression is something other than a single diagnostic entity, the complex interactive nature of the body chemicals involved, and the somewhat inconsistent clinical and experimental psychopharmacological findings would not be unexpected in terms of the differential emotion theory of depression. In brief, the theory maintains that depression is a variable pattern or combination of discrete but interacting fundamental emotions and feelings, each of which may have different neural and biochemical substrates. It follows that depression involves a variable pattern of emotion-related neural and biochemical mechanisms on the one hand and a variable pattern of emotions, feelings, and emotion-related attitudes on the other. Our empirical data on depression, to be presented in Chapters Ten and Eleven, were derived from self-report scales that focus on the phenomenology or subjective experience of depression and the separate fundamental emotions related to it.

IV. SUMMARY

Neurophysiological and biochemical research is contributing to our understanding of the emotion process, and this knowledge has immediate implications for the management and control of emotions and behavior. The current status of this field suggests the need for neurophysiology, biochemistry, pharmacology, psychology, and the social sciences to join in collaborative and more comprehensive efforts toward the solution of emotion problems.

As indicated in Chapter One, we are still faced with a scarcity of data on the neurophysiology of discrete emotions and patterns of emotions such as depression. If we assume that distress, defined in terms of sadness and dejection, is the key emotion in depression, then it seems safe to conclude that depression involves the trophotropic system. In the case of dominance by the trophotropic system, there would also be parasympathetic dominance, cortical synchronization, and a tendency toward sleeplike EEG potentials.

If we assume that depression involves a combination or pattern of emotions, including anger, both inner- and outer-directed, then we would have to allow for the possibility that the ergotropic system is also involved. With ergotropic dominance, there would be increased sympathetic activity, cortical desynchronization, and indices of behavioral and EEG arousal.

Differential emotion theory holds that depression represents a particular interactive balance between the trophotropic and ergotropic systems. Such a balance implies either a certain level of simultaneous functioning in these two systems or an alternation of dominance by the two systems. In either case, the assumption that both systems are involved highly complicates the neurophysiology and biochemistry of depression.

Research on the biochemistry of depression has focused on the biogenic amines and on water and electrolyte balance. To date, the biogenic amine hypothesis has received the greatest attention. This hypothesis states that the synthesis and metabolism of the biogenic amines are importantly related to depression and mania. More specifically, depression is associated with a low level of amines in the brain, mania with a high level. The amines receiving most attention are norepinephrine, dopamine, and serotonin. At present, most of the evidence indicates that norepinephrine deficiency in the brain and sympathetic nervous system is the single most critical factor in the biochemistry of depression. One recent study produced evidence that the mechanism for the influence of steroids on depression may be one that mediates an increase in norepinephrine in the nervous system (Maas & Mednieks, 1971).

Recent research has suggested that cyclic AMP is also involved in emotion processes, including depression. This possibility is enhanced by the fact that cyclic AMP has been rather well established as an intracellular mediator of the effects of some of the catecholamines, and possibly some electrolytes and body fluids.

Basic research on the biochemistry and neurophysiology of depression has led to clinical use and investigation of a number of antidepressant drugs. One class of drugs is the monoamine oxidase inhibitor which blocks the catabolism of naturally occurring amines and thereby provides an increase in the level of norepinephrine in the brain and the sympathetic nervous system. Unfortunately, MAOI drugs have not only proved ineffective with many depressives but may also lead to a number of side effects, especially when taken in conjunction with certain foods and beverages. A second class of antidepressant drugs is the tricyclic type, of which the most frequently used are inipramine and amitriptyline. Though the biological mechanism for the action of tricyclic drugs is different from that of the MAOI drugs, the net effect is the same—increasing the amount of free functional norepinephrine in the nervous system. The tricyclic drugs also have been found limited in effectiveness and also may lead to serious complications and adverse side effects.

The problems with antidepressant drugs do not rule out their use with some patients. However, authorities in biochemistry and psychopharmacology caution that the use of antidepressant drugs requires an extensive knowledge of their effects, of the patient's history, and of the particular type of depression being treated.

The latter requirement may prove to be the most difficult by far. There is considerable evidence from the neurophysiological, biochemical, and psychological levels that suggests that we must cease to view depression as a single diagnostic entity or unitary concept.

I have hypothesized that depression is a pattern or combination of discrete but interacting fundamental emotions and feelings and that assessment and treatment of depression will require a knowledge of the relative prominence of each of these conponents in the particular individual. This hypothesis will be elaborated and evaluated in subsequent chapters.

CHAPTER EIGHT

Psychoanalytic Theories of Depression

I. INTRODUCTION

As is the case with so many other human problems that reach clinical significance, the first psychodynamic explication of depression came from psychoanalytic theory. The history of psychoanalytic thought on depression has two points of considerable interest. First, Karl Abraham, the German psychoanalyst, preceded Freud in developing a psychoanalytic view of depression. It was the only time a psychoanalytic investigator found a significant clinical problem not already explored by Freud.

The second point may be of more historical interest. Abraham drew an analogy between anxiety and depression, then proceeded to distinguish the one from the other. He saw anxiety and depression as having a relationship analogous to that between fear and grief. According to Abraham, anxiety results when an instinct strives for gratification and repression prevents the attainment of satisfaction. Depression follows when a sexual aim has to be given up without having obtained gratification; therefore, the depressed individual "feels himself unloved and incapable of loving, and therefore, he despairs of his life and his future [Abraham, 1968, p. 27]."

The depressed cannot love because hostility feelings (or hatred) interfere. The hostility that was once part of an ambivalence toward a love object becomes both inner- and outer-directed hostility upon the loss of the love object.

In this brief but poignant picture of depression, Abraham laid not only the groundwork for Freud's later and more detailed comparison between mourning (grief) and melancholia (depression) but also a foundation for a differential emotion theory analysis of depression. Abraham saw fear and anxiety as having a relationship similar to that of grief and depression. In the differential emotion theory analysis of anxiety, fear was found to be the key emotion of anxiety with which other important fundamental emotions interrelate and interact. Similarly, differential emotion theory posits distress–anguish, the emotion which predominates in grief, as the key emotion in depression and the one with which other fundamental emotions interrelate and interact.

We often say of Freud's analysis of a clinical problem that very little can be added that is really new and different. The same can be said of Abraham's analysis of depression. A careful reading of Abraham shows that most of the basic elements of depression, taking the collective judgment of clinicians and investigators as a criterion, were discussed to some extent in Abraham's original paper. Even Freud failed to add any really new insights to Abraham's conceptualization, though Freud as well as others added noteworthy theoretical refinements and elaborations. In addition, it should be noted that many of the seemingly sharp differences between the later formulations and those of Abraham are nothing more than a differential weighting of the components or elements of depression that Abraham delineated—and he delineated virtually every element ever to receive attention in discussions of depression: grief, distress (sadness, dejection), anger and hostility, feelings of inferiority (loss of self-esteem), guilt, loss of interest, mental and motor inhibition, fear (especially of losing sexual potency), and feeling incapable of giving and receiving love.

In some respects Abraham anticipated the cognitive theory of depression, having once described the basic conflict in depression as deriving from "an attitude of the libido in which hatred predominates." He also saw relationships between depression and certain neurophysiological conditions.

II. THE ORIGINAL PSYCHOANALYTIC MODEL OF DEPRESSION

According to Abraham, the predisposition to depression derives from problems in psychosexual development. Since Abraham saw hostility as an important factor in depression, he first thought that depression could be traced back to fixation at the anal–sadistic phase of development. However, his clinical experience convinced him of a strong oral component in depression, and he came to view the hostility in depression in terms of the cannibalistic characteristic of the oral–sadistic phase of libidinal development. Because of fixation at this point in development, the individual requires a kind of sensational sadism directed promiscuously at everything and everybody. The hostile sadistic impulses create feelings of guilt.

It was Abraham who first proposed that identification is carried out by the instinctual process of oral incorporation. In this way, the self-accusation seen in depression can be traced back partly to feelings of guilt and a need for self-punishment. More importantly, though, the inner-directed anger and guilt stem from aggressive feelings toward the object, which through identification also become aggressive feelings toward the self. Guilt and reality testing result in repression of the sadism. The repressed hostility, some of which is turned on the self, becomes a determinant of depression.

Abraham introduced the concept of primal depression as a result of severe injury of infantile narcissism from dissapointments in love. The primal disappointment was thought to occur in the oral–cannibalistic stage and to be perceived as oral frustration. With the predisposition to hate having been fermented in the oral–sadistic phase of psychosexual development, the depression-prone individual develops the attitude that he cannot love other people and therefore has to hate them. Through the mechanism of projection, the individual forms the attitude that he is not loved by others but rather hated by them. This love–hate ambivalence, according to Abraham, is first expressed toward parents and then eventually toward a wider circle of people. The incapacity to love may lead to a fear of losing sexual potency. The feeling of incapacity to love and the concomitant lack of love from others also cause the individual to feel other deficiencies, and general feelings of inferiority often follow. As I see it, Abraham's concept of inferiority feelings anticipated the idea of loss of self-esteem, which became very important in later psychoanalytic views of depression.

The depressed individual eventually develops the attitude that people do not love him; rather, they hate him because of his deficiencies and his inferiority. He responds, in effect, by saying: "I am unhappy and depressed, and because of this and because of people's hostility toward me I must fight back with hate."

It is easy to see how feelings of hatred or hostility would lead to feelings of guilt and self-reproach. The self-reproach may represent a form of inner-directed hostility that can be viewed as inner-directed anger and disgust, and self-contempt.

197

Once the depression sets in, the individual's usual energetic pursuits suddenly cease. His conflict between love and hate has an almost paralytic effect, and he shows an extreme loss of interest in the world about him.

Following loss of interest the individual shows a high degree of mental inhibition which makes rapport between the depressed person and the external world more difficult. The inhibition serves as a kind of negation of life and in its more extreme form represents a symbolic dying.

Abraham saw mania and depression as dominated by the same complexes. As with depression, Abraham saw anger as an important emotion in mania. He also pointed out that the manic's flight of ideas represented a consciousness or mental process that had lost sight of its aim. In terms of differential emotion theory the lack of rapport between the depressed and his world and the flight of ideas without aim in the manic could both represent a loss of interest. In this context, interest is thought of as an emotion that effects selective focusing of perception and attention and helps initiate and sustain sensible and constructive relationships with the world about us.

In summary, depression was seen as beginning with a loss, and Abraham thought mainly in terms of loss of a love object. All later psychoanalytic thinkers adopted the position that grief and depression follow from some kind of loss. The difference between these two conditions begins with the fact that in depression the loss is cathected with both love and hate, or has both a positive and a negative cathexis. In Abraham's view, it is the anger and hostility and the other feelings and attitudes generated by these emotions in relation to the original loss-determined grief or distress that turn what might be normal grief into depression. As we shall see later, other psychoanalytic thinkers differ with Abraham on the relative importance of the several components of depression, particularly with respect to the importance of anger and hostility.

III. FREUD'S VIEW OF DEPRESSION

Freud acknowledged virtually all Abraham's components of depression and gave additional emphasis and explicitness to some of them. Like Abraham, he considered distress (sadness and dejection) a prominent factor, and added the notion that this affect was a painful one. Freud placed greater emphasis than Abraham on the possible somatic or biogenetic factors in at least some depressions.

Freud (1968) was somewhat more explicit in his view of the role of self-regard or self-esteem as a factor in depression. In fact, he thought that the loss of self-esteem was the trigger for the inner-directed hostility that finds "utterances in self-reproaches and self-revilings, and culminates in delusional expectation of punishment [p. 51]."

Freud placed greater emphasis than did Abraham on the role of cognitive processes in grief, particularly memories and expectations. Memories and expectations psychically prolong the existence of the lost object and "each single one of the memories and expectations in which the libido is bound to the object is brought up and hypercathected, and detachment of the libido is accomplished in respect of it [p. 52]." It is as though the ego were weighed down by the flood of libidinal memories and expectations brought about by the lost object.

According to Freud (1968), at least two things distinguish depression from grief. First, if depression involves an object loss it is a loss at the unconscious level. Second, in distinction from the person in grief, the depressed individual suffers "an extraordinary diminution in his self-regard, an impoverishment of his ego on a grand scale. In mourning it is the world which has become poor and empty; in melancholia it is the ego itself [pp. 53–54]." Since the individual feels worthless, inferior, and incapable of any achievement, inner-directed hostility begins to mount.

Of particular interest for differential emotion theory, Freud thought that the depressed individual differed in another significant fashion from a normal person suffering remorse. He thought that the depressed person lacked shame in social interactions. Freud saw the depressed person's insistent communicativeness and his apparent satisfaction from self-exposure as a trait of the depressive which is opposite that of shame or shyness.

Nevertheless, Freud (1968) pointed to the presence in depression of inferiority feelings and the loss of self-respect. The depressed do not feel ashamed or need to hide themselves "since everything derogatory that they say about themselves is at bottom said about someone else [p. 57]." The apparent inner-directed hostility in the depressed is in fact a reproach against a love object which has been transformed. Although Freud saw hostility as having an important role in depression, he viewed guilt or "dissatisfaction with the ego on moral grounds" as the most outstanding feature in the clinical picture of depression.

Following Abraham, Freud explained the dynamics of inner- and outer-directed hostility and guilt by means of the mechanisms of identification and introjection. For an object loss to be capable of triggering a depression, it is necessary to have an established identification of the ego with the abandoned or lost object. Through introjection of an object with which the ego identifies, an object loss may be transformed into an ego loss.

After identification with the object, the ego wants to incorporate the object into itself. As Abraham pointed out, it is during the oral –sadistic or cannibalistic phase of libidinal development that the ego wants to incorporate by devouring. Incorporation of a love object about which there has been some ambivalence—both love and hate—can now become ambivalence towards the self and result in the inner-directed hostility component of depression. The more ambivalence there was in the love relationship, the more likely is the loss of that loved object to bring about a depression.

> In melancholia, accordingly, countless separate struggles are carried on over the object, in which hate and love contend with each other; the one seeks to detach the libido from the object, the other to maintain this position of the libido against the assault [Freud, 1968, p. 67].

These struggles were seen by Freud as confined to the unconscious.

In summary, Freud added refinements to the analysis of depression. In the way of new emphases, the explication of hostility and guilt by way of identification and subsequent introjection stand out. A couple of Abraham's components were made more explicit and were elaborated. Of most importance, perhaps, is Freud's emphasis on the loss of self-regard or self-esteem that distinguishes depression from grief. Freud also added the note that the mood of mourning is a painful one. Finally, he made the point that though the depressed individual is at times overwhelmed with guilt, he is not ashamed or shy. The lack of shame was accounted for by the fact that the depressed person's self-reproaches are unconsciously attributed to others. Despite the fact that Freud saw the depressed as lacking in shame, he pointed to feelings of inferiority and lack of self-esteem as part of the clinical picture.

IV. NARCISSISTIC LOSS AND FIXATION

Fenichel (1946, 1968), too, recognized most of the major elements of depression that were first delineated by Abraham. According to Fenichel, depression occurs in some degree in nearly every neurosis. Like Abraham, and in the classical psychoanalytic tradition, Fenichel traced the dynamics of depression to fixations at the oral–sadistic level of psychosexual development. Thus, either the depressed person is one who is fixated at a level where his self-esteem is regulated by external supplies, or he is a person whose guilt feelings cause him to regress to that level. Interestingly, Fenichel compared the depressive to an addict. The depressed is a "love addict" who goes through the world in a condition of perpetual greediness.

Expanding somewhat on the earlier notions of oral fixation, Fenichel emphasized the dependency of the depressed. Simple or mild depression may be a rather normal reaction to a long period of deprivation and frustration. The severely depressed individual sees such deprivation as a signal that the vital and necessary ego supplies are being cut off. Hence, depressive behavior is a desperate attempt to force others to give the necessary supplies for the narcissistic needs.

Fenichel recognized that both grief or simple depression and more severe depressions have in common a loss of self-esteem. According to Fenichel, the differences between the sad or grieved person and the severely depressed person are partly differences in techniques or mechanisms used for the recovery of self-esteem. The grieved person is more readily satisfied with "narcissistic supplies" from external objects. The depressed person begins a desperate struggle to restore self-esteem, not only in the outside world but at the intrapsychic level. Intrapsychically, the depressed individual attempts to get his narcissistic support or supplies from the intro-jected object, or from the superego, partly by turning object-directed aggression toward the self. This is a way of accounting for the self-accusations and self-hatred seen in the severely depressed person.

V. DEPENDENCY, EMPTINESS, AND SHAME

Fromm-Reichmann departed from the traditional psycho-analytic view of depression in a number of ways. Though she saw distress–anguish as the most prominent affect in depression, she definitely relegated anger and hostility to a minor role. She emphasized the importance of dependency feelings in the depressed and thought that dependency could be traced to some extent to the same phases of psychosocial development that give rise to hostility; that is, the anal– and oral–sadistic phases. Fromm-Reichmann (1953) thought that anxiety or fear of abandonment was a factor in depression. The inner feeling of the depressed is one of emptiness and need. "The patient incessantly hopes for and strives for a dependency relationship in which all his needs are met by the other [p. 63]." The depressive's complaining and whining behavior is intended to enlist the needed gratification. In psychosis, the depressive loses hope and the pattern of emptiness and need becomes fixed.

Fromm-Reichmann differed from Freud on one possibly important point. Whereas Freud felt that the depressive's complaining and whining stem from a need for communication with others and consequent self-exposure, Fromm-Reichmann saw the depressed as a person who wants to disappear, to annihilate himself. By implication, Fromm-Reichmann saw the depressed as one ashamed, while Freud saw the depressed as lacking in shame and shyness.

VI. LOSS OF SELF-ESTEEM AND EGO CONFLICTS

Bibring (1968) challenged the standard psychoanalytic distinction between a normal grief and an abnormal depression. In his view, all depressions have a single common component, a loss of self-esteem. He described his analysis as an ego–psychological one.

Bibring described several cases of depression in which he saw a common denominator: The depressed were helplessly exposed to superior powers; they felt doomed to being lonely, isolated, unloved, and to feelings of weakness, inferiority, and failure. In fine, all of them suffered a loss of self-esteem. Depression, then, is the emotional expression of a state of helplessness and powerlessness of the ego.

Despite feelings of helplessness and powerlessness, the depressed person maintains one of three kinds of aspirations: (1) the wish to be worthy, to be loved; (2) the wish to be strong, secure; and (3) the wish to be good and loving. The dynamics of depression can be summarized as the tension between these highly charged narcissistic aspirations to be worthy, strong, secure, good and loving, on the one hand, and the ego's acute awareness of its seeming unworthiness, unlovableness, weakness, insecurity, badness, and hatefulness on the other. The ego has high aspirations and feels incapable of meeting them. These three sets of conditions are not mutually exclusive but coexist in varying combinations.

As Bibring (1968) described depression, it is not primarily a conflict between ego and id or between ego and superego, but rather a conflict stemming primarily from tension within the ego itself. "Thus depression can be defined as the emotional correlate of a partial or complete collapse of the self-esteem of the ego, since it feels unable to live up to its aspirations (ego ideal, superego) while they are strongly maintained [p. 164]."

Bibring placed considerable emphasis on another characteristic of depression that has been noted by earlier writers—the intensive and extensive inhibition of functions. He considered this dimension of depression as one in common with depersonalization and boredom. In the depersonalized individual there is the complaint of not having any feelings, of being blocked emotionally, and of being frozen—all these adding up to a feeling of unreality of the self and leading to automaton-like behavior. Somewhat similarly, boredom has been defined in psychoanalytic theory as a "painful feeling originating in a tension between a need for mental activity and the lack of adequate stimulation [p. 167]."

Bibring noted that Fenichel's conception of depression added the idea that, while the need for activity was felt, the aims were repressed. This would leave the individual incapable of developing purpose and direction. Thus in both boredom and depression, high goals and aspirations are maintained. In boredom, goal-directed activity is blocked and interfered with by repression of true goals; and in depression, the ego feels incapable of living up to its goals and narcissistic aspirations. Because of this similarity, depression may follow from boredom when a sense of helplessness and inescapability develop. In depression the inhibition of goal-directed activity is strong and pervasive, since some of the strivings of the person become meaningless in the face of the ego's incapacity to gratify them.

Bibring considered anxiety as diametrically opposed to depression. In anxiety, the ego perceives danger and uses the anxiety as a signal to prepare for fight or flight. In depression, any signal of "danger" tends to paralyze the ego because of its weakness and vulnerability. However, Bibring thought that individuals could suffer anxiety and depression concomitantly or that depression could follow anxiety in cases where the individual lost confidence and felt helpless in the face of danger.

Bibring agreed with Abraham and with Freud in considering the orally dependent person constantly in need of narcissistic supplies as the type most likely to develop a predisposition to suffer from depression. However, Bibring (1968) emphasized that his definition of depression was not dependent on the concept of oral fixation. "I should like to stress the point that the emphasis is not on the oral frustration and subsequent oral fixation, but on the infant's or little child's shocklike experience of and fixation to the feeling of helplessness [p. 173]." The feeling of not being independent and not being loved can contribute to the primary feeling of helplessness. Since the oral stage is the earliest chronologically, the individual is subject to feelings of helplessness and loss of self-esteem in critical phases of anal as well as phallic stages of development.

The individual at the anal stage is already capable of saying "no" and of marshaling some defensive aggressive forces in defying grownups. It is this stage that is most likely to give rise to the feelings of aggression and the subsequent feelings of guilt that characterize depression. In the phallic stage the individual's narcissistic aspirations to be strong and to be admired tend to make the individual susceptible.

Bibring implied that oral and aggressive strivings are not as universal or as important in depression as was often assumed in earlier theories. Most critical of all the dimensions of depression is the blow to self-esteem or the loss of self-esteem, the "narcissistic core of the ego." Only in certain cases does the ego's awareness of its helplessness force it to turn aggression from the object against the self. Bibring seems to have acknowledged here that some aggression toward the "object" remains a fairly consistent dimension of depression.

Bibring thought that his conception of depression as essentially a loss of self-esteem had implications for therapy. According to his conception, therapy should consist of facilitating the recovery of self-esteem. This may be brought about by bringing the goals and aspirations within reach, by techniques directly bolstering self-esteem, or by defenses directly aimed at the depression as such.

Bibring (1968) pointed out that depressive individuals usually attempted to obtain narcissistic supplies by demonstrating their suffering. However, they may exploit the depression, using it to justify their aggressive impulses toward external objects, "thus closing the vicious circle [p. 181]." In general, Bibring saw aggression as secondary to loss of self-esteem. He pointed out that there are some depressions that are not accompanied by any self-aggression and some cases in which angry self-hatred is not manifested in depression. However, he conceded that occasionally, "On recovery from depression by regaining self-esteem and the feeling of strength, aggressive impulses are released and directed against the object world [p. 179]."

VII. DEPRESSION INDEPENDENT OF LOSS

Though it was made implicit in a number of the psychoanalytic views of depression, particularly those of Rado (1968) and Bibring (1968), Gaylin (1968) underscored the point that depression can occur independent of the loss of a love object or even the loss of something that symbolizes a love object. It is only when a love object is invested with the lover's self-esteem that depression results from its loss. Loss of a love object is more likely to produce depression when the object is perceived as essential to the esteem and the survival of the lover. What the person actually mourns is loss of self-esteem; of course, self-esteem may be symbolized by a love object. In fine, it is the loss of self-esteem or any symbol of self-esteem that produces depression, not the loss of a love object or something that symbolizes the love object. The fact that the love object may be the symbol of self-esteem and security, particularly so for women, accounts for the fact that women are more likely to go into depression over the loss of a loved one than men.

VIII. DEPRESSION AND THE DISRUPTION OF SENSORY AND PERCEPTUAL FUNCTIONS

Schachtel (1959) has proposed that boredom and depression, which he sees as related phenomena, disrupt sensory and perceptual processes. The disruption is not brought about by environmental forces, but originates in the personality of the individual. The depressed person's inability to establish contact with persons and objects outside himself causes the world to appear dull and empty. Along with the disruption of sensory and perceptual processes and the lack of communication with the outside world, there is a loss of the sense of selfhood and aliveness. In effect, the bored and the depressed, because of their inability to establish contact with the outside world, suffer from a lack of stimulation. Schachtel explained the outer-directed hostility of the depressed person as his effort to reproach the world for not giving him the stimulation that he craves. The hostility is in vain since it is not the outside world that has ceased to be stimulating: It is the depressed who has lost the ability to turn to the world with interest. Schachtel thought that a full understanding of depression must await a comprehensive analysis of the changes and differences in perception that are brought about by changes and differences in moods and emotions.

IX. A PSYCHOANALYTIC VIEW INVOLVING DISCRETE EMOTIONS AND EMOTION DYNAMICS

Although much of the work of Sandor Rado preceded that of Fromm-Reichmann, Bibring, and others, he is reviewed last because he comes closer than any other theorist to dealing directly with discrete emotions and emotion dynamics in the manner of differential emotion theory. Rado's description of depression includes clear indications of the emotions of distress, anger, guilt, and fear. Depression is also characterized by a loss of self-esteem and self-confidence and by retardation of mental and motor processes that render the individual incapable of sustained effort. The depressed is preoccupied with feelings of failure and unworthiness and demonstrates a loss of interest in his work and his world. Depression may result from serious loss, failure, or defeat, or may occur without apparent cause.

Depressive behavior may be viewed as a cry for love, a cry precipitated by an actual or imagined loss perceived as endangering emotional security. According to Rado (1968), the depressive blames and punishes himself for the loss and strives to reconcile himself with the mother image and to reinstate himself in her loving care. "The aim-image of the patient's repentance is the emotional and alimentary security which he, as an infant, enjoyed while clinging to his mother's feeding breast. The patient's mute cry for love is patterned on the hungry infant's loud cry for help [p. 98]."

The depressive's dominant motivation is for repentance, but his situation is complicated by a simultaneous presence of a strong resentment. What Rado calls "guilty fear" creates humility and a desire for repentance. However, the lost beloved person, or whatever it was that threatened his security, evoked his anger by letting him down or deserting him. This anger leads to resentment and a desire to force the other person to love him. When such coercive rage is defeated, the patient feels repentant and the rage turns inward against the self. "As a superlative bid for forgiveness, the patient may thus be driven to suicide [p. 99]." The painfulness of depression may be due in part to the fact that the dependent individual is employing conflicting methods—coercive rage and submissive fear—in an effort to regain the "mother's love."

Rado saw the balance between fear and rage as the clinical distinction between retarded and agitated depression. "If rage is sufficiently retroflexed by the prevailing guilty fear, the patient is retarded; if the prevailing guilty fear is shot through with straight environment-directed rage, he is agitated [pp. 100-101]." Apparently Rado felt that, in most cases in which depression was maintained over a period of time, submissive fear had the upper hand over coercive rage.

In summary, Rado saw depression as characterized by a mood of "sustained, gloomy repentance; the regressive yearning for alimentary security of the infant; and the struggle between the excessive emergency emotions, in which submissive fear defeats coercive rage [p. 102]." Although cloaked for the most part in the language of psychoanalysis, Rado more clearly than any other psychoanalytic theorist recognized what we term discrete or fundamental emotions as components of depression and saw conflict or competition between such emotions as fear and rage as essential in explaining the motivational organization of the depressive.

Rado was perhaps the first of the psychoanalytic thinkers to emphasize the need for collaborative effort with other disciplines. He thought that a comprehensive analysis of depression would require research in genetics, pathologic anatomy, physiology, biophysics, and biochemistry.

X. EMPIRICAL STUDIES OF PSYCHOANALYTIC CONCEPTS

Two of the concepts of psychoanalytic theory have been put to empirical test: loss of love object and inner-directed anger. The former has been studied primarily in terms of childhood bereavement.

A. BEREAVEMENT AND DEPRESSION: EMPIRICAL EVIDENCE

Empirical studies of the importance of personal loss in the etiology of depression have mainly relied on information collected from depressed patients or their families. Gregory (1961) reviewed the systematic studies on early parental loss, and summarized them as "meager and inconclusive." He reported some positive correlations between adult depression and incidence of childhood bereavement, but noted that problems of definition and lack of comparisons with normal groups make the studies very difficult to assess.

Beck (1967) also reviewed the literature on early bereavement and, in combination with results from his own study, concluded that ". . . the death of a parent in childhood may be a factor in the later development of a severe depression in a significant proportion of psychiatric patients. The precise nature of this relationship cannot be determined without further research [pp. 226–227]." In his study, Beck used results on his Depression Inventory to divide 297 patients into high-depressed, medium-depressed, and nondepressed groups of roughly 100 each. Incidence of loss of either or both parents prior to age 16 was 27% for the high-depressed group, 15.5% for the medium-depressed group, and 12% for the nondepressed group. These differences were significant at the .01 level. Roughly the same findings obtained when bereavement was related to clinical ratings of depression ($p < .02$).

Spitz (1946) studied hospitalism and anaclitic depression in children under 5 years of age. He concluded that a child deserted by its mother for more than .5 months (once the child has formed some clear conception of the mother) was almost certain to become severely depressed. This suggested that loss alone, at least maternal loss at this young age, was a sufficient condition for the development of severe depression. He noted that the deprived children went through essentially the same three stages of alarm, resistance, and exhaustion as in the general adaptation syndrome. During the first month, children displayed restlessness, irritability, searching behavior, and sleep disturbance. In the second and third months they became withdrawn, disinterested, and displayed loss of appetite. If the mothers did not return shortly thereafter, children became severely apathetic, and many died.

Brown (1961) investigated the incidence of childhood bereavement in 216 hospitalized depressives, and found that 41% had lost a parent by death before age 15. This was reported to be significantly greater than the incidence of orphanhood in England (12%) and among 267 medical students (19.6%). The comparability of these control groups has been questioned (Silverman, 1968).

It should be mentioned that studies by Pitts, Meyer, Brooks, and Winokur (1965) and Gregory (1966a,b) failed to indicate a significant relationship between adult depression and early bereavement. The latter studies involved careful actuarial comparisons of groups of 321 and 1000 psychiatric patients with a similar number of controls. Neither depressives nor any other psychiatric group was associated with bereavement to any significant extent.

Psychoanalytic theories hypothesized early loss in combination with personal immaturity or fixation as the necessary and sufficient conditions for development of predisposition to depression, but not either of these by itself. Thus none of the studies reviewed constitutes a critical test of the hypothesis. It is possible, in fact, that the conflicting results obtained in some studies may be due to failure to consider both of these variables in combination. Also, most studies considered early bereavement as parental loss occurring up to age 15, whereas the psychoanalytic theories imply that the critical ages are between 1 and 6 years. It is reasonable that youths 12 to 16 years of age would have developed a variety of defenses and coping techniques applicable to bereavement that have not been learned by children under age 6.

Overall, the evidence relating depression to early parental loss must be regarded as tentative. Results of empirical studies are often conflicting, and nearly all are weakened by problems of diagnosis, demographic differences in mortality rates, and lack of comparable control groups.

B. INNER-DIRECTED HOSTILITY AND DEPRESSION: EMPIRICAL EVIDENCE

Evidence relating to the role of inner-directed anger in depression comes from a variety of sources. Malerstein (1967) noted that many psychotherapists assume that "the" approach to depression is to "get the anger out." Barnard and Banks (1967), Klauber (1966), Lampl-de Groot (1964) and other authors have argued that treatment of depression revolves around the patient's becoming aware of, and learning to control, his anger and hatred. However, this does not constitute support for the psychoanalytic position, even assuming for the moment that such a treatment mode is effective. Learning to understand and control one's aggressive feelings and behavior is an important part of the treatment of a number of emotional disorders.

Kendell (1970) and Silverman (1968) presented some epidemiological findings which suggested that countries where there is a high incidence of self-reproach and a low tolerance of other-directed aggression tend to show relatively high rates of depression, though there were a number of exceptions. They also studied suicide rates and depression in combat troops and prisoners of war, with results tending in the same direction. Although the investigators planned specifically to test the psychoanalytic hypothesis relating inner-directed hostility to depression, they actually did so only tangentially. The studies were concerned with general hostility and self-reproach, which may have very little to do with the sort of anger engendered by the loss of something basic to one's emotional well-being.

Wessman, Ricks, and Tyl (1960) studied inner-directed and outer-directed hostility in 25 female college students. Rosenzweig's Picture-Frustration Test was used to collect daily ratings on intropunitive, extrapunitive, and impunitive hostility over a period of six weeks. Daily ratings by subjects were concurrently made on a 10-point rating scale to determine mood state. Results showed that subjects recorded more extrapunitive responses and fewer intropunitive responses during depression than during normal and elated moods ($p < .05$ in both cases), contrary to the authors' hypothesis. The generality of these findings is questionable, since the Radcliffe girls studied may be at variance with the general population with respect to style of self-reporting or degree of self-awareness. No control group was studied.

Gershon, Cromer, and Klerman (1968) intensively studied six hospitalized female depressives. Hamilton's (1960) Depressed Symptom Scale was used as an index of severity of depression, and Gottschalk, Gleser, and Springer's (1963) technique for scoring three minutes of free association was used to rate patients on hostility-in, hostility-out, and ambivalent hostility. No control group was used; instead, the authors relied on Gottschalk's normative data for comparisons. The first analysis showed a significant positive correlation between hostility-in and level of depression, but no correlation with hostility-out. On the basis of observed patient differences and previous empirical differentiations (Friedman, Cowitz, Cohen, & Granick, 1963; Grinker, Miller, Sabshin, Nunn, & Nunnally, 1961), the six patients were divided into two groups in an effort to clarify the data. One group was primarily "hysterical" with overt expressions of hostility and demanding, pleading behavior. The other group showed more subdued expressions of sadness, guilt, and intropunitive behavior. Given this distinction, a small but negative correlation ($r = -.11$) was found, as predicted, between level of depression and

210

hostility-out. The correlation with hostility-in remained roughly the same ($r = .45$).

Several factor-analytic studies have found hostility to be a component of depression. (Factor-analytic investigations will be reviewed comprehensively in Chapter Ten.) Grinker *et al.* (1961) and Overall, Hollister, Johnson, and Pennington (1966) found factors interpreted as "provocative anger" and "hostile depression," respectively. Marshall and Izard (Chapter Ten) found factors interpreted as "inner-directed anger/disgust/contempt" and "outer-directed anger/disgust/contempt." Beck (1967) found factors interpreted as "self-debasement" and "pessimism-suicide." The Marshall and Izard study was the only one in which inner-directed and outer-directed hostility items were delineated. It is notable that in this study (in which normal subjects recalled their feelings in a past depression) scale means were consistently higher for inner-directed than for outer-directed hostility.

Empirical studies provide some degree of support for the psychoanalytic position of the importance of inner-directed anger or hostility in depression. However, the number of studies is too small and the populations sampled too limited to draw any firm conclusions at present. Furthermore, all analyses except the last were derived from questionnaires answered either by depressed patients or by psychiatrists. Gershon, Cromer, and Klerman (1968) have cautioned that self-reports from depressed patients are frequently misleading. These authors observed that patients with high hostility-out verbalized significantly fewer manifest expressions of depressed affect, although they had as many symptoms of depression as the hostility-in group. Marshall and Izard also observed that the high scale scores for inner-directed hostility may simply reflect a greater awareness of hostile impulses on the part of normal subjects, or a greater ability to accept and deal with them.

XI. SUMMARY

In the original psychoanalytic model of depression, Abraham described most of the features that are found in all the later psychoanalytic formulations. He drew the analogy between grief and depression, an analogy that Freud later discussed in terms of mourning and melancholia. Abraham's original analysis included most of the major components of depression: distress, anger and hostility, feelings of inferiority (loss of self-esteem), guilt, loss of interest, mental and motor inhibition, fear (especially of losing sexual potency), and inability to give and receive love. He even anticipated the cognitive theory of depression by describing it as an attitude of the libido in which hatred predominates. As indicated by this phrase, Abraham saw hostility feelings as a highly prominent dynamic in depression.

Abraham maintained that the predisposition to depression begins with frustration and subsequent fixation at the anal–sadistic and oral–sadistic phases of libidinal development. Fixation at this level results in hostile, sadistic impulses that in turn create feelings of guilt. This combination of negative affects leads to loss of interest, mental and motor inhibition, and a feeling of incapacity to give and receive love.

Typically the lost love object is one toward whom the individual has both positive and negative feelings and one with whom he has identified. The identification was effected by oral incorporation; thus the love object becomes a part of the self and the hostility once felt toward the love object is turned upon the self.

Freud essentially agreed with Abraham's analysis of depression. He placed somewhat greater emphasis on biogenetic factors on the one hand and on the cognitive processes of memory and expectations on the other. Freud thought that if depression involved an object loss, it was a loss at the unconscious level.

Interestingly, Freud saw the depressed individual as lacking in shame and shyness. Self-abasement does not seem to cause him much suffering. Essentially he is dissatisfied and angry with significant others and the outside world. Even the inner-directed hostility is in reality reproach against the lost love object that has been introjected.

Fenichel emphasized the notion of narcissistic loss and underscored the importance of fixation at the oral–sadistic level. He saw the depressed as a love addict, always greedy for narcissistic supplies. He interpreted depressive behavior as a desperate attempt to force others to fulfill narcissistic needs.

Fromm-Reichmann relegated anger and hostility to a minor role and emphasized the importance of dependency and feelings of emptiness. In contrast to Freud, she saw the depressed as a person ashamed, wanting to disappear and ultimately to annihilate himself. Fromm-Reichmann thought that anxiety or fear of abandonment was a factor in depression.

Bibring drew no essential distinction between grief and depression and considered loss of self-esteem as the essential dynamic in both. In his ego-psychological analysis of depression, he maintained that the depressed essentially suffers not from conflicts between superego and id, but from conflicts within the ego. The basic conflict is between the ego's highly charged narcissistic aspirations to be worthy, strong, secure, good, and loving on the one hand, and the ego's acute awareness of its seeming unworthiness, unlovableness, weakness, insecurity, badness, and hatefulness on the other. The ego suffers from inordinately high aspirations and concomitant feelings of incapacity to meet them.

In contrast to Fromm-Reichmann, Bibring considered anxiety as diametrically opposed to depression. While the anxious individual may use anxiety as the signal to prepare for fight or flight, in depression any signal of danger tends to paralyze the ego because of its weakness and vulnerability. Bibring agreed with Fromm-Reichmann in relegating aggressive strivings to a lesser role.

Gaylin underscored the point that depression can occur independent of the loss of a love object or even the loss of something that symbolizes the love object. Elaborating Bibring's point, he held that depression follows the loss of a love object only when the love object is invested with the lover's self-esteem.

Schachtel described the depressive as a person with defective sensory and perceptual functions. The depressed person becomes unable to make the sensory and perceptual discriminations that provide effective communication with others and the world about him. Loss of sensory and perceptual powers results in a state of sensory deprivation and a severe deficiency in stimulation. He explained outer-directed hostility as the depressed person's reproaching the world for not providing the stimulation that he needs.

Rado came closest of any of the psychoanalytic theorists to dealing with discrete emotions and emotion dynamics in his analysis of depression. He dealt rather clearly with the emotions of distress, anger, guilt, and fear. He saw depressive behavior as a cry for love, a cry precipitated by an actual or imagined loss perceived as endangering emotional security. The depressive blames and punishes himself for the loss. Blaming himself leads to what Rado called a mood of sustained, gloomy repentance. This mood is complicated by a simultaneous presence of guilt and of strong resentment toward the love object for deserting him. There results what Rado described as a conflict between guilty fear and coercive rage. The balance between guilty fear and rage provides the basis for the clinical distinction between retarded and agitated depression.

The psychoanalytic concepts of loss (particularly bereavement in childhood) and the role of inner-directed hostility have been studied empirically. A number of studies have found a correlation between childhood bereavement and depression. Other studies have found minimal or no evidence for such a relationship. The somewhat controversial findings and the vast problems of control leave the question unsettled.

Some investigators have also found fairly substantial evidence for a relationship between inner-directed hostility and depression. Others have failed to find such a relationship. However, it should be noted that inner-directed and outer-directed hostility were operationally defined and separated in only one study. In general, the evidence tends to support the hypothesis that inner-directed hostility is associated with depression.

CHAPTER NINE

Biogenetic, Sociocultural, and Cognitive Factors in Depression

In recent years, knowledge of depression has been increased substantially by three lines of research in addition to the biochemical and psychoanalytic traditions. These research approaches are aimed toward delineating biogenetic, sociocultural, and cognitive factors. Investigators in one or the other of these areas sometimes emphasize one set of factors almost to the exclusion of others. Nevertheless, each approach has discovered potentially important aspects of depression that should be considered along with other contributions.

I. A BIOGENETIC THEORY OF DEPRESSION

Perhaps the most comprehensive theory of depression that places strong emphasis on biogenetic factors is that of Kraines (1957). Kraines distinguishes between the mechanism of depression and the etiology of depression. He defines the mechanism of depression as dysfunction of the diencephalon, rhinencephalon (including the limbic lobe, the thalamus, and the hypothalamus), and the reticular formation. In some respects, Kraines's theory is compatible with the neurophysiological and biochemical research reviewed in Chapter Seven.

While Kraines acknowledges that psychogenic factors play a role in depression, he holds that the etiology is essentially physiological–hereditary and hormonal influences. Psychogenic factors play their role largely by modifying and prolonging the condition and in determining symptoms. Thus, a great deal of Kraines's analysis focuses around physiological pathology or, as he terms it, physiopathology.

A. CRITICISMS OF PSYCHOANALYTIC AND COGNITIVE THEORIES

Kraines prefaces his position with a rather severe criticism of Freud and the psychoanalytic theory of depression. He characterized the psychoanalytic view as imaginative, metaphorical fantasy. Some of his criticism is well taken, as is his criticism of the seeming circularity of some psychoanalytic thinking. For example, the patient cannot love because he hates his narcissistic love object. Because of this hate, he feels hated and, consequently, depressed. Other aspects of his criticism are ill founded or unwarranted. For example, he incorrectly attributes to all schools of psychoanalytic thinking the notion that a psychic trauma in early childhood is an essential part of the etiology of all manic-depressive illnesses.

Although Kraines's work preceded much of the literature that emphasizes cognitive factors in depression, his theory has an implicit critique of cognitive theory. First, he considers cognitive and intellectual changes as secondary and as events that follow from the more essential physiopathological conditions. Second, much of his critique of psychoanalysis holds equally well for cognitive theory.

Kraines pointed out several characteristics of depression that he thought could not be explained by psychoanalytic theory (nor could they readily be explained by cognitive theory).

1. Many persons become depressed without any discernible precipitating factor.
2. Even some psychogenic factors considered to be precipitating factors may have occurred on numerous previous occasions in the person's life without bringing on a depression.
3. There are often several decades between a childhood trauma and the onset of a depression.
4. Many people suffer a "serious ego trauma" without developing a serious depression.
5. Age, sex, and climatic change have been shown to be related to depression.
6. Psychodynamic factors are idiosyncratic and highly varied, yet depression tends strongly toward a patterned process of onset, course, and termination.

216

7. Depression is typically time-limited and often cyclic.
8. Radical therapies such as electric shock often prove therapeutic.

Kraines considers most of the above criticisms of psycho-analytic and cognitive theory as positive argument for a biogenetic theory of depression. In addition to the foregoing argument, he lists three other types of evidence for the nonpsychogenic etiology of depression: the marked influence of heredity, the relationship of depression to physique, and the frequent onset of depression after childbirth, even in women with stable personalities.

B. HEREDITY AND DEPRESSION

In support of his proposition that heredity is a significant factor in the eitology of depression, Kraines summarized the work of a number of investigators who have studied the hereditary incidence of manic-depressive psychosis. According to the data presented, manic-depressive psychosis occurs in only .4% (1 in 250) of the general population. Yet if one parent has had the disease, it will occur, according to different investigators, in 24–33% of the children of this parent; and another 17% of the offspring may have a mild affective disorder. If both parents have had manic-depressive psychosis, as many as 67% of the children will have a definite manic-depressive disorder, while the other 33% may have a mild affective disturbance. About 17% of half-siblings of manic-depressive patients are likely to have the disorder, while 23–24% of full-siblings have been found to suffer from manic-depressive psychosis. Different investigators have found that if one member of monozygotic twins has manic-depressive psychosis, between 70 and 96% of the other members will also suffer from manic-depressive psychosis.

C. RELATIONSHIPS BETWEEN BIOLOGICAL FACTORS
AND DEPRESSION

Kraines further developed his biogenetic view by pointing out the relationships between biological factors and depressive symptoms—considering, in the process, a number of commonly observed symptoms in depression. He attributed aching and twitching muscles and feelings of weariness and fatigue to disturbances in homeostasis that result in erratic functioning of the nervous system. The erratic functioning can result in bursts of neural discharge and

217

consequent muscular jerking and twitching. Such muscular activity can actually bring about real fatigue.

Kraines attributed visual paresthesias (e.g., blurred vision) to disturbance in the optic thalamus. The feeling of unreality (in the visual sense) is explained in psychodynamic theory as conflict between reality and the patient's own repressed needs and frustrations. According to Kraines (1957), the unreality sensations stem from physiological dysfunction of the integrative action of the optic thalamus. Feelings of unreality in the visual or physical realm "are related to emotional and intellectual reality and have the same physiologic basis [p. 183]."

Kraines discusses three other classes of sympoms which are of undisputed importance in depression. The first of these is emotional isolation or the lack of what Kraines terms "emotional identification." He defines emotional identification as "the capacity to feel emotional warmth for and appreciation of one's self and others; the ability to 'relate' one's self to another; to have appropriate emotional responses to persons, situations, and even to things and ideas; to project one's own feelings into as well as to appreciate the emotional content of others [p. 226]." Emotional isolation is the lack of these processes which constitute emotional identification. Kraines maintains that emotional identification develops from both psychic and physical sources. Psychogenic factors include the giving of affection and emotional support in infancy and childhood. The psychogenic factors that contribute to emotional well-being and ego strength usually contribute to emotional identification. However, in addition to these psychogenic factors, emotional identification varies with conditions such as fatigue, hunger, pain, and premenstrual tension. More generally, the physiological basis of emotional identification is rooted in the functioning of the diencephalic—rhinencephalic area of the brain.

According to Kraines, sensory impressions are the foundations for the emotions, and intact emotion processes are necessary for emotional identification. When sensory impressions are inappropriately transmitted or ineffectively integrated in the diencephalic—rhinencephalic area of the brain, emotional isolation results. The symptoms that follow may include emotional poverty or the inability to feel any emotion, inability to feel love, a feeling of aloneness, an overdetermined need for sympathy with an accompanying inability to appreciate it, and a sense of emotional unreality which amounts to defective emotion perception or recognition as applied to both self and others.

Another major symptom discussed by Kraines is that of irritability, defined as overreaction to stimuli, major irritation over mild annoyances, and temper outbursts. Apparently Kraines's concept of irritability is quite similar to the psychoanalytic notion of rage or hostility. Kraines argues that irritability is frequently caused by physical disturbances such as bodily states of toxicity and various forms of brain injury that affect the diencephalon. In general, it is diencephalic physiopathology that produces irritability. At the neuronal level, irritable responses have their basis in dysrhythmic, erratic, inconstant, and weak or excessive functioning.

The fearfulness seen in depressives also has its basis in physiological instability, according to Kraines (1957). "In the first place, the neuronal response (diencephalic) to danger is so rapid that the cultivated, conditioned attitudes of the cerebral cortex have minimal opportunity to modify a basic, primitive response (like fearfulness) to new or certain stimuli: hence sudden uncontrolled 'fear' [p. 240]." Further, instability of hypothalamic neurons causes erratic and excessive stimulation of the sympathetic and endocrine systems, thus adding to the physical aspects of fear. The patient's inability to understand what is happening to his insides results in what Kraines calls psychic fearfulness. Although Kraines was apparently unaware of it, his concept of uncontrolled fear is essentially similar to Freud's concept of innate anxiety, as discussed in Chapter Four.

D. BIOCHEMISTRY AND BODY TYPE
AS BIOGENETIC FACTORS

Some investigators have interpreted the work on the biochemistry of depression, discussed in Chapter Seven, as evidence for hereditary factors in depression and as general support for the biogenetic position. Hurst (1969) has discussed this work under what he terms the enzyme block hypothesis. He considers phenylketonuria (PKU) as the paradigm of genetically determined enzyme blocks that results in mental or emotional disorders. In the case of PKU, the error in metabolism is transmitted by simple recessive genes. The aberrant gene blocks the metabolism of phenylalanine to tyrosine, and this problem is thought to result from the absence or inactivity of the enzyme phenylalaninehydroxidase. Neither Hurst nor anyone else claims such precise chemical detail for depression or any of the endogenous psychoses.

The role of hormonal dysfunction as an etiolgical force in depression is supported by the differential rate of depression in men and women. According to Kraines, the cyclic variations in activity of the gonads is associated with the relatively greater frequency of depression in women.

Evidence which has been interpreted by a number of investigators (Kraines, 1957; Silverman, 1968) as support for the biogenetic view is the theory and research of Sheldon and his colleagues (Sheldon, Stevens, & Tucker, 1940). In Sheldon's view, manic-depressives are more frequently mesomorphs or have a body type which is a combination of endomorphy and mesomorphy. In this framework the depressive would be more likely to have a body build somewhere between the stocky, athletic type, and the rotund type.

II. SOCIOCULTURAL FACTORS IN DEPRESSION

There are a number of factors which may be considered as predominantly sociocultural in nature. These are family background, ethnic membership, social class, and urban versus rural residence. However, such factors as family background and ethnic membership may be confounded with a biogenetic component.

A. FAMILY BACKGROUND

Family background characteristics of 12 manic-depressive patients have been studied intensively by Fromm-Reichmann (1953). She noted that each of the families of these 12 manic-depressive patients was set apart from the social milieu by some factor that singled it out and made it different. The particular factor varied from family to family. In some cases it was minority-group membership. In others it was an economic factor such as a deteriorating social position and, in still other cases, other family members had been hospitalized with a psychotic condition. The predepressive person felt the social difference keenly and reacted to it with intense concern and effort to correct it. The need to change the family image or status was frequently in the picture. In most of the cases, the mother was pictured as an aggressive, intensely ambitious person who tended to devalue the father and blame him for the family's bad luck. Fathers were perceived by these patients as weak but loveable.

Most of the manic-depressive patients that Fromm-Reichmann (1953) studied had apparently experienced normal infancies. The mothers seemingly found the child more acceptable and loveable in infancy than in later childhood, when the vicissitudes of socialization brought about problems and conflicts.

Our impression is that it was the utter dependence of the infant which was pleasurable to the mother, and that the growing independence and rebelliousness of the early stage of childhood were threatening to her. Unconforming or unconventional behavior on the part of the child was labeled as "bad" by the mother, and she exerted great pressure to stamp it out [Fromm-Reichmann, 1953, p. 50].

This behavior on the part of the previously altogether-loving mother created emotional problems for the child and laid the groundwork for the manic-depressive's later ambivalence.

Perhaps due to the mother's ambition and aggressiveness, the depressives as children were frequently pushed into responsible roles in the family group at a very early age. In later life, the depressives remained extremely sensitive to competition.

Fromm-Reichmann argued that the depressive patients had different appraisals of one or both of their parents than did other members of their family. As a result of their different view of these significant others (parents), the manic-depressives were extremely lonely even during early childhood.

Fromm-Reichmann described the adult character of the manic-depressive as a person who is typically conventional, well-behaved, hard-working, and conscientious. He is usually involved with one or more people on whom he is extremely dependent.

B. ETHNIC MEMBERSHIP

As Fromm-Reichmann noted, membership in a minority group may be a factor that sets a family apart and helps create a climate for the development of depression. A number of other investigators have found some relationship between ethnic membership and depression. Prange and Vitols (1962) found a greater frequency of depression among whites than among blacks. Tonks, Paykel, and Klerman (1970) compared blacks and whites in terms of type of symptoms reported and severity of depression. They found no evidence for the notion that depression in blacks is more often associated with physical symptoms than in whites. They did find that black depressives reported a lower frequency of guilt feelings, pessimism and hopelessness, helplessness, and insomnia. They thought that most of these differences were related to a significant difference between the blacks and whites on their measure of severity of depression, with whites reporting more severe symptoms. This difference in reported severity held up even when investigators controlled for differences in social class. Their data were obtained by way of interviews and classified by means of a rating scale for depression. The authors speculated that the difference in ratings of severity of illness might possibly be attributed to differences in quality of communication between the black patients and the white psychiatrists who did the interviews and obtained the basic data. They also thought that the difference in severity might be real and based on the possibility that Negro families may be less tolerant of depressive behavior and depressive symptoms.

Silverman (1968) has reviewed a number of studies relating ethnic membership and depression. In commenting on the differences found among blacks and whites, she suggested that the lower incidence of depression among blacks may be associated to some extent with relatively less availability of treatment facilities for the black population. She indicated that some changes in patterns of psychiatric problems among blacks have been noted since the recent increase in racial integration.

Silverman noted that depression has been reported to be completely absent among the Anabaptist sect of Hutterites. Depression has also been found very infrequently in Africa and Ireland and reported to be high in England.

C. SOCIAL CLASS, URBAN–RURAL, AND SEASONAL FACTORS

The relationship between social class and mental disorder remains unsettled. There have been a number of studies that implicate social class as a determining variable in a number of psychopathological problems. However, according to Silverman, the relationship between depression and social factors is generally lower than in the case of other disorders.

Two other factors that have been studied in relation to the epidemiology of depression are urban–rural differences and seasonal variation. Silverman has reported that depression is not as sensitive to urban–rural differences as is schizophrenia. However, there seems to be more seasonal variation in depression than in other disorders.

Kraines (1957) has reported that the highest incidence of depression occurs in the spring and fall, with peaks in March and September.

III. COGNITIVE FACTORS AND A
DETAILED COGNITIVE THEORY

As Beck (1967) has pointed out, a number of classical and contemporary writers have placed emphasis on the role of cognitive factors in psychopathology in general and in depression in particular. More than 40 years ago, Jelliffee (1931) attributed depression to a series of false conceptions. More recently Kelly (1955) developed the concept of personal constructs and described problems of adjustment in terms of the way the individual construes the world about him. Similarly, Harvey, Hunt, and Schroder (1961) introduced the notion that concepts have the status of personality structures. They argue that individuals differ markedly in terms of certain identifiable, conceptual styles that explain the person's adjustment or his psychopathology.

Jacobson (1967) suggested that depression may be triggered by visual imagery that might be clear or vague, steady or fleeting. Jacobson introduced the fascinating notion of subvisualization, which he considered to be a missing link in the psychology of imagery. Subvisualization occurs when visual imagery becomes so diminished or fleeting as to pass beyond the threshold of identification.

Arieti (1970) began his discussion of depression by distinguishing between three levels or orders of emotion. The first order is stimulus-induced emotion. The second is image-induced emotion, and the third order is even further removed from objective stimuli. Arieti considered depression to be a third-order emotion, an emotion that involves language and more "cognitive work" than second-order and first-order emotions. Thus, while Arieti defines depression as an emotion, it is an emotion linked closely with language and cognitive processes. In contrast to the anxious person who anticipates the future occurrence of a situation fraught with danger, the depressive feels that the dangerous or bad thing has already happened and now dominates the thinking of the individual. Arieti considered depression as adaptive in the sense that it stimulated the person to reject the troublesome emotion and attempt to remove it.

Arieti followed cognitive theory very closely in his ideas of psychotherapy for the depressive. Psychotherapy, according to

Arieti (1970), consists of reorganizing the person's thinking. In spontaneous remissions, the individual is forced by his sadness and dejection and other depressive affects to reorganize his thinking. While the anxious individual may find relief by getting away from the painful stimulus, for the depressive the moving away is strictly psychological, a matter of getting away from depressive thoughts. "The escape from depression can only occur through cognitive means [p. 142]." For the most part, Arieti's analysis of depression could be derived from the principle of cognition–emotion interaction, but differential emotion theory views the emotions as primary and advocates dealing with them directly in psychotherapy (Izard, 1971).

A. CRITICISMS OF PSYCHOANALYTIC THEORY

Beck pointed out that psychoanalytic writers variously viewed depressive symptomatology in terms of gratification of drives or as defenses against these drives, while yet others emphasized the adaptive aspects of symptomatology. Many psychodynamic writers ascribe some purpose to the symptoms, such as sadness being an attempt to manipulate people. Beck criticized the notion that symptoms were purposive on the grounds that this was a teleological concept. Beck noted that teleological concepts have sometimes limited progress in science, but he failed to note that total abandonment of the concept of purposiveness in behavior made for an oversimplified mechanistic model that may place even greater limitations on the human sciences.

Beck made two quite telling criticisms of the psychoanalytic formulations of depression. First, some of the conceptualizations are so remote from observable behavior that they defy validation. He gave as examples the notion that in depression, the sadistic part of the ego attacks the incorporated love object and the notion that adult depression is a reactivation of early infantile depression. Second, Beck pointed out that the psychoanalytic hypothesis, which holds that depression is characterized by increased orality and repressed hostility, has been applied to numerous other psychological disorders. Beck also indicated that psychoanalytic theories often account for only some aspects of the complex picture of depression and correctly pointed out that any adequate theory would have to account for a wide variety of psychopathological phenomena.

B. BECK'S PRIMARY TRIAD OF COGNITIVE DETERMINANTS

Beck described as the three major cognitive patterns in depression the individual's way of viewing himself, his world, and his future. In describing this "primary triad" of cognitive determinants, Beck assumes that cognition is the principal determinant of emotion, mood, and action. Differential emotion theory considers the emotions as primary determinants, with subsystem interactions as complementary determinants. According to Beck, the first component of the primary triad—viewing himself in a negative way—causes the depressive to see himself as inadequate and unworthy and to attribute his miserable existence to physical, mental, or moral defects in himself. The second component—construing experience in a negative way—leads the depressive to interpret his interactions as failures, as leading to defeat and disparagement. Life is seen as a series of burdens and obstacles. The third component—viewing the future in a negative way—causes the depressive to anticipate that suffering, frustration, and deprivation will continue indefinitely in the future.

The depressive's negative view of himself, his world, and his future are seen by Beck as causes of depressed mood, paralysis of will, avoidance wishes, suicidal wishes, and increased dependency. As a result of the depressive's negative interpretation of experience, he may take a neutral attitude on the part of a friend or loved one as complete rejection. As this attitude becomes severe, it can lead to distorted conceptualizations and deviations from logical thinking, such as arbitrary inferences and overgeneralizations. A single difficulty may cause him to generalize an impossible barrier between himself and his goal. The result is a feeling of being aborted or defeated. He may interpret trivial setbacks as major losses, and neutral remarks as insults or ridicule.

Beck considers the negative view of self as the determinant of self-devaluation and self-blame. Other investigators have shown that the paranoid patient may see others as thwarting or rejecting him, but he somehow manages to maintain a positive concept of himself (Havner & Izard, 1962). While the paronoid will blame others for his deprivation, the depressed patient, because of the negative view of self, will blame himself. He may generalize for a single mistake to an undesirable character trait. Failure to get a date on a single occasion may lead him to feel that he is repulsive to the opposite sex. Beck, like the psychoanalytic thinkers, sees the negative self-concept as associated with self-rejection and self-dislike, but he does not place much emphasis on the component of hostility. Differential emotion theory maintains that it is essentially the patient's distress (sadness, dejection, and discouragement) that leads to a negative view of the world and that it is inner-directed hostility (inner-directed anger, disgust, and contempt) that leads to a negative concept of self. My difference with Beck is essentially in what is to be considered cause and what effect. While there are undoubtedly circular–feedback relations between emotion and cognition, much of the evidence presented for the biogenetic view and some of the evidence considered in the biochemistry of depression support the differential emotion theory position that emotions and the associated neural and biochemical processes are the determinants of cognitive as well as motivational and physical–vegetative symptoms.

The depressive's negative view of the future causes him to continually expect the worst. His present miserable state is not expected to improve or to have any limit in time. While the anxious patient may find some relief in the possibility of avoiding danger or in the passage of an unpleasant situation in time, the depressive sees himself as already hurt and the future as a continuation of his misery.

C. COGNITIVE THEORY IN RELATION TO DIFFERENTIAL EMOTION THEORY

Beck takes essentially the same position in regard to emotion as the cognitive theories discussed in Chapter Four. He sees affect or emotion as a consequence of cognitive processes, particularly as a consequence of the way the individual views himself and his world. Thus if a depressive thinks he is rejected or is a social outcast, he will feel lonely. If he thinks he will never get better, he will feel sad and hopeless. But surely the opposite conclusion is equally plausible: The emotions determine the depressive's way of thinking. Distress and inner-directed hostility tend to isolate a person and lead to loneliness, and distress and guilt lead to pessimism.

Beck also sees cognition as a determinant of changes in motivation, such as paralysis of the will and escape and dependency wishes. In this respect, Beck's failure to delineate the motivational properties of emotion and cognition creates considerable difficulty for his theory. Loss of motivation is viewed as the result of the patient's pessimism. His continual expectation of negative outcomes, from all effort, strips him of internal stimulation to do anything.

Loss of motivation and lack of internal stimulation may not be really characteristic of the depressive at all. Conflicts between emotions and inappropriate emotion–cognition interactions or relationships appear a more likely set of determinants of the apparent paralysis of will, or loss of motivation for conventional pursuits and achievement.

Avoidance and escape wishes, including suicidal thoughts, are seen by Beck as following from the depressive's expectations of a dire future, but a more parsimonious explanation would be that the patient is responding directly to the overwhelming negative emotions (distress, inner-directed hostility, and guilt) of depression. Increased dependency, seen by Beck as a result of the patient's negative view of himself and his consequent feelings of inadequacy and undesirability, can well be interpreted as a direct result of the distress (sadness, dejection, and misery) and the crippling effects of the other negative emotions.

Beck admits that the physical symptoms of depression present difficulties for his cognitive theory. He sees retardation as passive resignation and agitated depression as frantic search for relief from misery. Differential emotion theory interprets retardation as a result of the overwhelming distress and emotion–emotion conflicts that are paramount in all severe depressions. As already indicated, both psychoanalytic theory and differential emotion theory relate agitated depression to inner- and outer-directed hostility on the one hand and to anticipated fear and guilt on the other.

By far the most serious question to be put to Beck's theory is this: How does the depressed individual come to have persistently negative views of self, world, and future? According to Beck, these concepts of the individual are drawn from his experience, his perceptions of the attitudes and opinions of others, and his identifications with the important others in his life—parents, siblings, friends. When one asks what causes others' perceptions and attitudes toward the depressive or predepressive person, it becomes obvious that Beck's reasoning is circular. Also, one of Beck's criticisms of the psychoanalytic position seems now to hold for this aspect of his own theory. A negative self-concept and a negative view of the world and the future might well relate to a number of adjustment and psychopathological problems. This phenomenological or perceptual view of personality and self-concept development, systematically presented by Combs and Snygg (1959), makes for an excellent description of one aspect of the person and his behavior. However, it fails to account adequately for the role of the emotions in personality development and personality functioning.

227

The case has been made for considering fundamental emotions as innate and universal (Tomkins, 1962; Izard, 1971). The position represented by these authors holds that while cognition may trigger emotion, emotion may be viewed as an even more fundamental determinant of cognition. Furthermore, emotion may be triggered by other emotions, by innate releasers, perception, and imaging. The individual's personal experiences may well influence the patterning of emotions in his personality organization. Experience may well contribute to the development of a pattern of emotions that constitutes depression, but genetic and biochemical factors can contribute to the same result.

Instead of seeing a pattern of emotions as defining and determining depression, Beck (1967) sees a matrix or schema. A schema is a cognitive structure, a component of cognitive organization, which combines with the properties of a stimulus object to determine how the object or idea will be perceived and conceptualized. "A schema is a structure for screening, coding, and evaluating the stimuli that impinge on the organism . . . the schema condenses and molds the raw data into cognitions [p. 283]." The schemata of depression involve themes of personal deficiency, self-blame, and negative expectations, according to Beck. Again the critical question to put to this aspect of Beck's theory is: What determines the necessary selectivity of perception and cognition that go into the making of a schema? The answer, according to differential emotion theory, would be a fundamental emotion or some pattern or combination of them.

In the concluding paragraphs of the statement of his theory, Beck acknowledges the possibility that a circular feedback model would make a more adequate theory of depression. In the circular feedback model, he would see not only cognition causing emotion but emotion influencing thought content. Thus, schemata would influence affective structures and affective structures in turn would influence schemas. Here Beck has come close to one of the key concepts in differential emotion theory which holds that emotion, cognition, and action systems all have motivational properties and that feedback and interactive processes among these systems characterize much of complex human behavior.

IV. THE SYMPTOMATOLOGY AND PHENOMENOLOGY OF DEPRESSION

Though not an integral part of his theory, Beck's description of the symptomatology and phenomenology of depression is exceptionally clear and complete, and warrants review here. He described depression as characterized by a set of interesting paradoxes: The depressed person's image of himself frequently does not fit the objective facts; objective evidence or logic has little effect on the depressive's misconception of himself; behavior is often apparently in conflict with the pleasure principle; psychogenic determinants seem evident in some cases and not in others (frequently no discernible precipitating factor); finally, depression seems to have some characteristics in common with normal moods and feelings (e.g., grief), yet appears to have distinct qualities also. Beck indicated that one of the problems in understanding depression was a semantic one—the fact that depression has been used to indicate a symptom, a symptom complex or syndrome, and a well-defined disease entity.

Beck suggested that describing depression as an affective disorder was as misleading as designating scarlet fever as a disorder of the skin. Affective problems constitute only one of four distinct sets of attributes: affective, cognitive, motivational, and physical—vegetative.

It should be noted that Beck's summary of the symptomatology of depression is supported by extensive clinical and empirical investigations of 288 mildly depressed patients, 377 moderately depressed patients, 86 severely depressed patients, and a control group of 224 nondepressed patients. The data consisted of clinical interviews, psychotherapy content, and objective data obtained by means of his Depression Inventory. The inventory, usually completed by one or more psychiatrists, consisted of ratings in 21 categories of symptoms and attitudes:

1. Mood	12. Social withdrawal
2. Pessimism	13. Indecisiveness
3. Sense of failure	14. Distortion of body image
4. Lack of satisfaction	15. Work inhibition
5. Guilty feeling	16. Sleep disturbance
6. Sense of punishment	17. Fatigability
7. Self-dislike	18. Loss of appetite
8. Self-accusations	19. Weight loss
9. Suicidal wishes	20. Somatic preoccupation
10. Crying spells	21. Loss of libido
11. Irritability	

These categories, which fall into the four major groupings mentioned earlier, serve as something of a summary of the symptomatology of the depressive. Beck found that all 21 items in the inventory occurred more frequently in depressives than in nondepressed patients.

A. EMOTIONAL MANIFESTATIONS

The first major grouping of depressive symptoms described by Beck was emotional manifestations. The most prominent and frequent of these is a dejected mood, described by some patients with somatic terms such as a lump in the throat, an empty feeling in the stomach, or a heavy feeling in the chest. Other patients use more conventional affective adjectives such as sad, unhappy, lonely, miserable, hopeless, blue, down-hearted, humiliated, ashamed, worried, guilty. One can see in the adjectives summarized by Beck indicators of at least two fundamental emotions, distress and shame, the latter including guilt.

Beck (1967) found that not all the depressives reported a subjective change in mood. While the most moderately and severely depressed patients reported emotional distress, only 53% of his sample of mildly depressed patients reported feeling sad or unhappy. He found that such patients complained that they had lost their goals and direction, that they did not care, or that they did not see any point in living. It is difficult for the present writer to see how individuals could make such complaints and not feel any of the negative affects usually associated with depression.

The second type of emotional manifestation consists of negative feelings toward the self. Such feelings may be similar in tone to the ones mentioned above, but in this case they are inner-directed.

The third emotional manifestation is reduction in gratification or loss of gratification. This most common symptom was reported by 92% of the severely depressed patients in Beck's sample. Particularly, the person's social experiences lose their capacity to be pleasurable and gratifying. In differential emotion theory, the loss of pleasure relates more to the drive system than to the emotion system, but Beck does not make such distinctions as that between drive-pleasure and joy.

The fourth type of emotional manifestation is loss of emotional attachments. This manifests itself as loss of interest in other people and their activities and loss of affection or concern.

The fifth emotional manifestation of depression consists of crying spells or an increased tendency to cry. In very severe cases, Beck found patients who wept without tears, or who were no longer able to cry even when they felt extremely sad and wanted to cry. This seems to be a special case of the first emotional manifestation, an expression of sadness or dejected mood.

230

The final emotional manifestation discussed by Beck was loss of ability of the patient to enjoy humorous situations. In his study, 52% of the severely depressed patients, as opposed to 8% of nondepressed, reported that they had lost their sense of humor. This would contribute to low scores on the enjoyment–joy factor of the Differential Emotion Scale (Izard, 1969).

B. COGNITIVE MANIFESTATIONS

The second major set of symptoms was described by Beck as cognitive manifestations, characteristics which differential emotion theory interprets as the result of emotion–cognition interactions. The first of these is low self-evaluation, the tendency of the person to see himself as deficient in attributes that are particularly important to him. Such attributes may include intelligence, health, personal attractiveness, or financial resources. The patient tends to describe himself as inferior and inadequate. Perhaps due to the fact that Beck does not think in terms of personality subsystems and subsystem interactions, he does not clearly distinguish between low self-evaluation as a cognitive manifestation and negative feelings toward self as an emotional manifestation. Nor does he consider the possibility that both are results of subsystem interactions.

Beck termed the second cognitive symptom negative expectations and saw it as related to the affective manifestation of feelings of hopelessness. The depressed patient always thinks that things will get worse while, in contrast, the anxious patient may temper his negative anticipations with the possibility that he may avoid them or that they will pass in time.

The third cognitive manifestation consists of self-blame and self-criticism. The depressed feels he is deficient, then blames and criticizes himself for the alleged deficiencies. It appears that this is another cognitive manifestation that is closely related to the emotional manifestation of negative feelings toward self. This manifestation is as close as Beck comes to recognizing a factor of inner-directed hostility.

The fourth type of cognitive symptom is indecisiveness, seen on the one hand as anticipation of making the wrong decision and on the other as "paralysis of the will," avoidance tendencies, or increased dependency. The present writer sees indecisiveness, as defined by Beck, as another consequence of conflicts between emotional tendencies; for example, anger toward self versus anger toward others, or outer-directed anger versus feelings of guilt or fear.

The last type of cognitive symptom in Beck's system is distortion of body image. The patient often sees himself as physically unattractive. This was the case with 66% of the severely depressed patients in Beck's sample.

C. MOTIVATIONAL MANIFESTATIONS

The third major set of depressive symptoms consists of motivational manifestations, other characteristics which differential emotion theory interprets as primarily the result of emotion–cognition interactions. Beck pointed out that the characteristic motivations of the depressed are regressive in nature. The depressive tends toward more childlike roles, preferring passivity to activity and dependence to independence, and tends to have difficulty postponing gratification and seeking long-term goals, preferring immediate though transient gratification.

The second type of motivational manifestation, as characterized by Beck, is similar to the psychoanalytic concept of paralysis of the will, a characteristic also discussed as indecisiveness under cognitive symptoms. The depressed patient appears to lack self-direction or the inner stimulus to activity. Positive motivation is lacking. This motivational manifestation was described by Beck as avoidance, escapist, and withdrawal wishes. The patient seeks diversion or escape through passive recreation such as going to the movies, watching television, getting drunk, using drugs, or day-dreaming.

The third motivational manifestation is the suicidal wish. This symptom was reported by 74% of the severely depressed in contrast to only 12% of the nondepressed patients in Beck's sample. Beck considered the suicidal wish as highly diagnostic of severe depression and cautioned clinicians to take the threat of suicide seriously. In his experience, a substantial proportion of those who threatened suicide eventually attempted it, and a fair percentage of those who attempted it continued these attempts until they succeeded.

The fourth motivational manifestation was termed increased dependency by Beck. This was described as a desire to receive help, guidance, or direction and was distinguished from the actual process of relying on someone elso as seen in the cognitive manifestations of indecisiveness.

232

D. VEGETATIVE AND PHYSICAL MANIFESTATIONS

The fourth and last major set of symptoms discussed by Beck was vegetative and physical manifestations. In terms of differential emotion theory, these manifestations result from the interactions of bodily feelings, cognition, and emotion. The first of these manifestations was loss of appetite, reported by 72% of the severely depressed patients in contrast to only 21% of the nondepressed patients. The severely depressed sometimes have an aversion to food with a subsequent substantial loss in body weight.

The second physical manifestation in Beck's scheme was sleep disturbance, a symptom noted by almost all students of depression. While only 40% of nondepressed patients reported this symptom, 87% of the severely depressed patients reported it. Loss of libido, or of interest in sex, was reported by 61% of depressed patients and only 27% of nondepressed patients. The last physical or vegetative change noted by Beck was fatigability, which was found in 79% of depressed patients and only 33% of nondepressed patients. This symptom is often described as a feeling of heaviness in the limbs and body, as loss of pep or energy, or as listlessness and weakness. Beck noted that fatigability was often difficult to distinguish from loss of motivation and avoidance wishes.

Beck thought that depression is fairly easily diagnosed by inspection. The depressed person typically has a distressed, sad, or dejected expression and is either retarded or agitated. Occasionally depressives will conceal their distress behind a cheerful face, but careful interviewing will evoke the distressful facial expression. In retardation, the depressed shows a reduction in spontaneous activity, a tendency to stay in one position longer than usual, and to use a minimum of expressive and gestural cues. His movements are slow and deliberate. The agitated depressive is almost continuously active, finding it difficult to remain still for any length of time. He seems to be responding to his inability to accept or tolerate the gloomy state in which he finds himself and the continual worsening of the situation that he anticipates in the future.

In my view, Beck's system does not do a very effective job of accounting for his four major classes of symptoms. For example, cognitive determinants and physical–vegetative symptoms have little relationship, as Beck acknowledges. The great generality and flexibility of the fundamental emotions, with respect to their activation and their association or attachment to a multiplicity of stimuli, and their interactions with cognition, drives, and other bodily states, make it possible for differential emotion theory to develop a better account of the multifaceted clinical picture of depression.

V. SOME PERSONALITY (TEST) CHARACTERISTICS OF DEPRESSION

Hoffman (1970) has studied the personality characteristics of depressives using Jackson's Personality Research Form. He found depressed patients to be significantly higher in abasement, harmavoidance, and succorance. Depressives were significantly lower in achievement, dominance, endurance, exhibitionism, sentience, understanding, and desirability. Hoffman thought the depressives' profile on these traits, as defined by their item content, was consistent with the clinical picture of depression. He also found that depressed patients exhibited an acquiescence response set that was specifically related to and dependent upon the content of the personality dimension involved. For example, depressives endorsed "true" items more frequently in achieving their elevated means on abasement, harmavoidance, and succorance. In scales where the depressives had significantly lower scores than normals (achievement, dominance, endurance, and exhibition), they endorsed the "false" items less frequently.

VI. SUMMARY

The picture of depression is not complete without a consideration of biogenetic, sociocultural, and cognitive factors. Theory or research in each of these areas has contributed something to our understanding of the subject.

Kraines (1957) presented a rather detailed biogenetic theory of depression. He considered the etiology of depression to be essentially physiological (hereditary and hormonal influences). Kraines defined the mechanism of depression as dysfunction in three areas of the brain: the diencephalon, rhinencephalon, and the reticular formation. He maintained that biogenetic theory could explain the cyclic nature of depression and the efficacy of radical therapies, phenomena that are inexplicable in terms of psychoanalytic or cognitive theory.

Kraines summarized some rather convincing evidence for the role of heredity in depression. For example, when one member of monozygnotic twins has manic depression, between 70 and 96% of the other twins will also suffer from manic-depressive psychosis.

Kraines pointed out the relationship between biological factors and a number of depressive symptoms. He attributed visual paresthesias to disturbance in the optic thalamus and emotional isolation to inappropriate transmission or ineffective integration of the sensory processes involved in emotion. The research on the biochemistry of depression and on body types and depression are compatible with Kraines's biogenetic theory. To my knowledge no theories altogether rule out neurophysiological, biochemical, or biogenetic factors in depression.

A number of studies have found apparent relationships between sociocultural factors and the occurrence of depression. Depression has been reported less frequently in Africa and Ireland than in England. Some studies have suggested that blacks suffer less frequently and less severely from depression. However, some sociocultural factors such as family background and ethnic membership may be confounded with hereditary factors.

Fromm-Reichmann (1953) made an intensive study of the families of 12 manic-depressive patients and found that each family was set apart from the social milieu by some factor—minority group membership, deteriorating social position, high status need. She found that depressive children tended to perceive their parents differently from their normal siblings and, as a result, different parent–child relationships obtained.

Beck (1967) has presented a comprehensive cognitive theory of depression. His central theses are very similar to those of the cognitive theorists reviewed in the study of anxiety. Essentially he maintains that cognition is the primary determinant of emotions, moods, and behavior. He described as the primary triad of cognitive determinants the individual's way of viewing himself, his world, and his future. The negative view of self causes the depressive to see himself as inadequate and unworthy and to attribute his misery to personal defects. His negative view of the world leads him to interpret his interactions as failures, steps toward defeat and disparagement. His negative view of the future causes him to anticipate an indefinite continuation of his suffering. Beck explains most of the typical depressive symptoms such as paralysis of will, suicidal wishes, and self-devaluation as the result of one or the other of these cognitive determinants.

Differential emotion theory raises a number of critical questions for Beck's theory. The most important of these is the question as to how the individual comes to have persistently negative views of self, world, and future. To say that these are built up through experience and the reaction of others seems to be circular reasoning.

Instead of seeing a pattern of emotions as defining and determining depression, Beck sees a cognitive organization or schema that determines how an object or idea will be perceived and conceptualized. The schemata of depression involve such themes as personal deficiency and negative expectations. Beck does not address himself to the problem as to the determinants of the necessary selectivity of perception and cognition that go into the making of a schema. Differential emotion theory holds that such schemata develop from emotion–cognition interactions, with fundamental emotions or patterns of emotions serving as the primary determinants.

Beck presents a rather complete picture of the symptomatology and phenomenology of depression. Although his analysis has a cognitive theory bias, it is quite comprehensive and useful. He summarizes the attributes of the depressive in four major groupings. Emotional manifestations are exemplified by the frequently observed sadness or dejected mood. Cognitive manifestations are exemplified by the depressive's tendency to see himself as deficient in attributes that are particularly important to him. Motivational manifestations are exemplified by passivity, dependence, withdrawal wishes, and paralysis of the will. Vegetative and physical manifestations are exemplified by loss of appetite and sleep disturbance.

From the standpoint of differential emotion theory, Beck's groupings are rather arbitrary and overlapping. Surely emotional manifestations and motivational manifestations have common roots in emotion processes. Cognitive manifestations and physical and vegetative manifestations are also undoubtedly influenced in some way and to some extent by one or more of the fundamental emotions.

CHAPTER TEN

Depression as a Pattern of Emotions and Feelings: Factor-Analytic Investigations *

I. INTRODUCTION

The differential emotion theory conception of depression as a combination of components is explicitly or implicitly supported by two disparate approaches—the psychoanalytic and the factor analytic. Although there are some differences among psychoanalytic theorists, they all agree that depression involves a number of different emotions. Similarly, factor-analytic investigators derive somewhat different sets of factors for depression, which follow from differences in the item content of their instruments, but most of them find a common core of factors. The psychoanalytic conceptions were presented in Chapter Eight; the present chapter will present the results of factor-analytic studies.

One purpose of factor-analytic investigations was the development of better measures for differentiating among subtypes of depression. Overall, Hollister, Johnson, and Pennington (1966) observed that the apparently contradictory results obtained in many drug studies may be due in part to failure to differentiate subtypes of depression, or depressions with different components. In an earlier study comparing a tranquilizer and an antidepressant, the authors obtained puzzling results from a heterogeneous group of depressives

*This chapter was written in collaboration with Alan G. Marshall as first author.

(Overall *et al.*, 1966). In order to clarify these results, they rated 160 hospitalized depressives on the Brief Psychiatric Rating Scale, factor-analyzed the data, and used scores on the resulting factors to assign the 77 patients in the original study to hostile, anxious, or psycho-motor-retarded groups. With this differentiation, they were able to demonstrate the superiority of the tranquilizer in treating anxious patients and the superiority of the antidepressant in treating the psychomotor-retarded patients.

Beck (1967) also noted the heterogeneity of the concept of depression and studied it from five vantage points, including cognitive patterns in dreams and in psychotherapy, and incidence of childhood bereavement. In a factor analysis of questionnaire data on 135 depressives (Delay, Pichot, Lemperiere, & Mirouze, 1963; Pichot & Lemperiere, 1964) Beck found four factors: *(a)* vital depression— lack of appetite, sleep difficulties, etc., *(b)* self-abasement, *(c)* pessimism–suicide, and *(d)* indecision–inhibition. The absence of more purely emotional factors such as distress and guilt found in most studies may be due in part to the fact that Beck's cognitive theory of depression, discussed in Chapter Nine, guided the selection of the questionnaire items.

In a study by Grinker, Miller, Sabshin, Nunn, and Nunnally (1961), psychiatric residents and graduate psychiatric nurses rated 120 hospitalized depressives on a "feelings and concerns" checklist and a "current behaviors" checklist. Five factors were extracted from "feelings and concerns": *(a)* "essential" depression— feelings common to nearly all depressions such as sadness, hopelessness, and self-recrimination; *(b)* the attribution of misery to external causes; *(c)* a predominance of guilt feelings over aggressive impulses; *(d)* a predominance of anxiety; *(e)* the clinging, demanding attitude. The first factor was considered to be the foundation of depression, while the other four were thought to be ways of dealing with the underlying misery by projection, restitution, anxiety, and compensation.

The "current behaviors" checklist yielded 10 factors: *(a)* isolation, *(b)* retardation (psychomotor), *(c)* disinterest, *(d)* provocative anger, *(e)* hypochondriasis, *(f)* cognitive disturbance, *(g)* agitation, *(h)* rigidity, *(i)* somatic disturbance, *(j)* clinging, pleading demands for attention.

An additional factor analysis employed the scores of each of the 96 patients on all 15 factors in order to determine which groups of patients had common factor patterns. This analysis yielded four groups: *(a)* classical depressives, who are dismal, self-deprecating, retarded in movement, and outwardly neither hostile nor demanding; (b) depressives who exhibit more anxiety and agitation, more clinging demands for attention and approval; (c) patients who show more blaming of the environment, more hypochondriasis, more cognitive disturbance, and less distress; (d) angry depressives who are explosive, narcissistic, and who feel less gloom and guilt than the others. The last group was thought to be highly suicidal.

Friedman, Cowitz, Cohen, and Granick (1963) factor-analyzed scores on the Philadelphia Psychiatric Hospital Depression Rating Scale for 170 depressed patients. From the 60 items on this scale, the 22 most reliable and frequently used were selected for use in the factor analysis. Varimax rotation yielded four interpretable factors: (a) the classical mood depression with guilt, loss of self-esteem, and doubting; (b) the retarded, withdrawn, apathetic depression; (c) the primarily biological reaction with loss of appetite, sleep disturbance, constipation, work inhibition, and loss of satisfaction; (d) the querulous, hypochondriacal, self-preoccupied, demanding, and complaining type. Both Friedman et al. and Grinker et al. noted the newness of this last type of depression, and suggested that it is peculiar to the 20th century and is being encountered with increasing frequency.

Cattell and Bjerstedt (1966) factor-analyzed scores on a 73-item depression questionnaire administered to 78 adult mental hospital patients and 61 controls. They then readministered the questionnaire one month later to 65 patients and 48 normal controls from the same original populations and factor-analyzed the data. They performed a third factor analysis on an extended 236-item questionnaire given to 163 young adult males. Seven factors replicated across the three analyses. The psychological interpretation of their content was as follows: (a) exhaustion, hypochondria; (b) suicidal disgust versus zest; (c) restless, brooding discontent; (d) anxious or agitated depression; (e) simple or low-energy depression; (f) guilt and resentment; (g) bored depression and withdrawal. The authors concluded that there was no general factor in depression, but rather, a diversity of component factors.

With the exception of the study by Cattell and Bjerstedt, the above factor analyses were performed on hospitalized depressed patients, and ratings were done by persons other than the patients themselves. The median ages of the patients were between 35 and 45. Most of these studies found an essential component of distress (sadness, discouragement, and dejection) in depression, often accompanied by sleep disturbance and psychomotor retardation. The

239

content of other common factors included hostility, anxiety, self-dislike, and guilt. Most authors agreed that depressives could be differentiated into subtypes on the basis of patternings of the above factors.

The present studies were designed to extend the factor-analytic investigation of depression to normal subjects of younger age and to obtain the data directly from the subjects themselves. The central hypothesis was that depression is multidimensional, involving a number of interacting fundamental emotions and feelings. The term "feelings" is used here to refer to the impressions derived from bodily feelings associated with changes in homeostatic and drive processes, such as sleep, sexual arousal, and appetite. Thus these feelings are nonemotional, but they may have important interactions with emotions as well as with cognition and action. This distinction between emotions and bodily feelings, apparently an important one in the study of depression, is discussed further in Chapter Eleven.

With regard to the emotions, we expected that mean scores in an imagined depression situation would be highest for the factor representing distress, next highest for the factors representing the emotions anger, disgust, and contempt (hostility), and next highest for the factors representing shame (guilt, shyness) and fear. We expected the means for the factors associated with bodily feelings to be less affected than the emotion factors.

It was also expected that the studies might throw light on some of the psychoanalytic notions of depression components, in particular the Freudian hypothesis of the centrality of inner-directed anger in depression. Freud (1917) postulated the importance of "retroflected rage," turning resentment and anger against the self. A hostility factor was elicited in three of the factor-analytic investigations cited above, but it was not identified specifically as inner-directed. In the present studies, separate sets of items were included for hostility toward self and hostility toward others. Furthermore, the rating scale included a wider range of better-defined fundamental emotions than in former studies in order to test more effectively the hypothesis that a variety of discrete emotions and feelings contribute importantly to the phenomena of depression.

Two studies were done, the second being an attempt to replicate the findings obtained in the first investigation. The initial study, with students in a private university, will be presented fully. The second, which used the same method in a different population (public high-school students), will be treated more briefly.

240

II. STUDY I

A. METHOD

1. Subjects. Subjects were 332 students in undergraduate psychology courses at Vanderbilt University. Participation in the experiment satisfied part of the class requirement for involvement in research projects. No student declined to participate.

2. Scales. The self-report scale used in the study of depression was designated the DES+D. The 33-item Differential Emotion Scale provided 35 items, some items being used in both inner- and outer-directed form. Several factor analyses of this form of the DES have yielded a rather consistent set of factors. These statistically derived empirical factors correspond quite closely with the theoretically defined (a priori) emotion factors, and both the statistical and a priori factors display good reliability. The DES a priori factors and their item content are shown in Table 10-1.

Thirty-two depression items were added from Zuckerman's (1960) Multiple Affect Adjective Checklist (MAACL) in order to represent more completely what previous studies have shown to be the essential component of distress. Seven items were adapted from Beck's (1967) Depression Inventory representing phenomena such as cognitive distortion, suicidal tendencies, and loss of sexual interest. Finally, three items were added by the authors on the basis of clinical hunches, making a total of 77 items.

TABLE 10-1
A Priori Factors and Items of the Differential Emotion Scale

A priori factor	Item
Interest	attentive, concentrating, alert
Enjoyment	delighted, happy, joyful
Surprise	surprised, amazed, astonished
Distress	downhearted, sad, discouraged
Disgust	feeling of distaste, disgusted, feeling of revulsion
Anger	enraged, angry, mad
Guilt	repentant, blameworthy, guilty
Shyness	sheepish, bashful, shy
Fear	scared, fearful, afraid
Contempt	contemptuous, scornful, disdainful
Fatigue	fatigued, sluggish, sleepy

The DES+D was broken down into 66 items relating to emotions or feelings within or toward the self and 11 items reflecting emotions or feelings directed toward others. The subjects rated each item on a 5-point scale, anchored by "very slightly or not at all" (1), and "very strongly" (5). The DES+D, along with the instructions for visualizing the depression situation, are presented in Table 10-2.

3. *Procedure.* Prior to completing the DES+D, subjects were asked to cooperate in an investigation of depression. It was explained that the results would be meaningful only if they would attend seriously to the task and try to reflect accurately on their emotions and feelings. It was emphasized that subjects were collaborators in the study, that it would hopefully be relevant to clinical problems, and that there was no deception as to its purpose. Subjects were guaranteed anonymity, and were told that they would get information on the outcome of the study after the data were analyzed.

Subjects were then instructed to try to recall a past occurrence of depression or to imagine a situation that made them depressed, to write a brief description of it, and to complete the DES+D as a means of describing their feelings in the depression situation (see Table 10-2). Later in the same session the subjects, after being divided into six subgroups, completed the DES+D a second time while recalling or imagining a situation that elicited one of the six fundamental emotions: distress, anger, disgust, contempt, guilt, and shyness. The subjects wrote brief descriptions of these emotion situations before taking the DES+D a second time. The numbers of subjects completing the scale for the six emotion situations were comparable.

B. RESULTS

The subjects' free-response descriptions of the depression situation suggested that they were genuinely involved and cooperative. Table 10-3 presents a summary of these data. Many of these descriptions look like rather typical precipitating factors for depression. Although psychotic and neurotic depressions can occur without an apparent precipitating factor, precipitating factors are often present, especially in normal depression. Events or situations which are often a part of the picture in clinical depression and which are listed in Table 10-3, include loss of loved one, separation or alienation from loved ones, loneliness, failure, and heterosocial problems that often involve loss of love or self-esteem. As would be expected

242

in a normal college population, the failures and disappointments were most frequently in the academic and heterosocial realms. The frequency of occurrence of the situations depicted in Table 10-3 is virtually identical to that of precipitating factors described by depressed students who go to the Vanderbilt-Peabody Psychological and Counseling Center for help (Larson, personal communication). The psychiatrist at Student Health gives a very similar picture of the presenting complaints of his depressed student-patients (Wilson, personal communication). He pointed out that academic failure may involve real or perceived failure to please parents and that heterosocial problems may involve violation of moral codes, both of which may result in guilt.

Since depression is considered a combination of emotions and feelings, we expected some overlap between the free-response descriptions of the depression situation and descriptions of the six fundamental emotion situations. The analysis of overlap was not

TABLE 10-2

Instructions for Visualizing the Depression Situation and for
Subsequent Completion of the Scales; and the DES+D Items

Depression

All of us have our own idea as to the meaning of psychological depression and the feelings that go with it. We would like you to use the attached Differential Emotion Scale to describe your personal experience, your own feelings, when you are depressed.

Please try to recall an experience or situation in which you were depressed. Without revealing any names or personal information you do not wish to disclose, identify below the situation or experience you are recalling.

Depression experience:_____

The first set of the Differential Emotion Scale items reflects only feelings *within* or *toward yourself* (items 1-66). The second set of items reflects feelings *toward others* (items 67-77). You will be reminded of this difference prior to completing the latter portion of the scale, which begins with item 67.

Keeping the above depression experience in mind and visualizing or imagining it as vividly as you can, complete the Differential Emotion Scale, indicating the degree to which each word describes your feelings while you are experiencing depression.

(Continued on pages 244-245)

TABLE 10-2 *(Continued)*

DES+D

1	2	3	4	5
very slightly or not at all	slightly	moderately	considerably	very strongly

The first set of items (1-66) refers to feelings *toward* (within, about) *yourself* in the_____situation.

Circle the number which best reflects the intensity of the feeling *toward* (within, about) *yourself* in the_____situation:_____

1.	enraged	1	2	3	4	5
2.	sleepy	1	2	3	4	5
3.	hopeless	1	2	3	4	5
4.	free	1	2	3	4	5
5.	joyful	1	2	3	4	5
6.	sunk	1	2	3	4	5
7.	healthy	1	2	3	4	5
8.	dissatisfied	1	2	3	4	5
9.	loss of sexual interest	1	2	3	4	5
10.	tearful	1	2	3	4	5
11.	sheepish	1	2	3	4	5
12.	tormented	1	2	3	4	5
13.	happy	1	2	3	4	5
14.	fearful	1	2	3	4	5
15.	suicidal	1	2	3	4	5
16.	indecisive	1	2	3	4	5
17.	alive	1	2	3	4	5
18.	shy	1	2	3	4	5
19.	feeling of distaste	1	2	3	4	5
20.	angry	1	2	3	4	5
21.	blameworthy	1	2	3	4	5
22.	alert	1	2	3	4	5
23.	peaceful	1	2	3	4	5
24.	astonished	1	2	3	4	5
25.	low	1	2	3	4	5
26.	lucky	1	2	3	4	5
27.	disgusted	1	2	3	4	5
28.	scornful	1	2	3	4	5
29.	bashful	1	2	3	4	5
30.	feeling of revulsion	1	2	3	4	5
31.	fatigue	1	2	3	4	5
32.	inspired	1	2	3	4	5
33.	young	1	2	3	4	5
34.	mad	1	2	3	4	5
35.	scared	1	2	3	4	5
36.	attentive	1	2	3	4	5
37.	miserable	1	2	3	4	5
38.	good	1	2	3	4	5

39. surprised	1	2	3	4	5
40. discouraged	1	2	3	4	5
41. awful	1	2	3	4	5
42. downhearted	1	2	3	4	5
43. delighted	1	2	3	4	5
44. lost	1	2	3	4	5
45. forlorn	1	2	3	4	5
46. afraid	1	2	3	4	5
47. guilty	1	2	3	4	5
48. sluggish	1	2	3	4	5
49. alone	1	2	3	4	5
50. blue	1	2	3	4	5
51. fine	1	2	3	4	5
52. amazed	1	2	3	4	5
53. lonely	1	2	3	4	5
54. destroyed	1	2	3	4	5
55. fit	1	2	3	4	5
56. terrible	1	2	3	4	5
57. repentant	1	2	3	4	5
58. gloomy	1	2	3	4	5
59. safe	1	2	3	4	5
60. strong	1	2	3	4	5
61. wilted	1	2	3	4	5
62. whole	1	2	3	4	5
63. suffering	1	2	3	4	5
64. clean	1	2	3	4	5
65. rejected	1	2	3	4	5
66. active	1	2	3	4	5

For the following items, rate the extent to which each word describes your feelings *toward* (with, at) *others* when in the_____situation:

67. angry at others	1	2	3	4	5
68. contemptuous of others	1	2	3	4	5
69. mad at others	1	2	3	4	5
70. revulsion toward others	1	2	3	4	5
71. disdainful of others	1	2	3	4	5
72. others as unattractive	1	2	3	4	5
73. disinterested in others	1	2	3	4	5
74. others as distasteful	1	2	3	4	5
75. bitter toward others	1	2	3	4	5
76. envious of others' joy	1	2	3	4	5
77. suspicious of others	1	2	3	4	5

TABLE 10-3

Classification of Free-Response Descriptions of the Depression Situation[a]

Category	Percentage of total	Examples of responses
1. Academic failure, pressure of school work and competition for grades, and related problems	22.3	(a) Failed a course. (b) Failed math exam, first one taken in college. (c) Poor performance on tests and quizzes. (d) Did poorly on exam for which I thought I was prepared. (e) Behind in schoolwork, trying to catch up, but it does little good. (f) Too much homework, too little time, seem to be under it all—super bleak.
2. Heterosocial (boy-girl) problems	21.0	(a) Being away at school, separated from boyfriend. (b) The aftermath of breaking up with a girlfriend. (c) Breaking of an engagement. (d) When my boyfriend dumped me. (e) No letter from girlfriend. (f) After a really terrible date, finding out that the boy I liked had a great time on his date with another girl. (g) My boyfriend found out that I had a "summer fling" and had been unfaithful.
3. Loneliness, separation from loved ones, being left out	14.7	(a) Nothing specific—just alone in a single room. (b) First two weeks at school, knowing no one. (c) Com-

246

No.	Category	%	Examples
			ship with father was poor. (d) Dropped from fraternity rush list. (e) Feelings of total failure and worthlessness when unable to find a date.
4.	Loss or failure in nonacademic competition—sports, campus elections, honors	5.7	(a) Losing an important athletic contest (baseball) that was ultimately "blown." (b) Lost a football game in which I didn't get to play, though I thought I was better than those who did. (c) Lost an election for an office in a club I really wanted.
5.	Death or illness of loved one or friend	4.7	(a) Death of my father. (b) Death of my brother and its impact on my family. (c) Death of a friend in combat. (d) When a teacher of mine became an alcoholic and lost his coaching job.
6.	Difficulties with parents	3.3	(a) Separation of my parents. (b) Parents still treating me like a child. (c) Constantly restricted by uncle, who replaced parents and behaved in totally opposite manner from that of parents.
7.	Categories with less than 3% of total responses: loss of friendship or contacts with people; personal failure; life itself and world situation	18.0	
8.	Responses combining two or more categories	10.0	

[a] College sample ($N = 332$).

done systemetically for all responses, as was done in the anxiety study (Table 5-19). However, inspection of the data showed that every one of the fundamental emotion situations had some descriptions that were identical to those of the depression situation. The free-response data support the differential emotion theory concept of depression as a complex phenomenon that may contain elements of hostility (anger, disgust, contempt), guilt, shyness, and distress. The statistical analyses comparing the a priori and DES+D factor scores in the depression and fundamental emotion situations will be presented in Chapter Eleven.

1. Factor Analysis of the DES+D. Scores on the scales completed in the depression situation were first subjected to a principal axis factor analysis. The factors and item loadings for the promax rotation are shown in Table 10-4. In both of the factor analyses for depression, as in the one for anxiety, the promax and varimax factor structures were virtually identical.

Of the 15 factors extracted, three were deleted on the basis of ambiguity and high secondary loadings of items on other factors. Individual items were deleted if the difference in their primary and secondary loadings was .20 or less. A total of 27 items was thus dropped.

As expected, the largest number of items loaded on a distress factor. This factor included all but three of the Zuckerman depression items and the two Izard distress items that were included in this study. Izard's third distress item (sad) was omitted by mistake. It had previously loaded consistently with the other two items. It was included in the DES+D for the second study, and its primary loading was on the distress factor.

Six of Izard's eleven DES factors emerged precisely as expected, the items matching exactly with the a priori factors. Four other DES factors were clearly interpretable in terms of the a priori emotion categories. An exception was the interest factor, all items of which were questionable in this analysis.

Also as anticipated, the A/D/C (anger, disgust, contempt) items produced two factors, inner- and outer-directed hostility. Differential emotion theory considers hostility as a complex concept similar in nature to anxiety and depression. In the present study, it is operationally defined by the DES+D items relating to anger, disgust, and contempt. Outer-directed hostility represents a new factor in the studies using various forms of the DES.

Two other new factors emerged from the Zuckerman items that did not load on distress. They were interpreted as

248

TABLE 10-4
DES+D Factors: Primary Loadings from Promax Rotation[a,b]

Loneliness	.88 afraid	.65 active
.78 alone	.81 fearful	.62 healthy
.76 lonely		Deleted item:
	Fatigue	.51 young
Distress	.80 fatigued	
.81 miserable	.72 sluggish	*Shyness*
.79 awful	.60 sleepy	.82 bashful
.77 terrible		.77 shy
.72 gloomy	*Sociality/Sexuality*	.70 sheepish
.72 suffering	.67 disinterested in others	
.69 forlorn	.54 others as unattractive	*Joy + D-minus*
.68 downhearted	.49 loss of sexual interest	.78 happy
.65 blue		.76 delighted
(sad, omitted	*Guilt*	.75 joyful
by error)	.83 guilty	.74 fine
Deleted items:	.80 blameworthy	Deleted items:
.65 lost	.70 repentant	.65 good
.62 low		.49 free
.59 tormented	*A/D/C: Hostility,*	.48 peaceful
.58 discouraged	*outer-directed*	.46 lucky
.56 wilted	.85 disdainful of others	
.55 sunk	.84 revulsion toward others	*Defeated*
.54 rejected	.83 mad at others	Deleted items:
.51 tearful	.80 angry at others	.72 destroyed
	.79 contemptuous of others	.64 feeling of
A/D/C: Hostility,	.78 others as distasteful	revulsion
inner-directed	.77 bitter toward others	.60 suicidal
.85 angry	Deleted item:	.56 hopeless
.81 mad	.51 suspicious of others	.46 indecisive
.71 enraged		
.67 disgusted	*Surprise*	*Interest*
Deleted items:	.88 astonished	Deleted items:
.68 scornful	.87 surprised	.67 alert
.57 feeling of	.84 amazed	.64 attentive
distaste		.55 inspired
.42 dissatisfied	*Physical well-being*	.52 alive
	.71 strong	
Fear	.69 safe	*Also deleted:*
.89 scared	.68 fit	envious of
	.68 clean	others' joy
	.67 whole	

[a]College sample, $N = 313$. The sample used in the factor analysis was overlapping but not identical with the total sample.

[b]77 Items: 35 DES (Izard) items, 32 MAACL (Zuckerman) items, 7 DI (Beck) items, and 3 new items.

loneliness and physical well-being. In the second study, the loneliness items had their primary loadings on the distress factor—not a very surprising development in view of the kinship of the two concepts. However, the physical well-being factor emerged in the second study essentially without changing. Sixteen Zuckerman items failed to meet the criteria for retention on any factor and were deleted.

Of the seven items from Beck, four were deleted for lack of difference between primary and secondary loadings. The other three items formed a factor interpreted as sociality/sexuality.

III. STUDY II

A. METHOD

The second study of depression was essentially a replication of the first, in a different population and with some revisions in the DES+D. A central aim of this study was to see if the statistical factors derived in the first study would hold up in a new sample. A second aim was to extend the study of depression to a more heterogeneous sample.

1. Subjects. Subjects were 330 students in civics and human relations classes at Two Rivers High School in Nashville, Tennessee. This school draws its students largely from the middle and lower-middle income groups, which contrasts with Vanderbilt students who more often come from upper-middle income families and who are highly selected in terms of academic aptitude. All students participated voluntarily.

2. DES+D Revised. The DES+D was revised on the basis of the results of Study I. Twenty items were deleted on the basis of ambiguous loadings in the first factor analysis, and one item (Izard's third distress item—sad) was reinserted. Seven questionable items were retained in the second study on the basis of their performance in several previous factor analyses of DES items.

3. Procedure. The procedure in the first and second studies was essentially the same, except for two things. The free-response description was omitted in the second study. Instead, the students were asked to complete four 5-point scales (the Depression Questionnaire) describing the intensity, frequency, duration, and effects of their own previous depressed (or sad, dejected) states. The Depression Questionnaire will be discussed in Chapter Eleven.

B. *RESULTS*

Scores on the DES+D were subjected to a principal axis factor analysis as in the former study. The factors and item loadings are shown in Table 10-5.

A discrepancy between the two analyses was the failure to replicate the loneliness factor and that of sociality/sexuality. The two loneliness items loaded on the distress factor in Study II, and two items of the sociality/sexuality factor were rendered questionable because of high secondary loadings on related factors. The third

TABLE 10-5

DES+D Factors: Primary Loadings from Promax Rotation[a]
(58 items: 36 DES items, 19 MAACL items, and 3 DI items)

Distress (+ Loneliness)	Surprise	Guilt
.54 lonely	.65 amazed	.61 blameworthy
.53 blue	.65 astonished	.56 guilty
.47 downhearted	.55 surprised	.44 repentant
.46 sad		
.45 discouraged	*Physical well-being*	*Fear*
.44 alone	*(+ Interest)*	.75 afraid
.42 gloomy	.53 alert	.75 fearful
.40 forlorn	.52 attentive	.48 scared
Deleted items:	.40 active	
.31 suffering	.39 fit	*Joy*
.25 miserable	.39 concentrating	.66 joyful
	.35 strong	.60 happy
A/D/C: Hostility,	.34 whole	.46 delighted
outer-directed	Deleted items:	
.67 revulsion	.32 fine	*Fatigue*
toward others	.30 safe	.51 sleepy
.62 bitter toward others		.37 sheepish
.58 mad at others	*Shyness*	Deleted items:
.56 angry at others	.76 bashful	.40 fatigued
.51 others as distasteful	.71 shy	.25 sluggish
.50 disdainful of others		
.49 contemptuous	*A/D/C: Hostility,*	*Sexuality*
of others	*inner-directed*	.49 loss of
Deleted items:	.64 mad	sexual interest
.43 others as	.64 angry	
unattractive	.56 enraged	*Other deleted items*
.40 disinterested	Deleted items:	clean, terrible,
in others	.32 scornful	awful, healthy,
	.21 disgusted	feeling of distaste,
		feeling of revulsion

[a]High-school sample (N = 330).

sociality/sexuality item, loss of sexual interest, emerged as a separate factor.

Generally, the factor structure and content in the two studies were highly consistent. Rigorous statistical comparison of the two factor analyses was not possible because of the changes in scale items. However, visual inspection of Table 10-6, which presents the factors and items common to the two studies, reveals a very substantial degree of consistency. Seven of the 10 common factors were either identical in item content or differed by only one item.

As in the first study, the DES factor of interest-excitement did not emerge as a separate factor. Instead, all items loaded on physical well-being. Thus, both studies case doubt on the relevance of interest, as defined in the DES, as a component of depression. It is quite possible that for the study of depression, interest was too narrowly defined on the DES.

TABLE 10-6
Factors and Items Common to Both High School and College Studies

Distress	*A/D/C: Hostility,*
discouraged	*outer-directed*
gloomy	disdainful of others
forlorn	revulsion toward others
downhearted	contemptuous of others
blue	mad at others
(sad)	angry at others
	others as distasteful
A/D/C: Hostility,	
inner-directed	*Physical well-being*
mad	active
angry	fit
enraged	strong
Fear	*Shyness*
scared	bashful
afraid	shy
fearful	
	Surprise
Fatigue	astonished
sleepy	surprised
fatigued	amazed
sluggish	
	Joy
Guilt	happy
guilty	joyful
blameworthy	delighted
repentant	

252

In our factor-analytic studies of anxiety, second-order factors sometimes emerged that had many of the hypothesized components of anxiety. Such was not the case in our depression studies, in which depression components divided among several second-order factors.

IV. SUMMARY

As in most previous studies, the distress factor emerged as the central component of depression. However, 11 other interpretable factors were also extracted, supporting the concept of depression as heterogeneous rather than unitary. Three non-DES factors emerged: (a) loneliness, a factor that may relate to childhood bereavement or other critical personal loss in depression, a possibility raised by a number of authors (Beck, 1967; Brown, 1961; Schmale, 1958); (b) physical well-being, which may relate to the commonly extracted factor of psychomotor retardation; (c) sociality/sexuality, which reflects the frequently observed decrease in sexual drive and an aspect of what psychoanalytic theorists have termed loss of interest (Bibring, 1968; Freud, 1968; Rado, 1968). The loneliness and physical well-being items are from Zuckerman. Only one of the three new factors, physical well-being, was replicated as a separate factor in the second study.

The results of the two studies indicated that the Zuckerman depression scale was multifactor in nature. The items contributed to three factors in the first study—distress, loneliness, and physical well-being. In the second study, the loneliness items loaded on distress, but the physical well-being factor repeated. The distress factor of the DES can be extended considerably and probably strengthened by addition of some of the Zuckerman items.

Only six of 35 items from the DES had to be deleted, reaffirming the reliability of the scale's factor structure. The poor psychometric characteristics of the interest items (alert, attentive, concentrating) in this analysis raises a question as to their relevance for the measurement of depression. However, the interest items have emerged as a distinct factor in several previous analyses.

The results of both studies affirmed the strategy of dividing the anger/disgust/contempt items into inner- and outer-directed scales. The items representing these three emotions tended to cluster as they have in several previous factor-analytic investigations. Since these three emotions are considered the most important in the complex concept of hostility, we have designated the two factors inner- and outer-directed hostility. Both factors repeated in the second study, attesting to their reliability. Inner-directed hostility has been a hypothesized component of depression since the first psychoanalytic description of depression was written by Abraham. The present studies show that this component can be singled out and measured, along with the factor of outer-directed hostility that apparently plays a role in the overall dynamics of depression.

According to the results of the present studies, the similarities in the factor structure of depression in normal and hospitalized patient populations are quite substantial. Factors common to both populations include distress, hostility, guilt, and some factors related to bodily feelings. All of these factors are also represented in one or more of the psychoanalytic conceptions of depression. The two studies confirmed the differential emotion theory conception of depression as a combination of interacting fundamental emotions and feelings.

CHAPTER ELEVEN

Differential Emotion Theory and the Empirical Analysis of Depression

I. INTRODUCTION

By way of review, consider the origin and role of the various discrete emotions in depression, as presented by the psychoanalysts. All agreed that distress (sadness, dejection, despair) is part of the picture of depression. According to psychoanalysis, the distress results from real or imagined loss that threatens the individual's self-esteem, self-confidence, and emotional security. The predisposition to distress may be laid in the oral (early) stages of infancy at the height of the individual's helplessness and dependency. As Rado put it, the patient's "mute cry for love is patterned on the hungry infant's loud cry for help."

Second, almost all the psychoanalytic theorists agreed that anger is part of the picture of depression. All the psychoanalysts agreed that the anger and hostility of depression stem from the early frustrations and the tendency toward fixation at the oral and anal sadistic stages of psychosexual development. However, Fromm-Reichmann and Bibring relegated anger and hostility to a lesser role.

Guilt figures prominently as an emotion involved in depression, and for Rado the mood of gloomy repentance is the predominant one. (In my view, Rado's phrase "gloomy repentance" implies some combination of distress and guilt.) Guilt arises, according to the psychoanalytic system, as a result of the depressed individual's relatively uncontrollable anger and rage and the behavior which the latter determines.

Fear or anxiety is mentioned by a number of psycho-analytic theorists, some viewing it as due primarily to the fear of losing sexual potency. By inference one could see fear resulting from the individual's feeling of inadequacy and incapacity in the face of threat or danger.

The emotion of shame figures in the dynamics of depression in some psychoanalytic views and not in others. Freud felt that the depressed person lacked shame, whereas Fromm-Reichmann emphasized that shame was present and important. Most of the psychoanalysts agreed that loss of self-esteem, self-confidence, and self-respect figures as a prominent dimension of depression. One could consider this loss of self-esteem and the accompanying feelings of inferiority as indices of the emotion of shame.

It appears that psychoanalysts have dealt with discrete emotions in the description of depression much more than they did in the case of anxiety. One or another of the psychoanalytic investigators has touched on most of the components of depression that are hypothesized by differential emotion theory.

A number of theorists have been much less inclined to deal with discrete emotions. Ewert (1970) described depression as a mood, defining mood as a background experience in which there is decreased differentiation between experienced self and experienced world. Wellek (1970) also defined depression as a mood, a directionless mood. Pribram (1970) considered depression as a mood that predisposes one to behave in certain ways, but he saw feelings rather than emotions as the elements of such a mood predisposition. He defined emotion as a "plan" or neural program which is engaged when the organism is "disequilibrated." He defined feelings as images that form the matrix within which plans are formed. Feelings function as monitors of "momentary states of mind." The latter apparently derive from changes in drive or body states, including brain processes. However, Pribram spoke of feelings of hunger, thirst, sexiness, salience, happiness, sadness, right or wrong; thus he failed, at least semantically, to distinguish among drives, emotions, and cognitions or among the feelings related to them. This semantic breakdown makes it very difficult to follow Pribram's analysis.

Plutchik (1970), like the psychoanalysts, interpreted depression as a complex involving more than one emotion. In particular he pointed to the role of sadness, anger, and disgust. He suggested that multidimensional emotion measures might provide a test of the hypothesis that the manic sees the source of his anger in the external world while the depressive sees the source of his anger as mainly within himself.

II. THE DIFFERENTIAL EMOTION THEORY OF DEPRESSION

Differential emotion theory holds that depression, like anxiety, is a variable combination or pattern of fundamental emotions. Depression is an even more complex pattern than anxiety. More emotions are activated and there are more possibilities for conflicts in the emotion–emotion dynamics. The fundamental emotions involved in depression are distress, anger, disgust, contempt, fear, guilt, and shyness.

It was hypothesized that anger, disgust, and contempt would be expressed both toward the self and toward others. Since anger, disgust, and contempt are the central emotions in hostility, I have termed these components of depression inner-directed and outer-directed hostility. Depression can be described more simply as a combination of distress, hostility, fear, and shame, remembering that shame is measured at the phenomenological level by the separate factors of guilt and shyness.

Distress is considered the key emotion in depression. Distress is defined aprioristically on the DES as sadness, discouragement, downheartedness. Since distress is the key emotion in depression and there are, in addition, components of inner-directed hostility and shame, it follows that the emotion of enjoyment is expected to be virtually nonexistent in the depression situation. Surprise and interest may be slightly elevated because of their dynamic relationship to fear. As already indicated, some degree of interest seems necessary for any adaptive effort.

Although the fundamental emotions are thought to be the primary and most important elements of depression, there are other factors which are frequently present—decreased physical well-being, decreased sexuality, and increased fatigue. These elements may be most properly considered as immediate effects or by-products of depression. Nevertheless, they have motivational properties and, consequently, influence the other components of the depression and its course.

Since the factors of physical well-being and sexuality were not included in the DES+A, it is not possible to say that these factors would not have occurred in the anxiety profile. Their exclusion was dictated in part by the choice of the STAI as the anxiety scale to be added to the DES+A and, in part, by the fact that clinical evidence does not show these factors to be as common in anxiety as in depression.

Recognizing nonemotion factors in depression is quite consistent with differential emotion theory, which postulates five personality subsystems—the homeostatic, drive, motor, cognitive, and emotion systems. Since each of these systems has motivational properties, any of them can play a role in the dynamics of depression. Thus, there are both theoretical and empirical grounds for considering the nonemotion factors of physical well-being, sexuality, and fatigue in the study of depression. These factors are most directly related to the homeostatic, drive, and motor systems, all of which are regularly and importantly influenced by the emotion system and vice versa.

There is a problem in describing or classifying the nonemotion factors in depression. They are nonemotional by at least one empirical criterion: they appear as separate primary factors in the factor analysis of the DES+D, which contains items representing each of the fundamental emotions. This is true even in the varimax rotation where all derived factors are orthogonal.

One possibility is to consider these factors as attitudinal, but attitude is traditionally defined as consisting of a cognitive and an emotional element. This definition would not be strictly correct for nonemotion factors. A second alternative would be to consider these factors as attitudinal, defining attitude as cognition plus feeling, and defining feeling as sensation or sensory processes that do not culminate in emotion. But to say that these factors contain a cognitive element may mean only that the feeling element influences cognition and/or that cognitive processes (self-report on a verbal scale) have been used in measuring them. In this sense, the fundamental emotion factors of the DES also contain, or are influenced by, cognitive elements.

At present the best solution seems to be to consider the additional factors operationally measured by the DES+D as representing feelings, in the same way that the other factors represent emotions. These feelings emanate from muscles, tendons, viscera, or other body parts. The concepts describing these three factors— physical well-being, sexuality, and fatigue—are logically consistent with the notion that they derive directly from bodily feelings. Thus, these feelings may be defined as impressions derived from sensory processes or bodily sensations.

Perhaps the easiest way to illustrate the distinction I am drawing between a fundamental emotion and a feeling as defined here is to consider the factor of fatigue in relation to an emotion. It is well known that fatigue arises from neurophysiological and biochemical processes that are quite distinct from emotion processes. Both fatigue and emotion have neurophysiological and biochemical substrates and, of course, both have quite distinct psychological effects. Even when we look at fatigue in relation to the emotion with which it is most likely to be confused—distress—there are still very clear distinctions. The feeling of tiredness and the feeling of sadness, discouragement, and dejection are different in important ways. Because of the addition of these three bodily feeling factors and the use of items for measuring both inner- and outer-directed emotion, the DES+D profile represents a more complete picture of depression than does the DES a priori profile.

III. EMPIRICAL ANALYSIS OF DEPRESSION

The empirical analysis of depression as a pattern of emotions parallels rather closely the empirical analysis of anxiety. However, there are several noteworthy differences. In modifying the DES for the study of depression, the items relating to anger, disgust, and contempt were included once for measurement of feelings toward self, and again for measurement of feelings toward others. As already indicated, this was an effort to measure the hypothesized inner- and outer-directed hostility components. A second significant difference in the study of depression was the addition of items that might be considered not as indices of a fundamental emotion but of a bodily feeling. These components—physical well-being, sexuality, fatigue—may well be some of the effects of depression or of the interaction of the emotions in the depression pattern, yet they are so intimately involved in the complex that they should be studied in relation to the fundamental emotion components.

The lack of sexual interest or concern over sexual adequacy may be determined in part by the combined effects of inner-directed hostility on the one hand, and the fear and guilt components of depression on the other. The concern over physical well-being may result in part from the elevated nonemotion factor of fatigue as well as from the feeling of debilitation and motor retardation that can result from emotion–emotion conflicts.

For a number of reasons, the DES nonemotion factor of fatigue is expected to be elevated in depression. As noted earlier, there are actually some physiological similarities between depressive and fatigue states. Similarities have also been frequently noted in the clinical picture of these two conditions. Fatigue may be partly determined by the great expenditure of emotional energies in the emotion conflicts inherent in the depression pattern.

In the study of depression, all subjects in the sample visualized the depression situation and completed the DES+D. On the same occasion, subgroups of the total sample visualized a situation for one of six depression-related emotions and completed the DES+D again. All the depression-related emotions except fear were studied in this fashion.

The patterns of anxiety and depression taken together include all the fundamental emotions except enjoyment. Thus the pattern of emotions in anxiety overlaps with the pattern of emotions in depression in a number of cases. Fear, distress, guilt, shyness, and anger are common to the two complex patterns, as hypothesized by differential emotion theory. In this framework only the emotions of disgust and contempt are unique to the depression pattern and, as reported in Chapter Five, the empirical study of anxiety showed disgust to be present in the anxiety pattern.

In view of the very considerable overlap among the fundamental emotion components of anxiety and depression, it is obvious that many of the differences between the two are to be found elsewhere. The chief difference is in the patterning, or the shape of the two profiles. First, and of greatest importance, they have different key emotions. Furthermore, the rank order (relative intensity) of the different fundamental emotions in the two patterns is quite distinct.

IV. PATTERNS OF EMOTIONS AND FEELINGS IN DEPRESSION

Table 11-1 presents the profile of emotions in depression. The profile for the emotions represented by the a priori scales is shown in column 1. The obtained profile is quite similar to that predicted by differential emotion theory. Distress is the key emotion and is elevated substantially above all other emotions in the pattern. Although the item context is different, the DES scales are identical in content with those used in the study of anxiety. The DES scales describe the subject's feelings toward or within himself.

The second-, third-, and fourth-ranking emotions in the a priori depression profile are disgust, contempt, and anger, the three emotions I have designated as the hostility triad. These elevated means represent hostility directed toward the self. The rank of this component in the pattern is indicative of its relative importance in the depression situation. The fifth- and sixth-ranking emotions are fear and guilt, two emotions that are related in complex ways to each other as well as to the other emotion components of depression. The nonemotion factor of fatigue is actually the sixth highest mean in the profile. The reasons for its presence in the pattern have already been discussed.

A somewhat more complete picture of depression is presented in column 2 of Table 11-1. Column 2 presents the empirical factors derived from the factor analysis of the DES+D. The empirical factors include the bodily feeling conponents in addition to the fundamental emotion components.

Looking at the empirical factors that correspond to or represent fundamental emotions, it can be seen that the rank order of the emotions as represented in the empirical factors is virtually identical with the rank order of the emotions in the pattern based on

TABLE 11-1
Rank Order of Scale Means of a Priori and Empirical Factors in a Recalled or Imagined Depression Situation[a]

A priori scales (from DES items)		Empirical factors (from DES+ D items)		
Factor	Scale $\bar{x}$	Factor	Scale $\bar{x}$	Alpha
Distress	4.24	Loneliness	3.9	.88
Disgust	3.14	Distress + D	3.8	.89
Contempt	2.86	A/D/C: Hostility, inner-directed	3.1	.86
Anger	2.85	Fear	2.8	.90
Fear	2.80	Fatigue	2.6	.77
Fatigue	2.64	Sociality/Sexuality	2.5	.61
Guilt	2.41	Guilt	2.4	.83
Surprise	2.23	A/D/C: Hostility, outer-directed	2.3	.93
Interest	2.20	Surprise	2.2	.92
Shyness	2.05	Physical well-being	2.0	.85
Enjoyment	1.14	Shyness	2.0	.80
		Joy + ¦D-minus	1.2	.78

[a] Depression situation (N = 332).
[b] A/D/C = anger/disgust/contempt.

a priori scales. The differences are due largely to the presence of the bodily feeling factors that hold positions among the emotion factors.

In the empirical factor profile, the first factor is loneliness, a two-item factor that, as shown in Chapter Ten, did not emerge as a separate factor in the high-school sample. In the high-school sample, the items relating to loneliness had their primary loadings on the distress factor.

Regardless of its place in the factor structure, loneliness is often reported to be a component of depression. The potential importance of loneliness and its relation to other components was effectively articulated by one of the students in the author's undergraduate course on the emotions.

> If I could label the condition which most frequently stimulated depression for me, I would say loneliness. The tendency to feel hopelessly lonely for no apparent reason has plagued me throughout my adolescent life. The roots of this lie, I am sure, in a rather stormy and insecure childhood environment. Nevertheless, the slightest indication of a possible loss of a love object, or the vaguest sign of lack of acceptance can send me reeling into utterly lonely depression. In these periods I have little desire to eat and am usually unable to sleep. I withdraw to my room, stare at the walls and ceiling and become dominated by my fears and anxieties. Inwardly I berate myself for being so worthless and undesirable. The feeling which develops can be likened to falling into a bottomless pit, deeper and deeper, darker and darker, until I lose sight of the original reasons, if there were any, for my state of mind. Then my depression becomes nameless and amorphous. Something seems to be pushing from within; at the same time I have the claustrophobic reaction that all the unpleasantness of the world is closing in on me. The slightest word from another person grates on my nerves. There have been numerous times when I have contemplated suicide, and even partially attempted it.

Between the emotions of fear and guilt in the empirical profile is the sixth-ranking factor, sociality/sexuality. The decreased sociability and loss of interest in sexual activity undoubtedly relates to the inhibiting emotions of fear and guilt and also to the feelings of incompetence and inadequacy brought about by inner-directed hostility. The decreased sexual involvement may also be related to the individual's lowered sense of physical well-being.

The physical well-being factor consists of items from the Zuckerman depression scale. The decrease in physical well-being is undoubtedly a function both of the factor of fatigue and the emotion–emotion conflicts, which make heavy demands on the energy of the depressed individual.

The eighth-ranking component in the empirical factor pattern for depression is outer-directed hostility. The outer-directed hostility may serve an adaptive function by keeping inner-directed hostility from mounting higher and higher. Outer-directed hostility may also serve to allay some of the guilt and fear in the pattern.

The presence of fear in the depression pattern may be adaptive in two ways. First it may continue to function as motivation for the depressed individual to remove himself from the situation or otherwise to change the scene. The fear may also serve as a check against excessive inner-directed hostility and thus decrease the chances of suicidal behavior.

The depression profiles of the college group and the high-school group are juxtaposed in Table 11-2. Except for the absence of the loneliness and sociality/sexuality factors in the high-school sample, the two profiles are remarkably similar. In the high-school study, the loneliness items loaded on the distress factor, which is not considered essentially different. Two of the three sociality/sexuality items (others as unattractive, disinterested in others) had their primary loadings on the outer-directed hostility factor, but both had large secondary loadings on other factors. The third item, loss of sexual interest, emerged as a separate factor with a mean rating of 2.12, suggesting that sexuality is a component of depression in both age groups. The essential similarity of the profiles from the college and high-school studies attests to the stability and meaningfulness of the concept of depression as a pattern or combination of fundamental emotions and feelings.

TABLE 11-2

Rank Order of Scale Means of Common Factors
in the High-School and College Studies

College group, $N = 313$		High-school group, $N = 330$	
DES+D factor	Scale $\bar{x}$	DES+D factor	Scale $\bar{x}$
Distress	3.8	Distress	3.9
A/D/C: Hostility, in	3.1	A/D/C: Hostility, in	3.2
Fear	2.8	Fatigue	2.8
Fatigue	2.6	A/D/C: Hostility, out	2.7
Guilt	2.4	Guilt	2.6
A/D/C: Hostility, out	2.3	Fear	2.4
Surprise	2.2	Physical well-being	2.3
Physical well-being	2.0	Shyness	2.2
Shyness	2.0	Surprise	2.0
Joy	1.2	Joy	1.4

TABLE 11-3

*Scale Means of Males and Females and the Severe and
Mild Depression Groups in the High-School Study*

| | Scale $\bar{x}$ | | | |
DES+D factor	Male $N = 138$	Female $N = 192$	High $N = 135$	Low $N = 143$
Distress	3.7	4.0	4.3	3.5
A/D/C: Hostility, in	3.1	3.3	3.5	3.0
Fatigue	2.8	2.9	2.8	2.6
A/D/C: Hostility, out	2.6	2.8	2.9	2.6
Guilt	2.6	2.6	2.9	2.4
Fear	2.1	2.6	2.8	2.0
Physical well-being/interest	2.6	2.6	2.1	2.4
Shyness	2.1	2.3	2.3	2.1

Two other kinds of evidence add to the validity of the concept of depression as a pattern of interacting emotions and feelings and to the validity of the DES+D as a means of assessing depression. The relevant data are presented in Table 11-3. Inspection of columns 1 and 2 shows that in the high-school study, females had higher means than males on every component (factor) of depression except one. The exception was the physical well-being/interest factor, which, being the only positive factor, should have yielded a lower mean for females; a male–female difference of .02 was inconsequential. The differences on the other factors are consistent with clinical evidence and the findings of several investigations of sex differences in depression (see Chapter Ten).

The mean scale scores in columns 3 and 4 of Table 11-3 were derived from subjects with Depression Questionnaire scale means above 4.00 (high group) and below 2.00 (low group). The Depression Questionnaire is presented as Chart 11-1. Table 11-3 shows that the group with high scores on the Depression Questionnaire had substantially higher means on every component of depression except for the positive factor of physical well-being/interest, which was reversed as expected.

V. ANXIETY VERSUS DEPRESSION

Figure 11-1 presents the profiles of emotions obtained in the anxiety and depression studies. As already indicated, there are certain differences between the anxiety and depression studies that

CHART 11-1
Depression Questionnaire

Please try to recall some time in your life when you were depressed, or, if that word is too strong, some time when you were dejected or sadder than usual. With that experience of depression or sadness in mind, please answer these four questions:

1. To what extent were you depressed? (Circle one number)

1	2	3	4	5
Not at all	Slightly	Moderately	Pretty Badly	Severely

2. How often have you experienced similar depressions?

1	2	3	4	5
Never	Seldom	Occasionally	Fairly Often	Frequently

3. How many days did the depressions usually last? 1 2 3 4 5

4. How much did it affect your everyday behavior and schoolwork?

1	2	3	4	5
Not at all	Slightly	Moderately	Pretty Badly	Severely

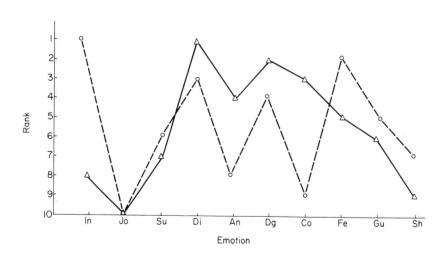

Fig. 11-1. *The profiles of emotions in anxiety (- - -) and depression (——). In = interest, Jo = joy, Su = surprise, Di = distress, An = anger, Dg = disgust, Co = Contempt, Fe = fear, Gu = guilt, Sh = shyness.*

265

may have had some effect on the DES scale scores. The item context was different in the two studies. The instructions were different in that the subjects in the depression study were instructed to rate the standard DES items specifically in terms of emotions within or toward the self. This was done to distinguish the DES items from the newly added items for measuring emotions toward others. While this separation was not made on the DES+A, the instructions and item format suggest that subjects respond in terms of emotions within and toward the self. Thus the difference in instructions was not considered to be of great importance. The items for the ten DES emotion scales were identical in the two studies. Differences in item context in previous studies has not appreciably affected factor structure.

The profiles for anxiety and depression are presented in terms of factor ranks rather than factor means. The emphasis here is on the patterning, as absolute differences in means in the different emotion situations would be difficult to interpret.

Interestingly, the shape of the anxiety and depression profiles is rather similar for the first six emotions listed—the two positive emotions, the emotion of surprise, and the hostility triad. The shape of the two profiles is also similar for the last three emotions—fear, guilt, and shyness. However, the profiles cross twice, and there is a difference in rank for nine of the ten fundamental emotions. The exception is the emotion of joy, which would be expected to be in the lowest rank for both of these complex emotion patterns.

The depression profile shows very clearly that distress is the key emotion and that this is followed by the hostility triad—anger, disgust, contempt. A comparison of the average rank for the hostility triad in depression and anxiety would show that the magnitude of hostility is much greater in depression. Aside from the emotion of interest, whose mean scale score was only very slightly larger than that for fear, the anxiety profile shows the expected pattern of emotions, and the expected differences in relation to depression. The emotions of fear, guilt, and shyness are higher in anxiety than in depression.

VI. MEASURES USED IN THE DEPRESSION STUDIES

Three different measures were used in the study of depression and its component emotions and feelings. The three measures were the depression score derived from the DES+D, the DES+D empirical factor profile, and the a priori profile derived from the DES items on the DES+D.

VI. Measures Used in the Depression Studies

The depression score derived from the DES+D comes from the items of Zuckerman's MAACL. In order to keep the studies of depression and anxiety parallel, the depression score was treated as a single variable in a number of analyses, although our factor analyses of the DES+D indicated that the depression score derived from the Zuckerman MAACL items is clearly a two-factor measure. The Zuckerman items that had unequivocal loadings in the factor analyses loaded either on the distress factor or the physical well-being factor. The two-factor nature of the DES+D depression score should be kept in mind in interpreting the analyses based on the depression score.

Also in order to keep the studies between anxiety and depression parallel, only six fundamental emotion situations were selected for study. The situations selected were those for distress, the key emotion; anger, disgust, and contempt—the triad which furnishes the basis for measuring inner-directed and outer-directed hostility; and guilt and shyness. A fear situation was not included. I thought that study of a fear situation would be relatively less important than study of situations related to distress, the hostility triad, and guilt and shyness. However, the empirical studies showed that the emotion of fear ranked fifth in the hierarchy of emotion components, above guilt and shyness. Although data on an imagined fear situation was not obtained in the depression study, it will be possible to discuss the role of fear in depression. The fear scale, which is one of the scales of the DES+D, was administered in the imagined depression situation and in each of the six selected fundamental emotion situations.

In most respects the procedures and analyses in the depression study parallel those of the anxiety study. Generally the findings from the depression study parallel those of the anxiety study and support the general hypothesis that depression, like anxiety, is a variable combination of fundamental emotions.

There were some substantial differences between the measures used in the anxiety study and the depression study. The anxiety instrument added to the DES to form the DES+A contained items representing several factors. All of its items except one loaded on one of the fundamental emotion factors. The depression instrument added to the DES to form the DES+D was essentially a two-factor measure. One group of items loaded on one of the fundamental emotion scales of the DES, the distress scale. The other group of depression items formed the physical well-being factor, a factor completely separate from the DES emotion scales. This factor, like the fatigue factor of the DES, is a nonemotion factor in that it does not overlap with any of the DES fundamental emotion scales.

267

Interestingly, the physical well-being factor was also separate and distinct from the fatigue factor.

Other items added to the DES+D from Beck's inventory produced another nonemotion factor, sociality/sexually. The three stable nonemotion factors that play a role in depression—physical well-being, sociality/sexuality, and fatigue—probably have different types of bodily sensations as their neurophysiological substrates. The perceptions or impressions of these bodily feelings produce the three factors.

The two new nonemotion factors make the DES+D a broader measure than the DES+A. The more complex DES+D profile is in part a function of the particular items added to the DES. The reasons which led to the selection of these items and the obtained results suggest that depression is more complex than anxiety or that there are more factors in depression that are relatively constant and stable. In summary, the principal differences between the anxiety and depression studies are due mainly to the fact that, by comparison with the DES+A, the DES+D contains more factors, and more factors are elevated in depression than in anxiety.

VII. THE DEPRESSION SCORES FROM THE DEPRESSION AND FUNDAMENTAL EMOTION SITUATIONS

As already noted, the depression score consists of what is essentially a distress component and a physical well-being component. Therefore, the depression score and the anxiety score do not relate in a comparable way to the DES a priori scales and the different recalled or imagined situations. In contrast to the analyses with the anxiety score, it was expected that the depression score from the depression situation would be significantly different from the depression score derived from the separate fundamental emotion situations. The different expectations for the two studies were due primarily to the differences in the STAI as an anxiety index and the MAACL depression items as an index of depression. According to the results of the factor analyses (Chapters Five and Ten), the STAI represents several fundamental emotions, while the MAACL depression items reflect only one—the emotion of distress. Table 11-4a presents the mean depression scores from the different emotion situations, and Table 11-4b presents the analysis of variance comparing the depression scores from the depression and the distress situations. As expected, the mean depression score from the depres-

TABLE 11-4a

*Mean Depression Scores from the
Depression Situation and the
Fundamental Emotion Situations*

Situation	N	Mean
Depression	332	96.90
Distress	68	90.13
Anger	54	83.33
Disgust	54	83.33
Contempt	46	87.49
Guilt	52	82.21
Shyness	58	87.19

TABLE 11-4b

*Analysis of Variance of the Depression Scores from the Depression
and Distress Situations*

Source	df	MS	F	p
Situations	1	1556.0000	16.3379	.0003
Subjects	67	364.5371	3.8276	.0000
Situations × subjects	67	95.2388		
Total	135			

sion situation is by far the highest of the seven mean scores. Since distress items form a major part of the depression score, it is quite reasonable that the second highest depression score is from the distress situation. The third highest score is from the contempt situation, one of the emotions in the hostility triad, and the third highest mean is that for shyness. Actually the rank order of mean depression scores among the six emotion situations is not as meaningful as was the case with the anxiety scores, since the depression scores contain the separate and distinct factor of physical well-being, a factor independent of the fundamental emotions.

The highly significant *F* due to situations, in Table 11-4b, indicates that the mean depression score from the depression situation is significantly higher than the depression score from the distress situation. This is as expected, and the difference is probably accounted for almost entirely by the presence of the physical well-being factor in the depression score. By this logic, physical well-being is a more important component in the pattern of the depression situation than in the pattern of the distress situation. The difference in importance of the physical well-being factor in the depression and distress situations is quite consistent with differential emotion theory, psychoanalytic theory, and other psychodynamic theories that recognize the complexity of depression.

An analysis of variance like that in Table 11-4b was used to compare the mean depression score from the depression situation with the depression score means from each of the remaining emotion situation shown in Table 11-4a. In every case a highly significant variance due to situations showed the depression mean to be significantly higher than the mean for fundamental emotion situations.

Table 11-5 presents the analysis of variance comparing the mean depression scores from the six fundamental emotion situations. The variance between emotion situations was not significant, although Table 11-4a shows that the mean in the distress situation is considerably higher than that in some of the other emotion situations.

VIII. THE DES+D PROFILES FROM THE DEPRESSION AND THE FUNDAMENTAL EMOTION SITUATIONS

The DES+D profile consists of the scores on the factors derived by the factor analysis of all the DES+D items on a sample of 313 college students. The criteria for selection of items as scorable for the various factors were explained in Chapter Ten. As shown in Table 10-4, poor items were deleted either because of low primary factor loadings or because loadings on the primary and secondary factors were not separated by .20 or more. The items that were retained constituted quite reliable factors as indicated by the alpha coefficients shown in Table 11-1. The sociality/sexuality factor was the only one with an alpha coefficent less than .77, and most of the alphas were in the 80s and 90s.

TABLE 11-5
Analysis of Variance of the Depression
Scores from the Six Emotion Situations

Source	df	MS	F	p
Between emotion situations	5	568.950	1.9193	.0898
Within emotion situations	326	296.433		
Total	331	300.550		

270

TABLE 11-6

Subjects × DES+D Factors × Situations Analysis of Variance: Depression Situation versus Distress Situation

Source	df	MS	F	p
Subjects	67	337.7014		
DES+D factors (A)	11	187.2727	1.7980	.0502
Situations (B)	1	2330.0000	25.0457	.0000
Factors × situations	11	151.5454	2.6458	.0028
A × subjects	737	104.1574		
B × subjects	67	93.0298		
A × B × subjects	737	57.2768		
Total	1631	94.3550		

Table 11-6 presents the analysis of variance of the DES+D factors from the depression and distress situations. The highly significant factors × situations interaction indicates that the subjects responded quite differently to the different DES+D factors in the two situations.

The two profiles that are analyzed in Table 11-6 are juxtaposed in Table 11-7. This table reports the means in terms of the 5-point scale used on the DES+D in order to make factors with different numbers of items comparable. One obvious difference between the profiles is the higher scale means in the depression situation. The higher means on the first eight factors indicate that the

TABLE 11-7

DES+D Empirical Profiles from the Depression and Distress Situations

Factor	Depression		Distress	
	Scale $\bar{x}$	Rank	Scale $\bar{x}$	Rank
Loneliness	3.9	1	3.4	2
Distress + D	3.8	2	3.6	1
A/D/C: Hostility, in	3.1	3	2.3	5
Fear	2.8	4	2.5	3
Fatigue	2.6	5	2.3	5
Sexuality	2.5	6	2.2	7
Guilt	2.4	7	2.1	8.5
A/D/C: Hostility, out	2.3	8	1.9	10.5
Surprise	2.2	9	2.3	5
Physical well-being	2.0	10.5	2.1	8.5
Shyness	2.0	10.5	1.9	10.5
Joy + D minus	0.9	12	1.2	12

emotions and feelings in a depression situation are more intense than in a distress situation.

The profile of factors in depression is more like the profile of factors in distress than in any other fundamental emotion situation. Yet as evident from inspection of Table 11-7, the profiles in depression and distress are distinct. Table 11-6 showed that the quantitative differences between the depression and distress profiles were statistically significant. Table 11-7 shows where the major differences occur. In comparing the two profiles, it is well to keep in mind that the loneliness factor, which was only a two-item factor, merged with distress in the high-school study. Thus the reversal in ranks of these two factors in the depression and distress situations is probably not as important as the difference in magnitude of the two pairs of means. As expected, the means for these factors are higher in depression than in distress.

One of the most remarkable differences between the profiles of the depression and distress situations appears on the inner-directed hostility factor. This factor occupies the third rank in the depression situation but only the fifth rank in the distress situation. The scale means for inner-directed hostility in the two situations are almost a full scale step apart. This finding supports the psychoanalytic hypothesis regarding the importance of retroflected anger in depression.

Fear and guilt were slightly higher in depression than in distress, and outer-directed hostility was moderately higher in depression. The profile for depression and the ways in which it differs from the profile for distress are quite consistent with differential emotion theory and are consistent with a number of propositions in psychoanalytic theory, as discussed in Chapter Eight.

IX. DES+D FACTORS IN THE FUNDAMENTAL EMOTION SITUATIONS

It was of some interest to see whether the DES+D profiles differed for the six fundamental emotion situations considered in the depression study. The analysis of variance for the DES+D profiles for the six emotion situations is presented in Table 11-8. The variance due to the interaction of situations × factors is highly significant. This analysis demonstrates that the DES+D can distinguish between the recalled or imagined situations in which the subject focuses on one of the fundamental emotions.

As was the case in the anxiety study, an emotion situation was defined as a situation in which a particular fundamental emotion

TABLE 11-8
*Analysis of Variance of DES+D Empirical Factors from the
Six Emotion Situations*

Source	df	MS	F	p
Subjects	331	7.982		
Emotion situations	5	18.916	2.4207	.0351
Between error	326	7.814		
Within subjects	3320	8.091		
Factors	10	178.850	24.2478	.0000
Situations × factors	50	20.574	2.7894	.0000
Within error	3260	7.376		
Total	3651	8.081		

was dominant in the subject's experience. And in both the anxiety and depression studies, each such situation produced a pattern or profile of emotions. This does not mean that the depression pattern should be viewed as a pattern of patterns. In the depression pattern the several fundamental emotions and feelings interact as distinct components. However, since a number of fundamental emotion situations elicit patterns containing several of the depression components, any of these emotion situations may trigger the depression pattern in a person with a predisposition to depression.

X. A PRIORI PROFILES IN DEPRESSION AND THE RELATED FUNDAMENTAL EMOTION SITUATIONS

The anxiety study included an analysis of the a priori emotion profiles for the fear, distress, guilt, shyness, anger, and interest situations. Each of these profiles, which were presented in Table 5-22, was distinct from the others. Four of the fundamental emotions that were studied by way of the recall or imaging technique in the anxiety study were also considered in the depression study. This provided the opportunity to check the reliability of the imaging technique, at least in a general way. Although the method of recalling or imaging the fundamental emotion situations in the anxiety and depression studies was the same, the measuring instruments in the two studies differed, as explained earlier. In spite of these differences the profiles of emotions in the overlapping fundamental emotion situations are quite similar in the two studies. The differences that do exist are probably easily accounted for in terms of the differences in the instruments.

Table 11-1 juxtaposed the a priori and empirical factor profiles in the depression situation. Although the empirical profile contains the additional bodily feeling factors, the ranks of the fundamental emotions in the two profiles were substantially similar. Any differences that exist are accounted for, in part, by the fact that the a priori profile contains only items related to emotions toward or within the self, whereas in the empirical profile, anger, disgust, and contempt are represented by both inner- and outer-directed items. The a priori profiles for depression and the depression-related fundamental emotions are valuable for showing the patterns of emotions within or toward the self.

Table 11-9 presents the analysis of variance of the a priori profiles from the depression and the distress situations. This analysis parallels that which compared the DES+D empirical profiles of the depression and distress situations (see Table 11-6). As expected, the a priori profiles of the depression and distress situations were highly different. The variance due to the interaction of factors × situations indicates that the subjects responded differentially to the various DES scales in the two situations.

The analyses for the a priori profiles parallel and confirm the analyses for the DES+D empirical profiles. Both clearly show that there is a distinct pattern of emotions and feelings in depression. Furthermore, each of the emotions related to depression has a distinct pattern in situations where it is the key or dominant emotion.

The a priori profiles of emotions in the recalled or imagined situations are represented in Table 11-10. This table corresponds to Table 5-22, which presented the a priori profiles of emotions

TABLE 11-9
Analysis of Variance of a Priori Emotion Profiles from the Depression Situation and the Distress Situation

Source	df	MS	F	p
Subjects	67	36.7332		
A priori factors (A)	10	573.7812	53.4585	.0000
Situations (B)	1	279.8125	23.4783	.0001
Factors × situations	10	30.0937	5.3015	.0000
A × subjects	670	10.7332		
B × subjects	67	11.9179		
A × B × subjects	670	5.6765		
Total	1495	13.7610		

TABLE 11-10
A Priori Profiles of Emotions in Imagined Situations Characterized by a Depression-Related Fundamental Emotion[a]

Distress situation (N = 68)		Anger situation (N = 54)		Disgust situation (N = 54)		Contempt situation (N = 46)		Guilt situation (N = 52)		Shyness situation (N = 58)	
Emotion	$\bar{x}$	Emotion	$\bar{x}$	Emotion	$\bar{x}$	Emotion	$\bar{x}$	Emotion	$\bar{x}$	Emotion	$\bar{x}$
Distress	11.09	Anger	12.89	Disgust	12.02	Contempt	12.52	Guilt	12.56	Shyness	12.34
Fear	7.52	Disgust	10.33	Anger	11.80	Disgust	12.11	Disgust	10.10	Fear	9.76
Interest	7.12	Contempt	9.94	Contempt	11.28	Anger	11.41	Distress	9.48	Interest	9.17
Disgust	7.02	Interest	9.72	Distress	10.07	Interest	9.02	Fear	9.15	Distress	8.14
Fatigue	6.87	Surprise	8.57	Surprise	9.00	Distress	8.91	Anger	8.42	Disgust	6.91
Surprise	6.75	Distress	8.26	Interest	7.76	Surprise	8.48	Contempt	7.90	Enjoyment	6.36
Anger	6.66	Fear	5.98	Guilt	6.43	Fear	5.65	Interest	7.42	Fatigue	6.12
Contempt	6.48			Fear	6.39			Shyness	7.15	Surprise	5.97
Guilt	6.15			Fatigue	5.56			Surprise	5.85	Contempt	5.69
Shyness	5.62							Fatigue	5.83	Anger	5.53

[a] A priori factors: minimum score 3, maximum score 15.

considered in the anxiety study. As already noted, the profiles for the emotion situations considered in both studies are substantially similar. Most of the differences are probably due to the differences in the DES+A and the DES+D. As was the case in the anxiety study, each of the emotion situations was characterized by a key or dominant emotion, the one which was in focus, and a number of related emotions. The patterns which differ most in the anxiety and depression studies are those for the shyness situation. The rank orders of the emotions are quite similar, but the magnitude of the means is considerably higher for the first four emotions in the profile for the shyness situation in the depression study. The reasons for this are not clear. It is apparent that the emotion means in the different emotion situations in the depression study tend to be generally higher than the emotion means in the emotion situations in the anxiety study. This may be due in part to the fact that inner- and outer-directed emotions were not separated in the anxiety study.

The analysis of variance comparing the a priori profiles from the six fundamental emotion situations is presented in Table 11-11. This analysis parallels that of Table 11-8, which compared the DES+D empirical factor scores from the six emotion situations. As expected, the a priori profiles differed significantly from situation to situation. Again, the evidence indicates that a situation recalled or visualized as one eliciting a particular fundamental emotion elicits that emotion as the dominant one, together with a number of dynamically related emotions. Life situations typically elicit patterns of emotions.

Evidence was presented in Chapters Five and Six that showed that the patterns of emotions in the different situations were

TABLE 11-11

*Analysis of Variance of a Priori Emotion Profiles
from the Six Emotion Situations*

Source	df	MS	F	p
Subjects	331	28.071		
Emotion situations	5	165.553	6.3768	.0001
Between error	326	25.962		
Within subjects	3320	14.848		
Factors	10	965.419	117.4909	.0000
Situations × factors	50	257.076	31.2860	.0000
Within error	3260	8.217		
Total	3651	16.047		

distinct. The emotion situations considered in the depression study yielded similar evidence. A Lindquist Type I analysis of variance compared all possible pairs of the a priori profiles from the six fundamental emotion situations. A typical analysis is presented in Table 11-12. There were 15 such comparisons and in each one the variance due to the situations × factors interaction showed that the a priori emotion profiles were significantly different. Life situations produce patterns of dynamically related interacting emotions, and each pattern is unique.

TABLE 11-12

Analysis of Variance of the DES a Priori Profiles
from the Distress and Disgust Situations

Source	df	MS	F	p
Subjects	121	29.758		
Situations	1	533.839	20.8877	.0001
Between error	120	25.558		
Within subjects	1220	13.656		
Factors	10	496.430	61.4938	.0000
Situations × factors	10	200.864	24.8814	.0000
Within error	1200	8.073		
Total	1341	15.109		

Although each emotion situation yielded an average profile that was distinct, it should be remembered that the specific content of a situation was always defined by each individual subject. Each subject recalled or imagined a situation of his own choosing, a situation necessarily related to his own personality and experience. There was no standard or average situation, yet for each situation there was a characteristic profile of emotions. This does not mean that all individuals had the same pattern of emotions in a given situation. There was considerable variability in profiles from individual to individual.

XI. PATTERNS OF EMOTIONS OF DEPRESSIVE CLIENTS
IN PSYCHOTHERAPY

Concurrently with the systematic studies of the DES+A and DES+D in anxiety, depression, and related fundamental-emotion situations, the Differential Emotion Scale was being used as a tool to facilitate psychotherapy. The Differential Emotion Scale II, a version of the DES that has both a frequency and an intensity scale for each of the 33 items, was also in use. The principal difference between the DES and DES II is in the temporal dimension. The DES is designed to obtain an assessment of emotions of the moment, emotions in a particular and fairly well-defined situation. The DES II is designed to obtain the full range of emotions that occurs over a period of time or in an interpersonal relationship. The period may be a psychotherapy session, a day, a week, a month, or the whole life experience.

Table 11-13 presents a DES and a DES II profile for two psychotherapy clients. Both of the profiles are basically similar to the profile of depression obtained from normal subjects recalling or imagining a depression situation. The fact that these profiles differ from each other and from the depression profiles is quite as expected in terms of differential emotion theory. The depression pattern may vary from individual to individual or from time to time within the same individual. The particular pattern as it exists at the time can be used to guide the therapist in his treatment of the client.

In the case of the first profile in Table 11-13, the housewife and her husband were having extramarital affairs with the knowledge and consent of each other. Actually the housewife could not fully consent and could never adapt happily to the quadrangle affair. Distress was the most prominent emotion in her pattern, but surprise was also high. She was continually astonished to find herself in the situation. Anger, guilt, and fear were also elevated.

TABLE 11-13
DES Profiles of two Depressed Psychotherapy Clients

Housewife suffering from marital upheaval (age 29)[a]		College male suffering from loss of father and feelings of personal inadequacy (age 20)[b]	
Distress	15	Distress	75
Surprise	7	Fear	70
Anger	7	Disgust	62
Guilt	7	Guilt	61
Fear	7	Shyness	52
Fatigue	5	Contempt	44
Interest	5	Fatigue	38
		Anger	22

[a] DES scores range from a maximum possible of 15 to a minimum possible of 3.

[b] DES II scores range from a maximum possible of 75 to a minimum possible of 3.

278

Consider the second profile in Table 11-13. The client was considerably more debilitated and retarded in his functioning than was the housewife. This could be inferred from the fact that fear, the most toxic and debilitating emotion, was second only to distress in the profile. For this client, the disgust and contempt were largely inner-directed. Guilt and shyness also played an important role in this young man's reactive depression.

XII. PATTERNS OF EMOTION AND FEELINGS IN HOSPITALIZED DEPRESSIVE PATIENTS

Marshall and Izard (in preparation) have administered a modified form of the DES+D to 30 female and 10 male hospitalized depressives. Table 11-14 compares the rank order of the DES+D factor scores for the depressed patients with that of the high-school sample described in Chapter 10. Considerable similarity obtained between the profile of emotions and feelings for the depressed patients and that for the high-school students describing a recalled and visualized period of depression. Differences of two or more were found between the ranks of three of the factors. One of these was not predicted, but the other two were quite as expected in a comparison of depression in hospitalized patients and normals. The patients reported relatively less fatigue than the high-school students. This was somewhat surprising, until we considered the differences in environmental conditions and treatment. The patients may not experience as much fatigue because of their confinement, freedom

TABLE 11-14
Rank Order of DES+D Factors for High-School
Students Recalling and Visualizing a Depression
Situation and for Depressive Patients

Factor	High school ($N = 313$)	Depressive patients ($N = 40$)
Distress	1	1
Inner-directed hostility	2	3
Fear	3	2
Fatigue	4	7
Guilt	5	4.5
Outer-directed hostility	6	8
Physical well-being	7	6
Shyness	8	4.5

from usual responsibilities, relative inactivity, and use of anti-depressant drugs.

The depressed patients reported relatively less outer-directed hostility. This is consistent with clinical observation and differential emotion theory, which suggests that outer-directed hostility could be adaptive in allaying inner-directed hostility and militating against the fear and guilt components of depression.

The largest difference between the depressed patients and the high-school students was on shyness, where the depressed patients had a considerably higher rank. This tends to favor differential emotion theory and Fromm-Reichmann's position that shame is important in depression. It disconfirms the Freudian notion that the depressive is one who lacks shame and shyness and makes defensive use of exhibiting his miseries and woes. The differences on shyness and outer-directed hostility could result in part from differences in severity of depression and overall psychological adjustment.

Despite these differences in relative rank order for three of the eight factors, it remains a fact that the two groups have quite similar profiles and that the depression profile is profoundly different from the profile in the anxiety situation and the profiles obtained in the various fundamental emotion situations.

It should be noted that the mean scores for the factors shown in Table 11-8 were not reported because they are not directly comparable. The version of the DES+D administered to the high-school students contained only an intensity scale for each item, while the version administered to the depressed patients contained both a frequency and intensity scale. The differences in both content and format of the two forms of the DES+D underscores the significance of the similarity between the emotion and feeling profiles of the normal subjects and depressive patients.

XIII. SUMMARY

Of all the theoretical approaches to depression, the psychoanalytic conception comes closer than any other to differential emotion theory in delineating the various components of depression. Although all psychoanalytic writers are not in complete agreement, one or the other has dealt with almost all the discrete emotions and bodily feelings described as components of depression by differential emotion theory. Other theorists have been less explicit and analytical, defining depression as a mood or predisposition.

Among contemporary psychologists, Plutchik's view is closest to that of differential emotion theory. At least, the two approaches are similar in structure. Plutchik defined depression as a complex involving several emotions and pointed in particular to sadness, anger, and disgust.

According to differential emotion theory, the components of depression are the fundamental emotions of distress, anger, disgust, contempt, fear, guilt, and shyness, and the bodily feelings of physical well-being, sexuality, and fatigue. The hostility component of depression, as measured in terms of anger, disgust, and contempt, has both an inner- and outer-directed element. The fundamental emotions are the primary and most important elements of depression, distress being the key or dominant emotion. The bodily feeling factors of physical well-being, sexuality, and fatigue are direct functions of the homeostatic, drive, and motor systems, but they have interactive relationships with the emotions. These bodily feelings may in part result from the emotion conflicts and emotion dynamics inherent in depression, but they in turn influence the emotions and emotion interactions.

The empirical analysis of depression as a pattern of emotions paralleled the empirical analysis of anxiety, although there were certain differences in the structure of the two studies. The empirical analyses in terms of the DES+D profiles and the DES a priori profiles supported the differential emotion theory conception of depression as a complex pattern of fundamental emotions and bodily feelings.

The profile of emotions in depression is quite distinct from the profile in anxiety. As expected, distress and the hostility triad are higher in depression while fear, guilt, shyness, and interest are higher in anxiety.

The MAACL depression measure, which was added to the DES, proved to be a two-factor instrument. Most of the MAACL depression items loaded on the DES distress scale or on the new and separate factor of physical well-being. The MAACL depression scores differentiated between the depression and the fundamental emotion situations. This result was predictable, since the physical well-being factor mean was expected to be low in the depression situation but not in the fundamental emotion situations. Further, the depression score contained a distinct distress factor on which one would expect scores to be higher in the depression situation than in any of the fundamental emotion situations, other than the distress situation.

The DES+D profiles distinguished between the depression situation and each of the fundamental emotion situations. The

DES+D profiles for the various fundamental emotion situations also varied significantly.

The aprioristically defined scales of the DES yielded a profile for depression essentially similar to that of the DES+D profile, except for the absence of the bodily feeling factors. As was the case in the anxiety study, the a priori profile differentiated between the depression situation and each of the fundamental emotion situations. The a priori profile also differed for each of the fundamental emotion situations.

Both the DES+D profiles and the a priori profiles were essentially similar for a college population and for a high school population. The relatively high alpha coefficients for the DES and DES+D factors and the replication of the results from the college study in a more heterogeneous and more representative high-school sample furnish evidence for the reliability and meaningfulness of the findings. Additional confirming evidence was found in the DES profiles of depressive clients in psychotherapy and in the profiles of hospitalized depressive patients.

The results of both the anxiety and depression studies indicate that life experiences are typically characterized by a pattern of emotions and feelings that direct or influence cognition and action. When the pattern is that of anxiety or depression, the person is faced with a highly complex set of motivational and cue-producing forces.

References

Abdulla, Y. H., & Hamadah, K. 3',5'-adenosine monophosphate in depression and mania. *Lancet*, I, 1970, 378-381.

Abraham, K. Notes on the psycho-analytical investigation and treatment of manic-depressive insanity and allied conditions. In W. Gaylin (Ed.), *The meaning of despair*. New York: Science House, 1968.

Abselson, R. P., & Sermat, V. Multidimensional scaling of facial expressions. *Journal of Experimental Psychology*, 1962, 63, 546-554.

Alexander, F. *Psychosomatic medicine*. New York: Norton, 1950.

Allport, F. H. *Social psychology*. Cambridge, Massachusetts: Houghton Mifflin, 1924.

Aquinas, Saint Thomas. Summa theologica. In A. C. Pegis (Ed.), *Introduction to Saint Thomas Aquinas*. New York: Random House, 1948.

Arieti, S. Cognition and feeling. In M. B. Arnold (Ed.), *Feelings and emotions*. New York: Academic Press, 1970.

Arnold, M. B. *Emotion and personality*. Vol. I. *Psychological aspects*. New York: Columbia University Press, 1960. (a)

Arnold, M. B. *Emotion and personality*. Vol. II. *Neurological and physiological aspects*. New York: Columbia University Press, 1960. (b)

Arnold, M. B. In defense of Arnold's theory of emotion. *Psychological Bulletin*, 1968, 70, 283-284.

Averill, J. R. Grief: Its nature and significance. *Psychological Bulletin*, 1968, 70, 721-748.

Averill, J. R. Autonomic response patterns during sadness and mirth. *Psychophysiology*, 1969, 5, 399-444.

Averill, J. R., Opton, E. M., Jr., & Lazarus, R. S. Cross-cultural studies of psychophysiological responses during stress and emotion. *International Journal of Psychology*, 1969, 4, 83-102.

Ax, A. F. The physiological differentiation between fear and anger in humans. *Psychosomatic Medicine*, 1953, 15, 433-442.

Barratt, E. Anxiety and impulsiveness: Toward a neuropsychological model. In C. D. Spielberger (Ed.), *Anxiety: Contemporary theory and research*. New York: Academic Press, 1972.

283

References

Barnard, G, & Banks, S. "Motoric" psychotherapy found effective for the depressed. *Frontiers in Clinical Psychiatry*, 1967, **4**, 1-4.

Bartlett, E. S. Comparison of two approaches to the understanding of emotion: Dimensional versus typological. Unpublished major area paper, Vanderbilt University, 1969.

Basowitz, H., Persky, H., Korchin, S. J., & Grinker, R. R., Sr. *Anxiety and stress.* New York: McGraw-Hill, 1955.

Bauman, M. J., & Straughon, J. H. BRS as a function of anxiety, stress, and sex. *Psychological Record*, 1969, **19**, 339-344.

Beck, A. T. *Depression.* New York: Harper & Row, 1967.

Bibring, E. The mechanism of depression. In W. Gaylin (Ed.), *The meaning of despair.* New York: Science House, 1968.

Block, J. Studies in the phenomenology of emotions. *Journal of Abnormal and Social Psychology*, 1957, **54**, 358-363.

Brady, J. V. Ulcers in "executive" monkeys. *Scientific American*, 1958, **199** (4), 95-100.

Brady, J. V. Emotions: Some conceptual problems and psychophysiological experiments. In M. B. Arnold (Ed.), *Feelings and emotions.* New York: Academic Press, 1970.

Brandt, K., & Fenz, W. D. Specificity in verbal and physiological indicants of anxiety. *Perceptual and Motor Skills*, 1969, **29**, 663-675.

Breggin, P. R. The psychophysiology of anxiety. *Journal of Nervous and Mental Disease*, 1964, **139**, 558-568.

Brown, F. Depression and childhood bereavement. *Journal of Mental Science*, 1961, **107**, 754-777.

Bull, N. The attitude theory of emotion. *Nervous and Mental Disease Monographs.* New York: Collidge Foundation, 1951, No. 81.

Buss, A. H. *The psychology of aggression.* New York: Wiley, 1961.

Bunney, W. E., Jr., & Fawcett, J. A. Possibility of a biochemical test for suicide. *Archives of General Psychiatry*, 1965, **13**, 232-239.

Bunney, W. E., Jr., Mason, J. W., & Hamburg, D. A. Correlations between behavioral variables and urinary 17-hydroxycorticosteroids in depressed patients. *Psychosomatic Medicine*, 1965, **27**, 299-308.

Cattell, R. B. Anxiety and motivation: Theory and crucial experiments. In C. D. Spielberger (Ed.), *Anxiety and behavior.* New York: Academic Press, 1966.

Cattell, R. B., & Bjerstedt, A. The structure of depression, by factoring Q-data, in relation to general personality source traits, in normal and pathological subjects. *Educational Psychology Interactions*, 1966, **16**, 1-13.

Cattell, R. B., & Scheier, I. H. *The meaning and measurement of neuroticism and anxiety.* New York: Ronald Press, 1961.

Cohn, C. K., Dunner, D. L., & Axelrod, J. Reduced catechol-o-methyltransferase activity in red blood cells of women with primary affective disorder. *Science*, 1970, **170**, 1323-1324.

Combs, A. W., & Snygg, D. *Individual behavior.* New York: Harper, 1959.

Darwin, C. *The expression of the emotions in man and animals.* Chicago: University of Chicago Press, 1965. (Originally published in 1872.)

Davis, J. Theories of biological etiology of affective disorders. *International Review of Neurobiology*, 1970, **12**, 145-175.

Davitz, J. R. A dictionary of grammar of emotion. In M. B. Arnold (Ed.), *Feelings and emotions.* New York: Academic Press, 1970.

284

Delay, J., Pichot, P., Lemperiere, T., & Mirouze, R. La nosologie des etats depressifs. *Encephale*, 1963, 52, 497-505.

Duffy, E. An explanation of "emotional" phenomena without the use of the concept "emotion." *Journal of General Psychology*, 1941, 25, 283-293.

Duffy, E. The psychological significance of the concept "arousal" or "activation." *Psychological Review*, 1957, 64, 265-275.

Duffy, E. *Activation and behavior*. New York: Wiley, 1962.

Duncan, D. B. Multiple range and multiple F tests. *Biometrics*, 1955, 11, 1-42.

Eccleston, D., Loose, R., Pullar, I., & Sugden, R. Exercise and urinary excretion of cyclic A.M.P. *Lancet*, II,1970, 612-613.

Ekman, P., Sorenson, E. R., & Friesen, W. V. Pan-cultural elements in facial displays of emotion. *Science*, 1969, 164, 86-88.

Epstein, S. The nature of anxiety with emphasis upon its relationship to expectancy. In C. D. Spielberger (Ed.), *Anxiety: Contemporary theory and research*. New York: Academic Press, 1972.

Ewert, O. The attitudinal character of emotion. In M. B. Arnold (Ed.), *Feelings and emotions*. New York: Academic Press, 1970.

Ey, H. Psychose periodique ou maniaco-depressive. Mimeographed copy of lectures given at l'Hopital St. Anne, Paris, France, 1949. Cited by F. Fromm-Reichmann, An intensive study of twelve cases of manic-depressive psychosis. Final Report, Office of Naval Research Contract Nonr-751(00), Baltimore: Washington School of Psychiatry, 1953.

Fehr, F. S., & Stern, J. A. Peripheral physiological variables and emotion: The James–Lange theory revisited. *Psychological Bulletin*, 1970, 74, 411-424.

Fenichel, O. *The psychoanalytic theory of neurosis*. London: Routledge & Kegan Paul, 1946.

Fenichel, O. Depression and mania. In W. Gaylin (Ed.), *The meaning of despair*. New York: Science House, 1968.

Fenz, W. D., & Epstein, S. Manifest anxiety: Unifactorial or multifactorial composition. *Perceptual and Motor Skills*, 1965, 20, 773-780.

Freud, S. Introductory lectures on psychoanalysis. London: Hogarth Press, 1917.

Freud, S. Inhibitions, symptoms, and anxiety. In J. Strachey (Ed.), *The standard edition of the complete psychological works of Sigmund Freud*. Vol. 20. London: Hogarth Press, 1959.

Freud, S. Mourning and melancholia. In W. Gaylin (Ed.), *The meaning of despair*. New York: Science House, 1968.

Friedman, A., Cowitz, B., Cohen, H., & Granick, S. Syndromes and themes of psychotic depression: A factor analysis. *Archives of General Psychiatry*, 1963, 9, 504-509.

Frijda, N. H. Emotion and recognition of emotion. In M. B. Arnold (Ed.), *Feelings and emotions*. New York: Academic Press, 1970.

Frijda, N. H., & Philipszoon, E. Dimensions of recognition of expression. *Journal of Abnormal and Social Psychology*, 1963, 66, 45-51.

Fromm-Reichmann, F. An intensive study of twelve cases of manic-depressive psychosis. Final Report, Office of Naval Research Contract Nonr-751(00), Baltimore: Washington School of Psychiatry, 1953.

Funkenstein, D. H. The physiology of fear and anger. *Scientific American*, 1955, 192, 74-80.

Gaylin, W. The meaning of despair. In W. Gaylin (Ed.), *The meaning of despair*. New York: Science House, 1968.

285

References

Gellhorn, E. Motion and emotion: The role of proprioception in the physiology and pathology of emotions. *Psychological Review*, 1964, 71, 457-572.

Gellhorn, E. The neurophysiological basis of anxiety: A hypothesis. *Perspectives in Biology and Medicine*, 1965, 8, 488-515.

Gellhorn, E. The tuning of the nervous system: Physiological foundations and implications for behavior. *Perspectives in Biology and Medicine*, 1967, 10, 559-591.

Gellhorn, E. (Ed.) *Biological foundations of emotion: Research and commentary*. Glenview, Ill.: Scott, Foresman, 1968.

Gellhorn, E. The emotions and the ergotropic and trophotropic systems. *Psychologische Forschung*, 1970, 34, 48-94.

Gellhorn, E., & Loofbourrow, G. N. *Emotion and emotional disorders: A neurophysiological study*. New York: Harper & Row, 1963.

Gershon, E., Cromer, M., & Klerman, G. Hostility and depression. *Psychiatry*, 1968, 31, 224-235.

Goodman, L. S., & Gilman, A. (Eds.) *Pharmacological basis of therapeutics*. (4th ed.) New York: Macmillan, 1970.

Goodwin, F. K., Murphy, D. L., Brodie, H. K. H., & Bunney, W. E., Jr. L-Dopa, catecholamines, and behavior: A clinical and biochemical study in depressed patients. *Biological Psychiatry*, 1970, 2, 341-366.

Gottschalk, L. A., & Gleser, G. C. *The measurement of psychological states through the content analysis of verbal behavior*. Los Angeles: University of Californis Press, 1969.

Gottschalk, L. A., Gleser, G. C., & Springer, K. Three hostility scales applicable to verbal samples. *Archives of General Psychiatry*, 1963, 9, 254-279.

Gray, J. *The psychology of fear and stress*. New York: McGraw-Hill, 1971.

Grinker, R., Miller, J., Sabshin, M., Nunn, R., & Nunnally, J. C. *The phenomena of depressions*. New York: Hoeber, 1961.

Grinker, R. R., Sr., & Spiegel, J. P. *Men under stress*. Philadelphia: Blakiston, 1945. (Also published by McGraw-Hill in paperback form, 1963.)

Gregory, I. *Psychiatry: Biological and social*. Philadelphia: Saunders, 1961.

Gregory, I. Retrospective data concerning childhood loss of a parent. *Archives of General Psychiatry*, 1966, 15, 354-361. (a)

Gregory, I. Retrospective data concerning childhood loss of a parent. II. *Archives of General Psychiatry*, 1966, 15, 362-367. (b)

Grossman, S. P. Modification of emotional behavior by intracranial administration of chemicals. In P. Black (Ed.), *Physiological correlates of emotion*. New York: Academic Press, 1970.

Hamburg, D. A. Emotions in the perspective of human evolution. In P. H. Knapp (Ed.), *Expression of emotions in man*. New York: International Universities Press, 1963.

Hamilton, M. A rating scale for depression. *Journal of Neurology, Neurosurgery and Psychiatry*, 1960, 23 56-61.

Harvey, O. J., Hunt, D. E., & Schroder, H. M. *Conceptual systems and personality organization*. New York: Wiley, 1961.

Hoffman, H. Personality pattern of depression and its relation to acquiescence. *Psychological Reports*, 1970, 26, 459-464.

Havner, P. H., & Izard, C. E. Unrealistic self-enhancement in paranoid schizophrenics. *Journal of Consulting Psychology*, 1962, 26, 65-68.

286

References

Hurst, L. A. Research implications of converging advances in psychiatric genetics and the pharmacology of psychotropic drugs. In M. Manosevitz, G. Lindzey, & D. D. Theissen (Eds.), *Behavioral genetics: Method and Research.* New York: Appleton-Century-Crofts, 1969.

Izard, C. E. On understanding and promoting human effectiveness. Unpublished manuscript, Vanderbilt University, 1965.

Izard, C. E. Differential emotion scale. Unpublished test, Vanderbilt University, 1969.

Izard, C. E. *The face of emotion.* New York: Appleton-Century-Crofts, 1971.

Izard, C. E. The emotions and emotion concepts in personality and culture research. In R. B. Cattell & R. M. Dreger (Eds.), *Handbook of modern personality theory.* In preparation.

Izard, C. E., Chappell, J. E., & Weaver, F. Fundamental emotions involved in black-white encounters characterized by race prejudice. *Proceedings,* 78th Annual Convention, American Psychological Association, 1970.

Izard, C. E., & Dougherty, F. *Manual for the Differential Emotion Scale.* In preparation.

Izard, C. E., & Tomkins, S. S. Affect and behavior: Anxiety as a negative affect. In C. D. Spielberger (Ed.), *Anxiety and behavior.* New York: Academic Press, 1966.

Izard, C. E., Wehmer, G. M., Livsey, W., & Jennings, J. R. Affect, awareness, and performance. In S. S. Tomkins & C. E. Izard (Eds.), *Affect, cognition, and personality.* New York: Springer, 1965.

Jacobson, E. *Progressive relaxation.* (Rev. ed.) Chicago: University of Chicago Press, 1938.

Jacobson, E. *Anxiety and tension control.* Philadelphia: J. B. Lippincott, 1964.

Jacobson, E. *Biology of emotions.* Springfield, Ill.: Charles C. Thomas, 1967.

Janis, I. L. Stress and frustration. Part 1, in I. L. Janis, G. F. Mahl, J. Kagan, & R. R. Holt (Eds.), *Personality: Dynamics, development, and assessment.* New York: Harcourt, Brace & World, 1969.

Jelliffee, S. E. Some historical phases of the manic-depressive synthesis. *Association for Research in Nervous and Mental Disease,* 1931, 11, 3-47.

Jolly, A. Lemur social behavior and primate intelligence. *Science,* 1966, 153, 501-506.

Katz, P. K., & Zigler, P. K. Self-image disparity: A developmental approach. *Journal of Personality and Social Psychology,* 1967, 5, 186-195.

Kendell, R. Relationship between aggression and depression. *Archives of General Psychiatry,* 1970, 22, 308-318.

Kelly, G. A. *The psychology of personal constructs.* Vol. I. New York: Norton, 1955.

Kety, S. S. Neurochemical aspects of emotional behavior. In P. Black (Ed.), *Physiological correlates of emotion.* New York: Academic Press, 1970.

Kierkegaard, S. *The concept of dread.* Translated by W. Lowrie. Princeton: Princeton University Press, 1944. (Originally published in Danish, 1844.)

Klauber, J. An attempt to differentiate a typical form of transference in neurotic depression. *International Journal of Psychoanalysis,* 1966, 47, 539-545.

Kline, N. S. *Depression: Its diagnosis and treatment.* New York: Brunner/Mazel, 1969.

Kraines, S. H. *Mental depressions and their treatment.* New York: Macmillan, 1957.

References

Lampl-de Groot, J. Depression and aggression. In R. Loewenstein (Ed.), *Drives, affects, behavior*. New York: International Universities Press, 1964.

Lazarus, R. S. *Psychological stress and the coping process*. New York: McGraw-Hill, 1966.

Lazarus, R. S., & Averill, J. R. Emotion and cognition: With special reference to anxiety. In C. D. Spielberger (Ed.), *Anxiety: Contemporary theory and research*. New York: Academic Press, 1972.

Lazarus, R. S., Averill, J. R., & Opton, E. M., Jr. Towards a cognitive theory of emotion. In M. B. Arnold (Ed.), *Feelings and emotions*. New York: Academic Press, 1970.

Levitt, E. E. *The psychology of anxiety*. Indianapolis: Bobbs-Merrill, 1967.

Lindsley, D. B. Emotion. In S. S. Stevens (Ed.), *Handbook of experimental psychology*. New York: Wiley, 1951.

Lindsley, D. B. Psychophysiology and motivation. In M. R. Jones (Ed.), *Nebraska symposium on motivation*. Lincoln: University of Nebraska Press, 1957.

Lindquist, E. F. *Design and analysis of experiments in psychology and education*. Boston: Houghton Mifflin, 1953.

MacLean, P. D. Psychosomatic disease and the "visceral brain": Recent developments bearing on the Papez theory of emotion. *Psychosomatic Medicine*, 1949, 11, 338-353.

MacLean, P. D. The limbic system and its hippocampal formation. Studies in animals and their possible application to man. *Journal of Neurosurgery*, 1954, 11, 29-44.

MacLean, P. D Contrasting functions of limbic and neocortical systems of the brain and their relevance to psychophysiological aspects of medicine. In E. Gellhorn (Ed.), *Biological foundations of emotion*. Glenview, Ill.: Scott, Foresman, 1968.

MacLean, P. D. The limbic brain in relation to the psychoses. In P. Black (Ed.), *Physiological correlates of emotion*. New York: Academic Press, 1970.

Maas, J. W., & Mednieks, M. Hydrocortisone-mediated increase of norepinephrine uptake by brain slices. *Science*, 1971, 171, 178-179.

Maher, B. A. *Principles of psychopathology*. New York: McGraw-Hill, 1966.

Malerstein, A. Depression as a pivotal affect. *American Journal of Psychotherapy*, 1967, 21, 202-217.

Mallama, A. D. Substantive definitions and descriptions of anxiety. Unpublished manuscript, Vanderbilt University, 1970.

Malmo, R. B. Studies of anxiety: Some clinical origins of the activation concept. In C. D. Spielberger (Ed.), *Anxiety and behavior*. New York: Academic Press, 1966.

Marshall, A. G., & Izard, C. E. An evaluation of cerebral electrotherapy for depressive patients. Vanderbilt University, in preparation.

Martin, B. The assessment of anxiety by physiological behavioral measures. *Psychological Bulletin*, 1961, 58, 234-255.

May, R. *The meaning of anxiety*. New York: Ronald Press, 1950.

McGeer, P. L. The chemistry of the mind. *American Scientist*, 1971, 59, 221-229.

Mikhail, A. A. Relationship of conditioned anxiety to stomach ulceration and acidity in rats. *Journal of Comparative and Physiological Psychology*, 1969, 68, 623-626.

Mosher, D. L. Differential influence of guilt on the verbal operant conditioning of hostile and "superego" verbs. *Journal of Consulting Psychology*, 1966, **30**, 280.

Nowlis, V. Research with the mood adjective check list. In S. S. Tomkins & C. E. Izard (Eds.), *Affect, cognition, and personality*. New York: Springer, 1965.

Nowlis, V. Mood: Behavior and experience. In M. B. Arnold (Ed.), *Feelings and emotions*. New York: Academic Press, 1970.

Osgood, C. E. Dimensionality of the semantic space for communication via facial expression. *Scandinavian Journal of Psychology*, 1966, **7**, 1-30.

Osgood, C. E. On the why and wherefore of E, P, and A. *Journal of Personality and Social Psychology*, 1969, **12**, 194-199.

Overall, J., Hollister, L., Johnson, M., & Pennington, V. Nosology of depression and differential responses to drugs. *Journal of American Medical Association*, 1966, **195**, 946-948.

Papez, J. W. A proposed mechanism of emotion. *Archives of Neurological Psychiatry*, 1937, **38**,725-743.

Papez, J. W. Correlation of the Papez mechanism of emotion with the attitude theory of emotion of Nina Bull. In N. Bull, The attitude theory of emotion. *Nervous and Mental Disease Monographs*. New York: Collidge Foundation, 1951, No. 81.

Paul, M. I., Cramer, H. & Bunney, W. E., Jr. Urinary adenosine 3′,5′-monophosphate in the switch process from depression to mania. *Science*, 1971, **171**, 300-303.

Paul, M. I., Ditzion, B. R., Pauk, G. L. & Janowsky, D. S. Urinary adenosine 3′,5′ -monophosphate excretion in affective disorders. *American Journal of Psychiatry*, 1970, **126**, 1493-1497.

Pichot, P., & Lemperiere, T. Analyse factorielle d'un questionnaire d'auto-evaluation des symptomes depressifs. *Revue de Psychologie Appliquee*, 1964, **14**, 15-29.

Pitts, F., Meyer, J., Brooks, M., & Winokur, G. Adult psychiatric illness assessed for childhood parental loss, and psychiatric illness in family members. *American Journal of Psychiatry*, 1965, **121**, (Suppl. i-x).

Plutchik, R. *The emotions: Facts, theories and a new model*. New York: Random House, 1962.

Plutchik, R. Emotions, evolution, and adaptive processes. In M. B. Arnold (Ed.), *Feelings and emotions*. New York: Academic Press, 1970.

Prange, A., & Vitols, M. M. Cultural aspects of the relatively low incidence of depression in southern Negroes. *International Journal of Social Psychiatry*, 1962, **8**, 104-112.

Pribram, K. H. Emotion: Steps toward a neuropsychological theory. In D. C. Glass (Ed.), *Neurophysiology and emotion*. New York: Rockefeller University Press, 1967.

Pribram, K. H. Feelings as monitors. In M. B. Arnold (Ed.), *Feelings and emotions*. New York: Academic Press, 1970.

Rado, S. Psychodynamics of depression from the etiologic point of view. In W. Gaylin (Ed.), *The meaning of despair*. New York: Science House, 1968.

Ramey, E. R., & Goldstein, M. S. *Psychological Review*, 1957, **37**, 155. Cited by J. W. Maas & M. Mednieks, Hydrocortisone-mediated increase of norepinephrine uptake by brain slices. *Science*, 1971, **171**, 178-179.

References

Robison, G., Coppen, A., Whybrow, P., & Prange, A. Cyclic A.M.P. in active disorders. *Lancet*, II, 1970, 1028-1029.

Sarason, S. B. The measurement of anxiety in children: Some questions and problems. In C. D. Spielberger (Ed.), *Anxiety and behavior*. New York: Academic Press, 1966.

Sarason, S. B., Davidson, K. S., Lighthall, F. F., Waite, R. R., & Ruebush, B. K. *Anxiety in elementary school children*. New York: Wiley, 1960.

Schachtel, E. G. *Metamorphosis*. New York: Basic Books, 1959.

Schachter, S. S. Pain, fear and anger in hypertensives and normotensives: A psychophysiologic study. *Psychosomatic Medicine*, 1957, **19**, 17-29.

Schachter, S. S. The interaction of cognitive and physiological determinants of emotional state. In L. Berkowitz (Ed.), *Advances in experimental social psychology*. Vol. 1. New York: Academic Press, 1964.

Schildkraut, J. J., Davis, J. M., & Klerman, G. L. Biochemistry of depressions. In D. H. Efron, J. O. Cole, J. Levine, & J. R. Wittenborn (Eds.), *Psychopharmacology: A review of progress 1957-1967*. Washington, D. C.: Public Health Service Publication, 1968.

Schlosberg, H. A scale for the judgment of facial expressions. *Journal of Experimental Psychology*, 1941, **29**, 497-510.

Schlosberg, H. The description of facial expressions in terms of two dimensions. *Journal of Experimental Psychology*, 1952, **44**, 229-237.

Schlosberg, H. Three dimensions of emotion. *Psychological Review*, 1954, **61**, 81-88.

Schmale, A. Relation of separation and depression to disease. *Psychosomatic Medicine*, 1958, **20**, 259-267.

Sheldon, W. H., Stevens, S. S., & Tucker, W. B. *The varieties of human physique: An introduction to constitutional psychology*. New York: Harper, 1940.

Silverman, C. *The epidemiology of depression*. Baltimore: Johns Hopkins Press, 1968.

Simpson, H. H. II. The emotional dimensions of the concept of death. Unpublished paper, Vanderbilt University, 1971.

Snyder, C. R., & Katahn, M. The relationship of state anxiety, feedback, and ongoing self-reported affect to performance in complex verbal learning. *American Journal of Psychology*, 1970, **83**, 237-247.

Spence, J. T., & Spence, K. W. The motivational components of manifest anxiety: Drive and drive stimuli. In C. D. Spielberger (Ed.), *Anxiety and behavior*. New York: Academic Press, 1966.

Spencer, H. *The principles of psychology*. Vol. I. New York: Appleton, 1890. (Originally published in 1855.)

Spielberger, C. D. Theory and research on anxiety. In C. D. Spielberger (Ed.), *Anxiety and behavior*. New York: Academic Press, 1966.

Spielberger, C. D. (Ed.), *Anxiety: Contemporary theory and research*. New York: Academic Press, 1972.

Spielberger, C. D., Gorsuch, R. R., & Lushene, R. E. *State Trait Anxiety Inventory Test Manual for Form X*. Palo Alto: Consulting Psychologists Press, 1970.

Spielberger, C. D., Lushene, R. E., & McAdoo, W. G. Theory and measurement of anxiety states. In R. B. Cattell & R. M. Dreger (Eds.), *Handbook of modern personality theory*. In preparation.

Spitz, R. A. 'Anaclitic depression.' *Psychoanalytic Study of the Child*. 1946, 2, 313-342.

Sprague, J. M., Chambers, W. W., & Stellar, E. Attentive, affective, and adaptive behavior in the cat. *Science*, 1961, **133**, 165-173.

Stanley-Jones, D. The biological origin of love and hate. In M. B. Arnold (Ed.), *Feelings and emotions*. New York: Academic Press, 1970.

Sullivan, H. S. *The interpersonal theory of psychiatry*. New York: Norton, 1953.

Sutherland, E. W. On the biological role of cyclic AMP. *Journal of the American Medical Association*, 1970, **214**, 1281-1288. (a)

Sutherland, E. W. The Sollmann oration. *The Pharmacologist*, 1970, **12**, 33-37. (b)

Sutherland, E. W., Robison, G. A., & Butcher, R. W. Some aspects of the biological role of adenosine 3',5'-monophosphate. *Circulation*, 1968, **37**, 279-306.

Tomkins, S. S. *Affect, imagery, consciousness*. Vol. I. *The positive affects*. New York: Springer, 1962.

Tomkins, S. S. *Affect, imagery, consciousness*. Vol. II. *The negative affects*. New York: Springer, 1963.

Tomkins, S. S. Affect as the primary motivational system. In M. B. Arnold (Ed.), *Feelings and emotions*. New York: Academic Press, 1970.

Tonks, C. M., Paykel, E. S., & Klerman, G. L. Clinical depressions among Negroes. *American Journal of Psychiatry*, 1970, **127**, 329-335.

Triandis, H. C., & Lambert, W. W. A restatement and test of Schlosberg's theory of emotion with two kinds of subjects from Greece. *Journal of Abnormal and Social Psychology*, 1958, **56**, 321-328.

Unger, S. M. On the development of guilt reactivity in the child. Unpublished manuscript, Cornell University, 1962.

Wehmer, G. M. The effect of a stressful movie on ratings of momentary mood, experienced anxiety, and plasma 17-hydroxycorticosteroid level in three psychiatric groups. Unpublished doctoral dissertation, Vanderbilt University, 1966.

Wellek, A. Emotional polarity in personality structure. In M. B. Arnold (Ed.), *Feelings and emotions*. New York: Academic Press, 1970.

Wessman, A. E., Ricks, D. F., & Tyl, M. M. Characteristics and concomitants of mood fluctuations in college women. *Journal of Abnormal and Social Psychology*, 1960, **60**, 117-126.

White, R. W. Motivation reconsidered: The concept of competence. *Psychological Review*, 1959, **66**, 297-333.

Williams, R. H. *Textbook of endocrinology*. Philadelphia: W. B. Saunders, 1968.

Wolpe, J. The conditioning and deconditioning of neurotic anxiety. In C. D. Spielberger (Ed.), *Anxiety and behavior*. New York: Academic Press, 1966.

Wolpe, J., & Lazarus, A. A. *Behavior therapy techniques*. London: Pergamon Press, 1967.

Woodworth, R. S. *Experimental psychology*. New York: Holt, 1938.

Wundt, W. *Grundriss der psychologie*. (C. H. Judd, translator.) 1896.

Zimmerman, W. B. Psychological and physiological differences between "light" and "deep" sleepers. *Psychophysiology*, 1968, **4**, 387.

Zuckerman, M. The development of an affect adjective check list for the measurement of anxiety. *Journal of Consulting Psychology*, 1960, **24**, 457-462.

Zuckerman, M., & Lubin, B. Measurement of experimentally induced affects. *Journal of Consulting Psychology*, 1964, **23**, 418-425.

Subject Index

A

Acetylcholine, 11
Activity
  as a dimension, 133, 144, 147
  and the fundamental emotion
    situations, 144
Acute fear, 29, 30
Addison's disease, 182
Adenosine $3',5'$- monophosphate
  (*see* Cyclic AMP)
Adenosine triphosphate, 184
Adenyl cyclase, 184
Adrenal gland, 37
Adrenalin (*see* Epinephrine)
Affect, as an hysterical attack, 65
Agitated depression, determinants of,
  227
Ambivalence, 195
Amines
  and depression, 179-182
  sympathomimètic type, 187
Amitriptyline, and the treatment of
  depression, 188
Amygdala, 15
Anger, 48, 52, 69, 74, 89, 95, 101,
  113
  and contempt, 14
  in depression, 255
  and the depression pattern, 261

inner-directed, 31, 38
  outer-directed, 37, 38
  predisposition to, 255
  sympathetic and parasympathetic
    activity in, 12
Anger-contempt combination, 4
Anger-in, 31
Anger-interest combination, 4
Anger-out, 31
Anger situation, instructions for
  visualizing, 97
Anterior thalamic nuclei, 15
Antidepressant drugs, types and uses,
  187-190
Anxiety, 29-33, 34, 74
  adaptive function of, 64
  as antagonistic ergotropic and
    trophotropic functioning, 32, 33
  as anticipatory reaction, 75
  as arousal, 75-78
  biochemical factors in, 37
  in relation to choice, possibility,
    and freedom, 76
  as chronic fear, 31, 32
  classical psychoanalytic theory of,
    61
  as a variable combination of
    emotions, 57
  as a combination of interacting
    fundamental emotions, 83, 102

293

and antidepressant drugs, 185
basic functions of, 184
and depression, 184, 185

D

Death, 90
Dejected mood in depression, 230
Deliberateness, as a dimension, 144, 147
Dependency in depression, 226, 232
Depression, 31, 74
  and aggressive strivings, 204
  and ambivalence toward love object, 195
  versus anxiety, 195, 203, 264-266
  biochemical aspects of, 178
  a biogenetic theory of, 215-219
  complexity of, 176
  criticisms of, 216
  dependency in, 201
  and discrete emotions, 206
  and disruption of sensory and perceptual functions, 205
  empirical analysis of, 259-272
  factor analytic investigation of, 237-254
  and fixation at the anal-sadistic and oral-sadistic levels, 196, 197
  Freud's view of, 198
  and grief, 196
  distinguished from grief, 199
  and feelings of guilt, 197, 199
  and heredity, 217, 218
  and feelings of hostility, 195, 199
  independent of loss, 205
  and feelings of inferiority, 197, 199
  and inhibition of functions, 203
  and inner- and outer-directed hostility, 195, 197, 209-211
  and interest, 206
  and love-hate ambivalence, 197
  mechanism of, 215
  need for a new concept of, 190-191
  narcissistic needs in, 201, 204
  neurophysiological factors in, 176-178
  and the role of oral fixation, 204
  and oral strivings, 204

  as a pattern of fundamental emotions and feelings, 257
  and the powerlessness of the ego, 202
  psychoanalytic theory of, 216, 224
  and psychosexual development, 196
  as reproach of the world, 206
  retarded versus agitated, 207
  and self-esteem, 201-202
  and self-reproach, 197
  and sexual potency, 197
  and shame, 199, 202
  and shyness, 199
  and the struggle between emotions, 207
  symptomatology of, 229-234
  as a third-order emotion, 223
  and feelings of unreality, 218
  and visual paresthesias, 218
Depression situation
  versus distress situation, 272
  free-response descriptions of, 246
  instructions for visualizing, 242
Depressives
  aspirations of, 202
  and the motivation for repentance, 206
  psychotherapy for, 204
  personality characteristics of, 234
  view of the future, self, and world, 225
Depressive behavior, as a cry for love, 206
Differential Emotion Scale (DES), 131
  and the assessment of anxiety experiences, 167
  combined with an anxiety scale, 91-95
  compared with the DRS, 165, 169
  and the comparison of anxiety situations, 156
  development of, 85
  and the differentiation of anxiety groups, 158
  and the differentiation of fundamental emotion situations, 147-152
  effective combination for differentiating emotion situations, 151
  factor analyses of, 86